QUEEN
VICTORIA'S
CHILDREN

ALSO BY JOHN VAN DER KISTE

Frederick III (1981)
Dearest Affie [with Bee Jordaan] (1984)
Queen Victoria's Children (1986)
Windsor and Habsburg (1987)
Edward VII's Children (1989)
Princess Victoria Melita (1991)
George V's Children (1991)
George III's Children (1992)
Crowns in a Changing World (1993)
Kings of the Hellenes (1994)
Childhood at Court 1819–1914 (1995)
Northern Crowns (1996)
King George II and Queen Caroline (1997)
The Romanovs 1818–1959 (1998)
Kaiser Wilhelm II (1999)
The Georgian Princesses (2000)
Gilbert & Sullivan's Christmas (2000)
Dearest Vicky, Darling Fritz (2001)
Once a Grand Duchess [with Coryne Hall] (2002)
William and Mary (2003)
Emperor Francis Joseph (2005)
Sons, Servants and Statesmen (2006)
A Divided Kingdom (2007)

QUEEN VICTORIA'S CHILDREN

JOHN VAN DER KISTE

Cover illustration: Queen Victoria and her Children *by John Callcot Horsley (1817–1903) (Forbes Magazine Collection / The Bridgeman Art Library).*

First published in 1986
This edition published 2009

Reprinted 2010, 2011, 2013, 2015, 2017, 2019, 2021

The History Press
97 St George's Place
Cheltenham, Gloucestershire, GL50 3QB
www.thehistorypress.co.uk

© John Van der Kiste, 1986, 2003, 2004, 2009

British Library Cataloguing in Publication Data.
A catalogue record for this book is available from the British Library.

ISBN 978 0 7524 5472 6

Typesetting and origination by The History Press
Printed and bound by Imak, Turkey

Contents

Preface to Second Edition

Queen Victoria's Children was first published in 1986, and minor revisions were made to the first paperback edition in 1990. Since then our knowledge of Queen Victoria's children has been added to immeasurably by further biographies and selections of letters. In addition to long-awaited comprehensive lives of Princess Louise, Prince Arthur and Prince Leopold, there has also been another major study of Princess Victoria, and the final volume in the series of letters between this eldest daughter and her mother. Add to these four major works on Queen Victoria herself, one taking the story up to 1861, the other three her complete life, and also a biography of her physician, Sir James Reid, and the sum total speaks for itself.

I have taken this opportunity to add to my text from these and other more recently published volumes, make a few small corrections, and undertake a thorough revision of the reference notes and bibliography.

In conclusion, I would like to dedicate this volume to Kim.

Foreword

Queen Victoria's children have been the subject, individually and collectively, of substantial biographical attention. The two eldest, the Princess Royal (later the German Empress Frederick) and King Edward VII, have been dealt with adequately by several writers from personal and political angles, and most of the seven younger princes and princesses have been accorded at least one biography each. In addition there are various works on Queen Victoria's family and children, even two on the Queen and her daughters.

Our knowledge of the children as individuals, however, is inevitably uneven. Queen Victoria and the Empress Frederick were among the most tireless correspondents and journal-writers of their time,* and it is largely thanks to the publication of so many of their letters that so much is known of their personalities, their likes and dislikes, their attitudes and relationships with the family. The Queen's other children did not inherit these literary gifts in such measure. Moreover, some of them are known to have left instructions that much of their correspondence was to be burnt after their death. King Edward VII ordered the destruction of vast quantities of private letters from the Queen to Disraeli, describing her family; Princess Beatrice transcribed her mother's journals, destroying the original manuscript as she went along. Many more letters – one

* When Conte Egon Caesar Corti was researching and writing his biography of the empress, an abridged English translation of which was published as *The English Empress* in 1957, he counted 4,161 letters from the empress to the Queen, in the Royal Archives at Windsor, and 3,777 from the Queen to her daughter, in the Kronberg Archives, all spanning the years 1858 to 1901.

can only guess at the quantity – are still sealed at present and may be made available in future years.

Most of the Queen's surviving correspondence has already been made available in some form, and the history of the family during her lifetime is thus reasonably well-documented. After 1901, the year in which she and the Empress Frederick died, there are still considerable gaps, and it is chiefly for this reason that Queen Victoria's longest-lived children have been comparatively little written about. The aim of this book is to examine the relationships between her, her sons and her daughters, and between each other after her death, as clearly as available material will permit.

My thanks for help, advice and information are due to Theo Aronson; Bee Jordaan; John May; Shirley Stapley; and in particular my parents, Wing Commander Guy and Nancy Van der Kiste, for their assistance with reading the manuscript and checking proofs.

I am indebted to the following copyright holders for permission to quote from published works: Bell & Hyman Ltd (*Dearest Child, Dearest Mama, Your Dear Letter, Darling Child, Beloved Mama*, all edited by Roger Fulford); John Murray Ltd (*King Edward the Seventh*, by Philip Magnus; *The letters of Queen Victoria*); and Weidenfeld & Nicolson Ltd (*Victoria R.I.*, by Elizabeth Longford; *Victoria and her Daughters*, by Nina Epton).

Prologue

Queen Victoria's grandparents, King George III and Queen Charlotte, had fifteen children, of whom twelve attained their majority. The five princesses were spinsters or childless. Of their seven brothers, only three were married in the eyes of the royal act of succession, passed by the King in 1772 as a safeguard against unsuitable alliances. Between them, they could only boast one legitimate or officially recognized grandchild – Princess Charlotte of Wales, offspring of the tempestuous marriage of the Prince Regent and his wife Caroline.

In May 1816 Charlotte married the good-looking, earnest Prince Leopold of Saxe-Coburg Saalfeld. The match was popular, for Leopold made an agreeable change from his wife's ageing, dissolute uncles, but their happiness was destined to be tragically brief. Within eighteen months she gave birth to a stillborn son, and died herself.

Rarely had the country grieved so unanimously for a royal death. The large family of King George III, now a blind and deranged shadow, was apparently heading for extinction. There was no chance of the Prince Regent and his wife having further children, and the Dukes of York and Cumberland were validly married but still childless. Tempted by the prospect of generous parliamentary allowances in return for performing their dynastic duties, three of the other dukes were prepared to jettison their mistresses and seek suitable wives.

In July 1818 Edward, Duke of Kent, married Leopold's elder sister Victoire, widowed Princess of Leiningen. The Dukes of Clarence and Cambridge likewise wedded German princesses that year, and in 1819 there were four royal births. All three duchesses, and the Duchess of Cumberland, presented their husbands with children that spring. In March Princess Charlotte of Clarence was born, but lived only a few hours. By contrast

Prince George of Cambridge was a healthy infant who would live to the ripe old age of eighty-five. These births were followed by two in May. The second of these was Prince George of Cumberland, a delicate child later smitten with blindness, destined to be the last King of Hanover.

Three days earlier, on 24 May, Princess Alexandria Victoria of Kent had been born at Kensington Palace.

Like her cousin Charlotte, Victoria was to be an only child. The penniless Duke and Duchess of Kent wintered that year at the seaside town of Sidmouth in Devon, where the cost of living was considerably less than in London. Ironically the Duke was solicitous about his family's health, but neglected his own. A cold turned to pneumonia shortly after their arrival in Devon. The prince who had frequently boasted he would outlive his brothers died on 23 January 1820, aged fifty-two. Six days later, King George III followed him to the grave.

The Prince Regent ascended the throne as King George IV. His heir was Frederick, Duke of York, whose wife died later that year. Second in line was William, Duke of Clarence. It was assumed that his wife Adelaide would present him with heirs in due course, for he was already the father of ten healthy children by his mistress, the late actress Dorothy Jordan. Sadly for the Clarences, none of their children survived infancy. In 1825, therefore, parliament acknowledged that Princess Victoria would almost certainly succeed Clarence on the throne, and voted the Duchess of Kent an annuity of £6,000 for the maintenance and education of her daughter.

In 1827, Victoria came one step nearer to the throne on the death of the Duke of York. Three years later, King George IV died and was succeeded by the Duke of Clarence as King William IV.

Princess Victoria's childhood was a lonely one, with few even remotely contemporary companions. Her half-sister Feodora, twelve years her senior, married Prince Ernest of Hohenlohe-Langenburg in 1828 and went to live in Germany. After this her only constant playmate was Victoire Conroy, daughter of the Duchess of Kent's controller. Yet this friendship was strained by Sir John Conroy's unprincipled behavior. His loyalty to the Duchess, it was widely believed – and perhaps even suspected by Princess Victoria herself – verged on the excessively familiar. It is unlikely that the two were ever lovers, but the ambitious Sir John certainly overreached himself in another direction. At the age of sixteen Victoria fell seriously ill with typhoid. While she was still convalescent, he attempted to force her to sign a document promising that she would appoint him her private secretary when she became Queen. Appalled that he and her mother should take advantage of her ill health to make such peremptory demands, she refused in no uncertain terms. The episode did incalculable harm to her relationship with her mother.

Victoria's only real friend during her formative years was Louise Lehzen, who had initially come to England as Feodora's governess. In 1824 she was appointed Victoria's governess as well, and six years later she became the Duchess of Kent's lady-in-waiting. The princess respected Lehzen as a trusted confidante, especially after Conroy's attempts at coercion made her life more troubled still. In her childhood journal – admittedly written for her mother's regular inspection, and therefore expressed in guarded terms – there were many more references to 'dear Lehzen' than to 'dear Mama'.

The only constant male influence was that of her uncle Leopold. Though he married a second time, to Louise, daughter of King Louis Philippe of France, and had been elected King of the Belgians in 1831, he maintained a regular correspondence with his twice-widowed sister and young niece. Each year he wrote her a long birthday letter of affection and sound avuncular if rather pompously expressed advice. When he visited England with Queen Louise in September 1835, the princess's delight knew no bounds: 'What happiness it was for me to throw myself in the arms of that *dearest* of uncles who has always been to me like a father and whom I love so *very dearly*.'[1]

That the princess enjoyed no real relationship with the eccentric but kindly King William and Queen Adelaide was not the fault of either. The Duchess of Kent and Conroy ostentatiously kept her from court as much as possible, apparently because they did not want her to associate with a monarch who had so many illegitimate children. Throughout the King's reign, Conroy organised a series of unofficial tours in which Princess Victoria could be formally presented to her future subjects. King William's permission was not asked, and he was infuriated at this setting up of what amounted to a rival court. Though these expeditions were useful to Victoria in giving her some first-hand knowledge of her country, she was undoubtedly embarrassed at knowing of the ill-feeling they caused.

This feud came to a head in the summer of 1836. The King invited his sister-in-law and the princess to Windsor for the Queen's birthday on 13 August, requesting them to stay for his birthday on 21 August and a celebration dinner next day. The Duchess ignored Queen Adelaide's birthday and sent word that she would arrive on 20 August. He was furious at this slight to his wife, and after his health had been drunk at his own dinner he rose to his feet and made an angry speech announcing his wish to be spared nine months longer, so that no regency would take place. He would then have the satisfaction of 'leaving the royal authority to the personal exercise of that young lady (pointing to his niece) . . . and not in the hands of a person now near me who is surrounded by evil advisers and who is herself incompetent to act with propriety in the station in which she would be placed.'[2] Having declared vehemently that the same person had continually insulted him and that he was determined his authority would be respected in future, he ended on a more affectionate note, but the damage was done. Queen Adelaide was embarrassed, Princess Victoria burst into tears, and the stony-faced Duchess remained silent. After dinner she collected her daughter and announced their immediate departure.

Despite failing health, the King's wish was granted. Victoria attained her majority on 24 May 1837, and with it went the prospect of a regency. King William offered her an annual income of £10,000 and an establishment independent of her mother. The Duchess and Conroy made a last desperate attempt to provide for a regency until she was twenty-one, on the grounds that she was too young, inexperienced and mentally unstable to rule. Further attempts to make the princess agree 'voluntarily' resulted in her refusing to speak to her mother for a while. Foolishly, they tried to secure Leopold's support for the scheme. Aware that some kind of conspiracy was afoot, he sent his confidential adviser Baron Stockmar to London. The baron spoke to both parties and saw at once that the princess was being bullied. Arguments and plots continued for nearly a month, with Conroy vainly trying to enlist senior members of parliament in his cause. Almost without exception, they sided with Stockmar and the future Queen herself.

On 20 June, shortly after two o'clock in the morning, King William IV died at Windsor Castle. The archbishop of Canterbury and the lord chamberlain, Lord Conyngham, drove to Kensington Palace, demanding to see 'the Queen'. Victoria was aroused from her sleep, and received the news in a hastily donned dressing gown.

The pressures of a difficult adolescence had left their mark on the young Queen Victoria, and overshadowed the first two years of her reign. 'Mama' and daughter appeared together at state occasions, but in private they had as little contact as possible. As confidantes she still had the devoted support of Lehzen and Stockmar, who had become a regular emissary from King Leopold, though these were soon surpassed by her relationship with her prime minister, Lord Melbourne. The cynical yet charming old aristocrat had led a tragic private life, blighted by the wild behaviour of his deranged wife and the epilepsy of their only son, both of whom had predeceased him. He and the young Queen, both starved of affection, found each other excellent company, and many happy hours were spent in long evenings of friendly conversation at Windsor Castle. On the day of her coronation, 28 June 1838, his support and encouragement were invaluable to her. Such solicitude was in marked contrast to the Duchess of Kent's endless fussing about her own precedence in the coronation procession.

By 1839 Queen Victoria, still not yet aged twenty, was

suffering from a reaction to the first eighteen months of her reign. Excitement and dedication to duty were taking their toll; and this, added to persistent unpleasantness with her mother and Conroy, led to two errors of judgement, one almost disastrous.

Melbourne resigned in May after defeat in parliament, and much against her will Queen Victoria summoned the Conservative leader Sir Robert Peel to form a government. He requested politely that she replace her Whig ladies of the bedchamber; she angrily refused. When he answered with regret that he could not therefore assume office, she triumphantly recalled Melbourne. The 'bedchamber crisis' had been a victory for the Queen, but at the risk of identifying the crown overwhelmingly with one political party.

Had this incident occurred in isolation, little harm would have been done to her reputation. Unfortunately it happened at the same time as the Lady Flora Hastings affair. Lady Flora was one of the Duchess of Kent's ladies, and as such a close friend of Conroy and bitter enemy of Lehzen. Early in the new year, after returning to London from Scotland in a railway coach with Conroy, she complained of feeling unwell. Rumours began to circulate that she was pregnant. The Queen and Lehzen were only too ready to believe the worst, and Melbourne did nothing to discourage them. Bravely Lady Flora submitted to a medical examination by the royal physicians, proving that she was still a virgin. A cancerous tumour of the stomach was diagnosed, and though the conscience-stricken young Queen sought to do what she could for 'poor Lady Flora', she died in July. The Queen's popularity plummeted, and a carriage she sent to the funeral was stoned by angry crowds.

After her crisis-ridden summer, Queen Victoria was temporarily exhausted. Late in July, she told Melbourne petulantly that the very subject of marriage was odious to her, and that if possible she would prefer never to marry at all.

Nonetheless it was not a problem to be put off indefinitely. The Queen was twenty years of age, and she was expected to marry and have heirs, no less than her father and uncles had been bidden to barely a generation earlier. At present her heir was Ernest Augustus, King of Hanover.* As Duke of Cumberland, he had been by far the most unpopular member of the family. Rumours that he was guilty of incest with his sister Sophie and had murdered his valet were certainly false, not to say libellous. But his violent temper, battle-scarred face, and reactionary politics had long made the British dread the possibility of King Ernest Augustus reigning over them as well as over his ancestral home.

There were also personal factors which made the contemplation of matrimony advisable. Inevitably Queen Victoria was beginning to find Lord Melbourne's company dull, and his flippancy mildly offensive. Starved of company of other young people throughout childhood, as she was later to admit, she had 'no scope for my very violent feelings of affection.' A visit to Windsor that summer by Alexander, Grand Duke of Russia,+ had delighted her, and she sorely missed him after he had gone. Her sudden transition from nursery to throne had been a joy at first, but the loneliness of her newly-found independence was beginning to take its toll. It would be much to the benefit of all if Her Majesty was to marry soon.

Princess Victoria had been delivered by the midwife Fraulein Charlotte Siebold, who left Kensington for Germany shortly after the Duchess of Kent's accouchement. The Duchess's sister-in-law Louise, Duchess of Saxe-Coburg Saalfeld, was expecting her second child. She and Duke Ernest already had one son, also called Ernest, destined to inherit his father's Dukedom. On 26 August 1819 she was delivered of another son, Albert.

Like Victoria, Albert had an unhappy childhood. His parents were an ill-matched couple. Ernest was seventeen years older than his wife, and by the time he had succeeded to the Dukedom

---

* Women were barred from the Hanoverian throne. With the death of King William IV, the link between Britain and Hanover had been broken.
+ Later Tsar Alexander II.

in 1826 they had drifted apart. Both found consolation in extra-marital affairs, and they divorced by mutual consent in 1824. Louise was bitterly distressed at parting with her children, whom she never saw again, and Albert was far more deeply affected than his brother. He never forgot his mother, who made a second marriage but died of cancer in 1831. After her death Duke Ernest married his niece Princess Marie of Württemberg. The boys were therefore without a mother for the greater part of their boyhood, and the greatest influences on their formative years were those of their grandmothers and their tutor, Herr Rath Florschutz.

Ernest and Albert were almost inseparable. They were, however, to grow up markedly different, the extrovert Ernest taking after his disagreeable father in his dissolute behaviour and spendthrift habits, sensitive Albert the complete opposite apart from a passion for practical jokes and mimicry. Yet nothing ever destroyed the fraternal bond between them, although Albert was later to become exasperated by Ernest's self-indulgence and marital infidelity.

Almost from his birth, the family intended that Albert should be the husband of Princess Victoria of Kent. When he was aged two their grandmother, Dowager Duchess Augusta of Saxe-Coburg, wrote to the Duchess of Kent that Albert was the 'pendant to the pretty cousin'. It was a scheme which the Duchess and King Leopold of the Belgians soon came to share, especially after it became clear that King William and Queen Adelaide would leave no surviving heir or heiress. Albert himself was aware of the plan from an early age, and Victoria knew before she became Queen.

The cousins met for the first time in May 1836, when Duke Ernest brought them to England for a short visit. Albert, it was immediately apparent, did not share Victoria's love of late hours. Perhaps nervousness had affected him as well, for he was ill on the eve of her birthday. He bravely attended a ball at St James's Palace with her the following night, but almost fainted and was sent to bed. Otherwise he made a good impression on her. Though she liked both brothers, finding them 'so very very merry and gay and happy, like young people ought to be,'[3] Albert's good looks, musical and artistic talents and witty conversation at the breakfast table, gave him a modest advantage over Ernest. After their departure she wrote prosaically to King Leopold that he possessed 'every quality that could be desired to make me perfectly happy.'[4]

Melbourne was distinctly unenthusiastic about the idea of a Victoria-Albert marriage, warning her of the unpopularity of foreigners in England. But he had to agree that there seemed to be nobody else suitable. For her to marry a British subject would lead to jealousy and problems of precedence. Tacitly they agreed that there was no need for a firm decision for perhaps another four years at least.

Yet King Leopold was not prepared to let the matter rest indefinitely. To see his scheme have any hope of success required careful handling. If he pressed it too strongly, he realised, Victoria's antipathy to marriage would prove an insuperable barrier. Not to do anything would be grossly unfair on Albert. The young man had dutifully consented to be patient as long as Queen Victoria agreed to marry him in the end, but if she delayed too long and turned him down in the end, his chances of finding an eligible princess as his wife would be slender.

In July 1839 she confessed to King Leopold to her 'great repugnance' of changing her present position as a single woman, and believed there to be no great anxiety in the country for her marriage. Did Albert realise that there was no engagement between them? Despite the favourable reports she had of him, 'I may like him as a friend, and as a cousin, and as a brother, but not more; and should this be the case (which is not likely), I am very anxious that it should be understood that I am not guilty of any breach of promise, for I never gave any.'[5]

It was with some trepidation that Queen and prince awaited the crucial meeting on 10 October 1839. She had been nervous at the prospect, evidently under strain. For his part, Albert had been warned of Victoria's stubbornness, and he was uncomfortable at being regarded as a future husband on approval. Yet as they met on the stairs at Windsor, she was immediately struck by the change in him since their last meeting. He had grown much taller and altogether more imposing. Though he had not quite recovered from a rough crossing, he still exuded a sense of confidence and charm.

'It was with some emotion that I beheld Albert – who is *beautiful*,'[6] she wrote in her journal that night. There was no mention of Ernest, who had accompanied him. Though she later acknowledged the elder brother in references to 'my two dear cousins,' it was clear that she only had eyes for Albert. When Melbourne praised Ernest's brains, she snapped that Albert was far more clever. The two went riding by day and dancing at court balls in the evening. On 15 October, she told him shyly that it would make her 'too happy' if he consented to marry her, and both embraced warmly. After the tension of the previous week, it was a relief for them to have decided on the outcome which their families had eagerly awaited. Albert and Ernest stayed in England another four blissful weeks, leaving on 14 November.

The three months before their wedding were filled with problems. King Leopold wanted Albert to be made a peer, thinking it inappropriate for Her Majesty's husband to have a foreign title, while she wished him to be King consort. Thanks to Melbourne's prudent advice that they should not act hastily, nothing was done. The Queen's declaration of marriage, made on 23 November to the privy council, nearly caused an uproar. No reference was made to Prince Albert's religion, and rumour spread that he was a Roman Catholic. The Queen's anger at these two tiresome disagreements paled beside her fury when the annual allowance of £50,000 generally voted to a reigning Queen's consort, and proposed by Melbourne's administration, was reduced in parliament to £30,000. She felt bitterly that the Tory opposition was making a scapegoat of him because of his foreign birth. If she had been betrothed to her 'odious' cousin Prince George of Cambridge, she declared coldly, he would have been granted the full amount without a murmur.

Albert bowed to his humiliation with good grace. He found it unreasonable, however, of his future wife to thwart some of his wishes herself. Ever mindful of his instruction from Stockmar that the British royal household should be above politics, and aware of harm done by the bedchamber crisis and Lady Flora Hastings scandal, he wanted his personal staff to be composed of Whigs and Tories in equal measure, and in order to help him assuage his loneliness in a new country, he pleaded for the inclusion of non-political Germans in key posts. Primed by Melbourne and his reminders of 'unpopular foreigners,' she would not be swayed. She was equally adamant that they could not spend a long honeymoon at Windsor, telling him bluntly that she was the sovereign, 'and that business can stop and wait for nothing.'

Albert arrived at Buckingham Palace from Coburg on 8 February 1840, and the wedding took place two days later at the Chapel Royal, St James's. At the ceremony, it was remarked that Queen Victoria's eyes were 'much swollen with tears, but great happiness in her countenance,' while His Royal Highness Prince Albert seemed very awkward, embarrassed and 'agitated in his responses'.

Back at Windsor, reaction to her nervous excitement and the bustle of the last few days set in, and the Queen had such a headache that she retired to her sofa, unable to eat any dinner; 'but ill or not, I NEVER NEVER spent such an evening!!! My DEAREST DEAREST DEAR Albert sat on a footstool by my side, and his excessive love and affection gave me feelings of heavenly love and happiness, I never could have *hoped* to have felt before!'[7]

Early next morning, Victoria and Albert were out walking in the park, the Queen almost breathless as she kept pace with her husband's brisk long strides. Watching them, the Duchess of Bedford thought Her Majesty was 'excessively in love with him, but he not a bit with her.' The cynical diarist Charles Greville thought it 'strange that a bridal night should be so short,' and this 'was not the way to provide us with a Prince of Wales.'

The Queen intended to take her time over the latter. She hated and dreaded the idea of childbearing, and wanted at least one year of 'happy enjoyment' with Albert. Yet providence had other ideas. Within weeks she was *enceinte*. The tragedy of Princess Charlotte was still fresh in the public mind, and a visit by Queen Victoria to Claremont soon after her condition was known gave rise to macabre rumours. The Queen believed she too would succumb in childbirth, it was whispered, and she was furnishing Charlotte's bedroom as it had been on that melancholy occasion in 1817. Victoria was mindful of her cousin's fate, but her doctors and Melbourne assured her that the late princess had been kept 'too low' on a starvation diet, lack of exercise and unnecessary blood-letting. They told her the Hanoverians needed plenty of food and wine. Her hearty appetite would surely preserve her health, and Albert became anxious at her exuberant craving for exercise and walks.

Just as the events of summer 1839 had plunged the crown into deep unpopularity, so did an episode in June 1840 raise the newly-married Queen's stock even higher. She and Albert were leaving Buckingham Palace for a carriage drive up Constitution Hill, when two shots rang out and narrowly missed them. The would-be assassin, a mentally defective lad of eighteen named Edward Oxford, was apprehended and confined to an asylum. Almost ready to believe wild theories that King Ernest Augustus of Hanover was the *eminence grise* behind this dastardly attempt on their pregnant sovereign, the nation was deeply grateful for her escape. But the grim lesson was learnt that there were other hazards than childbirth which could take her life. In July parliament passed a bill in which Albert was to be appointed regent in the event of her premature death.

The Queen's confinement was expected in December. She was revolted by the never-ending precautions necessary, resented her increasing girth being the subject of so much attention at drawing rooms and levees, and complained bitterly at having to forego her pleasures of dancing and riding. Yet Albert's attention to her every need was beyond reproach. He was always there, ready to lift her from bed to sofa, wheel her from one room to another, or write her letters and read to her in a darkened room, lest she found the light too dazzling.

On 21 November, three weeks prematurely, she went into labour. Albert, the Duchess of Kent and the Queen's medical attendants were all present in the same room, while in an adjoining room were the councillors, including Melbourne, Palmerston and Lord John Russell. The Queen described the birth in a letter to Feodora some three weeks later: 'the last pains which are generally thought the worst I thought nothing of, they began at half past twelve and lasted till ten minutes to two when the young lady appeared . . . I never had any pain, nor any fever.'[8]

'Oh, Madam, it is a princess,' the doctor announced gravely.

'Never mind,' she answered, 'the next will be a Prince.'[9]

1

A Family of Eleven 1840–61

Queen Victoria was delighted that her first child was a daughter. As she would write rather tactlessly to this same princess after she had given birth to her eldest son some eighteen years later, 'Boys cause so much suffering, and sometimes one buys experience with one's first child and therefore a girl is sometimes better.'[1] Prince Albert had initially wanted a son, but his feelings turned to sheer delight when the midwife brought him the baby girl for the first time. Even by the standards of the average closely-knit family, this father-daughter relationship was destined to be remarkably close.

The Queen recovered so rapidly from her confinement that the court was able to spend Christmas at Windsor – a sparkling, festive occasion in the German tradition, with fir trees, candles, present-tables and log fires, like those Albert had enjoyed at Rosenau. They returned to Buckingham Palace early in the new year, and it was in the palace throne room that the princess was christened with the names Victoria Adelaide Mary Louisa – the second after the Queen Dowager, the third and fourth in honour of the Duchess of Kent, both of whom were among the godparents. The others were King Leopold, the Duke of Sussex, the Duchess of Gloucester, and the Duke of Coburg (represented by the Duke of Wellington). Albert was quick to sing his daughter's praises: 'She was awake, but did not cry at all, and seemed to crow with immense satisfaction at the sights and brilliant uniforms, for she is very intelligent and observing.'[2] A few weeks earlier, on 19 January, the hereditary 'style and distinction' of Princess Royal had been conferred on her. The last Princess Royal, Charlotte, later Queen of Württemberg, had died in 1828.

The boudoir and the breakfast room at Buckingham Palace became the royal nursery, and the little princess saw her mother twice a day. Her father was much less restrained, so much that his continual visits to see her and get down on his hands and knees to play did not pass without comment – not always favourable – from the household. He was rewarded by catching his daughter's first smile, and hearing her first word, which was naturally 'Papa'.

Vicky, or Pussy, as she was known in the family till the age of seven, was indeed the delight of both her parents. The Queen had an aversion to babies; she thought them 'frightful when undressed' until about four months old, and the idea of feeding her children herself was quite repugnant to her. Yet she was most enthusiastic in her letters to King Leopold, telling him how his great-niece gained daily in strength, health and beauty, and how she would be very like her dearest father – no small compliment. She had the child in her dressing-room every evening while she changed for dinner, and so lively did Pussy become while being bounced up and down on the nurse's knee that she could not get to sleep at night. It was very foolish, the Queen admitted, 'but one is very foolish with one's first child.'[3]

The public were so unaccustomed to the birth of a royal heir that rumours were quick to circulate concerning the baby's ill-health, that she was either blind or deformed. One journalist suggested that the Princess Royal should be put on public display in a glass case. Yet somebody did find a way to see her. When she was less than a fortnight old, a youth was discovered under a sofa at the palace. He was recognised as 'the boy Jones' (soon called 'In-I-Go Jones' by the press), seventeen-year-old son of a tailor, who had found his way into the building before. He claimed with pride that he had lived off scraps from the royal larders, 'that he had sat upon the throne, that he saw the Queen and heard the Princess Royal squall.' He was sent to a house of correction, and the nursery was thereafter fitted with new locks, Albert keeping the key under his pillow at night.

Pussy's exclusive reign as heir to her mother's throne did not last long. The Queen was furious to find that she was 'in for it' again so soon for the second time, barely before the first was christened. She had not intended to fulfil her promise of a prince so quickly. On 9 November 1841 Albert Edward, prince of Wales, 'Bertie' in the family, was born. He was described by his mother as 'wonderfully strong, with a very large nose and pretty little mouth.' Devoutly she hoped he would grow up to be just like his father.

The tranquillity that followed Vicky's birth did not recur on the second occasion. Queen Victoria's post-natal depression coincided with a long-overdue climax to a power struggle inside the royal household.

Albert had been deeply saddened by the ill feeling between his wife and her mother, and as he gradually learnt more about the state of affairs for himself, his concern turned to resentment against Lehzen. Victoria, he felt, was 'naturally a fine character but warped in many respects by wrong upbringing,' while the baroness was 'a crazy, common, stupid intriguer, obsessed with lust of power, who regards herself as a demi-god.' Her possessive nature had secretly resented the marriage between Victoria and Albert, yet still she interfered in the household administration as if nothing had changed since the Queen's accession. After the birth of the prince of Wales, she proposed that the duchy of Cornwall revenues should be handed over to her for nursery expenses. The way in which Lehzen was becoming a barrier between husband and wife was alarming. What, Albert wondered, were the implications of this for the upbringing and character of their children?

Albert's possessive instinct as a father added another dimension to the nursery problem. Queen Adelaide had told him that her children had not survived infancy because they had never been healthy, chiefly through lack of interest in food and inability to gain weight. As a result, he watched the progress of his daughter with almost obsessive interest, and when her health deteriorated after a promising start, he became worried. His resolve to see the last of Lehzen was strengthened.

In January 1842 the Queen and Albert returned to Windsor from a visit to the Duchess of Kent at Claremont. On their departure, household relations had been uneasy. Pussy was teething and 'not at all pleased with her little brother,' the Queen was tired and irritable, and Lehzen was suffering from jaundice. They went straight to the nursery on arriving home to find their daughter looking very thin and white. An altercation between Albert and the nurse made the Queen lose her temper. She accused him of wanting to drive the nurse away while he as good as murdered their child. He crept away in stony silence, but later that evening they quarrelled again. While she wept with rage, he resorted to pen and paper: 'Doctor Clark has mismanaged the child and poisoned her with calomel and you have starved her. I shall have nothing more to do with it; take the child away and do as you like and if she dies you will have it on your conscience.'[4]

In desperation she turned to Stockmar for advice. After tempers had cooled and the views of Melbourne and others had been sought, a compromise was reached. Lehzen was asked to retire with a generous annual pension, and a new governess should be appointed.

The rest of 1842 passed more happily. With Lehzen back in Germany, relations between the young couple, and between the Duchess of Kent and the Queen, improved rapidly. A respite from childbearing gave the Queen an opportunity to enjoy watching the progress of her children as well as undertaking some travelling with Albert around the country houses of England. By the end of the year she was accepting her third pregnancy less grudgingly.

On 25 April 1843 she gave birth to a second daughter, Alice. Alfred ('Affie') followed on 6 August 1844, and after an interval of nearly two years they were joined by Helena ('Lenchen') on 25 May 1846, one day after the Queen's twenty-seventh birthday.

The children were a lively, high-spirited crowd. It was fortunate for them that their upbringing was not carried out strictly according to the plans of their parents. Within a few months of their marriage, they had composed a joint memorandum on the education and development of princes, full of lofty phrases about the 'moral and intellectual faculties of man,' and strict instructions on hours of work, exercise and relaxation. Stockmar read it and declared gravely that any child subjected to such a regime would surely succumb to brain fever. He insisted on two things. Firstly, their children must be educated in England. Although he was German himself, he realised that the unpopularity of most of King George III's sons had been on account of their foreign education. Secondly, a lady of rank, 'well-educated and of irreproachable character,' must be placed in charge of the nursery as governess.

In Lady Lyttelton, soon nicknamed 'Laddle' by the children, they could hardly have chosen better. Her conscientious attitude to her duties exemplified in the daily report on her charges' diet, health and mental progress, was thoroughly approved of by Queen Victoria and Prince Albert. At the same time, her views on discipline sounded remarkably liberal for the time. Punishments, she maintained, 'wear out so soon and one is never sure they are understood by the child as belonging to the naughtiness.' References to the children receiving a 'good whipping' for bad behaviour meant perhaps no more than a sharp smack. Physical chastisement had no place under her supervision. The most effective punishment was to be deprived of a treat. To be denied a ride with their Papa or a carriage drive with Mama meant much more to the youngsters than being sent to their room for the afternoon or a scolding.

Pussy was a precocious child, quick to learn and always chattering. At the age of four she was taught a poem by Lamartine, including the line: '*Voilà le tableau qui se déroule à mes pieds*'. Not long afterwards, she was taken on a pony ride, and surveyed the view from a hill, repeating the line proudly with a theatrical flourish of her hand. She adored showing off, and the amusement her extrovert ways caused doubtless encouraged her. When a governess refused to stop on a carriage drive and pick her some heather from the roadside, the princess frowned, 'No, you can't,' she muttered indignantly, then glanced at two young ladies-in-waiting, 'but *those* girls might get out and fetch me some.' She was easily bored with routine, and often frustrated. The Queen found her 'difficult and rebellious' but Albert was delighted with her agile mind and winning ways.

If the Princess Royal could do no wrong, the prince of Wales could barely put a foot right. From the first day of his life, he was overshadowed by his mother's resentment. Her annoyance at having two pregnancies so quickly, and the severe labour at his birth, had given him a bad start in life. The weight of his eventual inheritance was another overwhelming burden. Though he had found fault with Albert's high-minded memorandum on education, Stockmar still concluded that it was in the monarchy's interests for Prince Albert Edward to be brought up according to the strictest moral principles. Because children were bound to imitate their elders, they should only be surrounded by those 'who will teach not only by precept but by living example.' Such philosophy found more favour at court than Melbourne's succinct belief that 'this damned morality will ruin everything.'

Bertie was as apathetic and backward as Vicky was precocious and eager to learn. She teased him for being slow-witted and mimicked his stammer. Their parents were too ready to contrast them both, to his detriment. His childish tantrums were a disruptive influence in the nursery. When opposed he would scream violently, stamp his feet and throw things around until he was exhausted. Unfortunately his faults were magnified, and Laddle was at first the only one to appreciate his positive qualities. When cheerful he could be charming, 'with a frequent very sweet smile,' and he was less given to lying than his sister. It was evident to Laddle that he preferred people to books, and in this he was most unlike his father. Although she had to admit that he was 'uncommonly averse to learning and requires much patience, from wilful inattention and constant interruptions,' and could be 'passionate and determined enough for an autocrat,' the fact that he spoke three languages by the age of six proves that he was by no means stupid. It was his misfortune that he was always compared to Vicky, who was exceptionally bright. Only an uncommonly clever boy could have come anything but a poor second to her.

None of the remaining children gave their parents as much trouble as the two eldest. Alice was a plump, easily-contented child, given to occasional bursts of temper but generally more placid than her sister. Bertie was always deeply attached to her, the relationship between both uncomplicated by the sense of inferiority he generally felt with Vicky. When Alice was sent to her room one day for being naughty, Bertie was caught paying her a clandestine visit. His excuse, he confessed wistfully, was that he only wanted to bring her 'a morsel of news.'

Affie showed signs of growing up more like his father. He was cheerful, placid and industrious. Utterly fearless, as soon as he could walk unaided he thought nothing of climbing out of windows and balancing on ledges thirty feet or more above ground, leaping across streams before he could swim, or sliding down banisters. Many was the time he had a narrow escape from serious injury and was scolded severely for taking risks, but he was not deterred from doing the same thing again. Though he got on very well with his brothers and sisters, he was equally happy left to his own devices, experimenting with toys and later building his own. A quick learner who showed particular aptitude for geography and the sciences, he was certainly his father's favourite son. Albert was inclined to regret that the boy would never inherit the crown, unless anything happened to 'poor Bertie'. Yet he consoled himself with the thought that Affie would succeed one day to the family's inheritance in Germany, the duchy of Saxe-Coburg Gotha, should Duke Ernest II and his wife, Alexandrine, remain childless.*

---

* Duke Ernest I, Albert's father, had died in February 1844. Ernest II had several illegitimate sons and daughters, but all of Alexandrine's pregnancies ended in miscarriages.

In January 1847 the Queen and her husband drew up another joint memorandum concerning the education of their present and future children. The princes and princesses were to be divided into classes. The first would be a nursery class, for all up to six years of age. Lady Lyttelton would be in charge of this, and the children would learn English, French, German and religious instruction. At the age of six, they would move into Class II. A new governess, Miss Hildyard, would then be in charge of them. She and two further governesses, one German and one Swiss, would still be responsible to Lady Lyttelton. Religious instruction would be given to the Princess Royal by the Queen, to the prince of Wales by both senior governesses. It was important that all the children should be able to converse in foreign languages as well as learning grammar. All problems, outings and punishments, should be referred to the Queen. The Princess Royal and the Prince of Wales would begin in Class II at the end of February 1847. One hour a day each would be devoted to French and German. The Princess Royal was to have her own maid, and would remain under the supervision of Miss Hildyard until she was nine or ten, when she would have a 'lady governess' to remain with her until marriage. The prince would enter a third class a year or two later, by which time he would have a tutor and a valet.

Sunday was to be free from lessons. Prince Albert loved to get on all fours and play in the nursery with the children. Always shy with adults, he was never more at ease than with his ever-growing brood, playing hide-and-seek, giving them rides on his back, and building houses with wooden bricks so tall he had to stand on a chair to complete them. The governess swore that none of the youngsters were as thrilled as he was when the houses toppled over and scattered around the floor. 'He is so kind to them,' wrote the Queen, a little enviously, 'and romps with them so delightfully, and manages them so beautifully and firmly.' She took less interest in them, attributing this to the fact that she had been brought up almost exclusively in adult company.

When they were older, Albert planned plays and *tableaux* for them, taking charge of rehearsals and designing their costumes. One of the most ambitious was a *tableau* they performed in February 1854, representing the four seasons. Alice was spring, Vicky was summer, Affie was Bacchus (representing autumn) in a leopard skin and crowned with grapes, Bertie was winter as an old man dressed for bitter weather, icicles hanging from his coat and hat. The younger children took smaller roles, but the short blue frock of Arthur (born in 1850) so startled his mother that she ordered him to be taken away and dressed, despite a nurse's reassurance that he was wearing 'flesh-coloured decencies'. He came back after putting on a pair of socks that barely came above his ankles.

Prince Albert differed from Queen Victoria in preferring peaceful countryside to the bustle of town and city life. He firmly believed that it was essential to bring the family up with all the benefits of an outdoor life in which he had revelled as a boy. They required something better than the London setting of Buckingham Palace, and the pomp and formality of Windsor Castle, while building at fashionable Brighton had accelerated so much since the regency period that the Pavilion no longer afforded them any privacy.

In 1844 they purchased Osborne House on the Isle of Wight, demolished the existing eighteenth-century mansion, and replaced it with a new Italianate building. With its wooded views, spacious grounds and views across the Solent, it was ideal as a main holiday home for them all. Even the newest arrival in the nursery could enjoy yachting, and each fine summer day at Osborne would find them all aboard the grand *Victoria and Albert*, or in a small steam yacht *Fairy*. There was always something to keep everyone occupied on board, whether looking out to sea through Papa's telescope, sketching on deck, or pretending to steer. Later a small chalet, the Swiss cottage, was erected in the grounds as a den where the princes could learn carpentry and gardening, the princesses housekeeping and cooking. Garden plots were laid out for each child, miniature barrows, trolleys and tools marked with their initials. Albert accompanied them on rambles, imparting to them the delights of nature study and starting them on their collections of wild flowers, shells and fossils, all of which would be painstakingly labelled and arranged in the family museum.

After a visit to the Scottish Highlands, the Queen and Albert rented a property at Balmoral, and on purchasing it in 1852, they pulled down the small house and erected a larger one in its place. In the remote hills of Aberdeenshire there were long pony expeditions and picnics, deer-stalking, shooting and fishing excursions, caves to explore and wild flowers to collect and press by day. In the evening there was Scottish dancing to the sound of the bagpipes. Much as visiting ministers and distant relatives might grumble about the tedium of Osborne or freezing temperatures at Balmoral, the family were never happier than when relaxing at either of these homes.

Moreover, Osborne and Balmoral were both built along modern lines, with plumbing and sanitary systems well in advance of their time. Windsor and Buckingham Palace were notorious for their primitive drainage. It was no coincidence that all nine children lived to maturity. They always returned from holidays full of energy, refreshed and invigorated by outdoor life. Though prone to childhood colds and sometimes chilblains, they escaped the more serious diseases which carried off many an infant in the nineteenth century.

On occasion there was the added excitement of a cruise in *Victoria and Albert* around the coast of southern England, or in 1852 even further afield across the North Sea. The children, dressed as 'little tars', became seasoned travellers, mercilessly mimicking their mother's ladies. When asked how she was enjoying herself, Vicky would lie down and plead that she was very ill, feigning the groans and nauseated expressions of less fortunate members of their suite.

Despite their exalted status, they were certainly not indulged in a life of luxury. They generally ate plain food, and slept in sparsely-furnished bedrooms with little heating. Queen Victoria was unusually impervious to cold, and would not tolerate fires unless it was exceptionally chilly. Their daily clothes were the same as those worn by any other middle-class family of the time, except those kept for special or state occasions, and were handed down to the younger children when outgrown by the elder.

The first five children were all born in a relatively trouble-free era. In 1848 a threat arose.

'What dismal times are these!' Albert wrote gloomily to his stepmother on 29 February. 'France is in flames; Belgium is menaced.'[5] The French monarchy had been overthrown, ex-King Louis Philippe and his family were refugees, fleeing across the channel to the safety of England. With reports of unrest in Italy, Austria and the German confederation, it seemed as if the entire continent might be engulfed by revolution. To make matters worse, the Queen was approaching her sixth confinement. She was allowed barely a moment's rest, comforting her careworn husband one minute, organising accommodation for their destitute Bourbon guests at Buckingham Palace the next. Alice and Affie were of an age to appreciate the excitement of the occasion, thrilled to be playing with their young cousins and adapting at once to their temporary dormitories in the servants' quarters, but Vicky and Bertie were distressed at sensing from their parents' drawn expressions that something was seriously wrong.

The Queen had a painful labour, complicated by the tension she was undergoing. Fortunately the new baby princess, born on 18 March, was large and healthy. She was named Louise after Albert's mother. The Queen recovered quickly from her confinement, but their worries were not over. Within a fortnight, she and Albert were warned of a huge Chartist demonstration planned in London on 10 April. With the probability of riots and republican agitation, ministers advised the family to leave the capital for a while. They retreated in an orderly fashion to Osborne. Luckily the 'demonstration' was remarkably tame. Only a few thousand of the expected half million turned out for the march from Kennington Common to Westminster. The nervous leaders proceeded peacefully in cabs to parliament and handed in their charter, signatories to which included the Duke of Wellington, H.M. Queen Victoria and Mr Punch. The court soon returned to Buckingham Palace.

Because she entered the world at a time of upheaval, her mother feared Louise would 'turn out something peculiar.' On the other hand, omens for the future of the next royal baby could not have been more propitious. As her confinement approached in the spring of 1850, the Queen decided that if it was a boy she would name him Arthur, in honour of the Duke of Wellington. Much was made by the press of the new prince's arrival on 1 May 1850, the venerable Duke's eighty-first birthday. He was delighted to accept his sovereign's invitation to be the prince's godfather, declaring gallantly that this gave him even more pleasure than his many military decorations.

From the cradle, young Arthur was fascinated by anything to do with the army – the sight of a red uniform, the sound of a military band, or watching the changing of the guard at Buckingham Palace, had him spellbound. 'Arta is going to be a soldier,' he proudly informed the family. In every way, he seemed perfect. A strong, healthy baby, he was an even-tempered lad with none of the irritability or tantrums of the older children, the courage yet not the recklessness of Affie.

At the age of seven and a half, Albert and Stockmar agreed, the Prince of Wales was to be handed over to a tutor. They believed he needed another man to take him in hand and prepare him for his inheritance; and, in Queen Victoria's words, he 'had been injured by being with the Princess Royal (who) puts him down by a word or a look.' To be reminded constantly of his intellectual inferiority was undermining his confidence.

Unwittingly, Vicky was one cause of his childhood problems, though his natural capacity for affection for his sister was never soured by the mental differences between them. Stockmar was a far more malign influence. The prospect of this unsatisfactory boy succeeding to the throne if his mother should die suddenly with Prince Albert as regent until the son was eighteen, but with no officially-recognised title, was galling.

Too much has been made of the apparent antipathy of Victoria and Albert to their eldest son. When he was five, she was 'much touched by Bertie asking me to do his little Sunday lesson with him sometimes.' On his ninth birthday, she noted in her journal that there was 'much good in him . . . he has such affectionate feelings – great truthfulness and great simplicity of character.'[6] Sadly, the parents were swayed too easily by Stockmar's excessive fault-finding, his forebodings that the prince of Wales was the reincarnation of his reprobate great-uncles. They were quick to criticise his shortcomings, not ready enough to praise him where credit was due. 'He is my caricature,' the Queen remarked perceptively. In him she saw the extroverted Hanoverian spirits, hasty temper, and aversion to studying – qualities she herself possessed and tried hard to tame. Stockmar recognised it as well, calling him an 'exaggerated copy' of his mother. In no way, they regretted, did he resemble his beloved father.

His first tutor was Henry Birch, a former assistant master at Eton. He was engaged to teach the heir calculating, geography and English, while other masters taught languages, religion, handwriting, drawing and music. Six days a week the timetable was divided into five hourly or half-hour periods. Lessons were never discontinued for more than a few days at a time, but family birthdays were always holidays, and there was inevitably a relaxation in routine when the court moved from London to Windsor. Though Bertie resented this demanding regime, and was often sullen or temperamental, he became greatly attached to Birch.

Though he did not wish to prejudice his employment by saying so, the tutor saw that his charge was being worked too hard. In consequence, he used discipline in moderation, and rewarded the prince for good work with afternoon rambles in the countryside which turned into exciting games of make-believe, readily calculated to appeal to a boy's imagination. After he had taken holy orders and resigned his post, to be succeeded by Frederick Gibbs, Birch wrote a report for Prince Albert on the prince of Wales as a pupil. While the boy had been extremely disobedient, impertinent and selfish at first, a sensible amount of discipline had the right effect. He soon showed his 'very amiable and affectionate disposition.' Prophetically Birch spoke of his 'very good memory, very singular powers of observation.' He had already seen what Albert and Stockmar had failed to realise – that the future king of England would always learn more from people than from books.

Throughout 1850, Prince Albert's greatest preoccupation, apart from his family, was with the great exhibition at Crystal Palace, a monumental tribute to the industrial and artistic skills of peacetime Britain and her empire. Already he suspected that the nineteen-year-old Prince Frederick William ('Fritz') of Prussia might be a suitable candidate for his eldest daughter's hand. He and Queen Victoria had met the prince's parents, William and Augusta, and Stockmar suggested inviting the family to the exhibition's opening ceremony in May 1851. In order to make the implications of this less obvious, other European royalties should be asked to attend as well. After a curt refusal, William relented and brought his wife, Augusta, and children, Fritz and twelve-year-old Louise.

Fritz was captivated by the ten-year-old Vicky. At their first meeting, in Buckingham Palace, he spoke to her in halting English, and she replied in fluent German. She had visited the exhibition before it opened, and she knew so much about items on display that she astounded him with her knowledge as she conducted him on an improvised tour around the displays, full of energy despite the heat and dust which made his head ache. At the same time, with tact well in advance of her ten years, she neatly took him by the arm to show him something different every time his ill-matched parents began to bicker. After a short but very happy stay with the family at Osborne, and a brief visit to Liverpool, Fritz returned to Prussia spellbound by the glimpse of life in England he had just seen. That Christmas, he and Vicky began to exchange letters.

Queen Victoria's eighth confinement was the first to be eased by chloroform, the effect of which she found 'soothing, quieting and delightful beyond measure.' Prince Leopold was born on

7 April 1853; his birth was easy and she recovered rapidly. Unfortunately he failed to thrive. 'Little Leo' suffered from weak digestion which made him thinner than his brothers and sisters, and his cry was feeble. On learning to walk, he bruised easily when falling over and cried out as if in severe pain. The doctors diagnosed in him the grave and incurable condition of haemophilia, a hereditary bleeding disease.

Medical and scientific theory have singled Queen Victoria out as the first royal carrier of haemophilia. The gene may have originated in her by spontaneous mutation, or it may have been inherited through her mother, though no instances of it have been traced in the Duchess of Kent's relations. Leopold was the only victim among the Queen's children and therefore the only male carrier. Two of her daughters, Alice and (the as yet unborn) Beatrice, transmitted it to their children and grandchildren, with disastrous results for the Russian and Spanish dynasties into which their daughters married.

From then on, Leopold was his parents' 'child of anxiety'. The Queen tried to protect him from physical accidents with an obsessive anxiety which he resisted, wanting to behave and be treated like his older brothers. Albert did his best to make light of the boy's condition, hoping he might grow out of it in time.

In 1854 England and France went jointly to war with Russia. During the Crimean conflict, Vicky and Alice accompanied Queen Victoria on visits to the wounded in hospital in London. When Florence Nightingale, the heroine of Scutari, was invited to Balmoral, the children were captivated by her and the work she had done in assuaging the suffering of the troops. She had set an example which the two eldest princesses would follow faithfully during wars in Germany during the next decade.

England's ally, Emperor Napoleon, paid a state visit to England in spring the following year, and this was reciprocated in August 1855. Vicky and Bertie accompanied their parents to Paris, where they were introduced to the Prussian ambassador Bismarck among other people, and found their few days in the second empire an exhilarating experience. For Vicky, the greatest moment was a waltz with the emperor in the *Salle des Glaces* at Versailles. As for Bertie, this first sight of the glittering court was one he would never forget, and Paris remained secure in his affections to the end of his days. Before they left, he begged Empress Eugenie to ask his mother if he and his sister could stay a little longer; 'they (his parents) don't want us, and there are six more of us at home!'

By this time, Vicky's fifteenth birthday was approaching and it was time for her matrimonial future to be considered more seriously. The Queen and Albert therefore invited Fritz to Balmoral in September 1855. 'He wishes to see Scotland,' Albert coyly informed the Duchess of Kent, but neither the older royal family nor the press were deceived. On his train journey from London, Fritz recognised and stopped to talk to the Duke of Cambridge. 'So evidently that marriage is to be,' the Duke wrote to his mother that evening as he described the meeting.

Vicky was astonished at the change in this handsome young suitor, still the same gentle unaffected friend she had known before but more manly and far more handsome. He was struck by the way in which a lively, attractive little girl was maturing into such a beautiful young woman. Queen Victoria and Prince Albert had agreed beforehand that they would not force the issue. If their daughter and guest were not impressed with each other, so be it.

One day while they were briefly alone, Vicky took Fritz's hand and squeezed it tightly. He was so elated that he had his first good night's sleep since arriving in Scotland, realising that he would almost certainly be returning to Berlin with the good news expected of him. Next day after breakfast, he took his courage in both hands and asked her parents if he could 'belong to our family.' Proposal, he said, had long been his wish. The Queen thought Vicky too young to decide just yet, but she was due to be confirmed the following April. Fritz should attend the ceremony if possible and propose to her afterwards. But he could not wait that long. He asked for permission to give her a bracelet and the Queen consented, adding that 'something had to be told her and he had better tell her himself.'

Later that week, the family went out riding up the heather-covered slopes of Craig-na-Ban, pausing to admire the view from the summit before proceeding down again. Fritz and Vicky lagged behind the rest. When they reached the carriage both were glowing with happiness, she holding a sprig of white heather he had given her as he asked the most important question of their lives. It was an emotional farewell when Fritz had to take his leave two days later.

In recognition of her new status as a betrothed princess and future Queen of Prussia, from that time onwards mother, father and daughter dined together *à trois* in the evenings.

Queen Victoria and Prince Albert had almost acquired a son-in-law before their family was complete. On 14 April 1857 the Queen gave birth to her ninth and last child, Princess Beatrice. Though she could note triumphantly in her journal a fortnight afterwards that she 'felt better and stronger this time than I have ever done before',[7] Albert had been warned by Dr Clark the previous year that he feared for her reason if she bore another child. Even she had confided nervously to the doctor that she felt sure 'she would sink under it.' It was as well that she stopped six short of her grandmother Queen Charlotte's total.

The Queen's emotions were now complicated by mixed feelings at Vicky's imminent departure. She was tortured by misgivings at having let her eldest child commit herself so young to the prospect of 'going to Berlin, more or less the *enemy's den!*'[8] Yet she shared Bertie's sense of intellectual inferiority at Vicky's dazzling cleverness, and was jealous of the close bond between father and daughter. Both would converse on the most erudite subjects, scientific, political, literary and artistic, at a level which left the Queen totally out of her depth. Even Albert was driven to remonstrate with his wife on occasions that she seemed only too pleased at the thought of being rid of their child.

Fritz came to England regularly. He was not the only German visitor at court, for his physician Dr Wegner had been summoned to attend Queen Victoria's last confinement 'to see how things are managed here.' Vicky and Fritz attended Beatrice's christening in their capacity as godparents.

Another landmark was reached that summer. The last of George III's children, the Duchess of Gloucester, died in May 1857. Such a fuss had been made over Prince Albert's precedence in 1840, and his lack of a title still rankled. As he wrote to his brother Ernest, 'wicked people' might still wish to give the prince of Wales precedence over his own father. Informed by the prime minister Lord Palmerston that His Royal Highness could not be made Prince Consort by act of parliament owing to a legal technicality, the Queen conferred the title on him by letters patent on 25 June.

The nine children and their parents were together for the last time that Christmas. A family sojourn at Balmoral was saddened by the Highlanders' farewells to Vicky as they told her tearfully they would never see her again. The other royal children were no less affected themselves. On Fritz's regular visits to England, Alice was generally so overcome that she burst into tears at the merest sight of him. For her part, Vicky's affection for her home threatened to overwhelm her at the prospect of marriage and separation from the security of her childhood surroundings. While studying literature with her father, hard mental work being his antidote for homesickness, her mind would wander and she would lament through her tears that 'the little sister will never have known me in the house.'

Vicky and Fritz were married on 25 January 1858 at the chapel of St James's, where her parents had been married. Vicky's self-possession, which she maintained with no little effort, made a strange contrast to the Queen's nervousness and her father's grim expression, all three captured in a daguerreotype made that morning at the palace where the Queen's likeness was blurred as she trembled so much. Apart from the archbishop's bungling of the words, the ceremony was a great success, the dignity of bride and groom winning praise from all quarters. Even the Prussians, who had been disgruntled because Queen Victoria had firmly decreed that the marriage should take place in London and not Berlin, were quick to call it 'the event of the year.'

Like the bride's parents, the young couple were only permitted a two-day honeymoon before the court joined them at Windsor. On 2 February, a day of bitter wind and snow, the Queen and her children wept at the parting as Albert, Bertie and Affie joined the bride and groom on their journey to Gravesend. There Fritz led Vicky to her cabin, where she clung to her father in a last embrace, loath to leave him. He stood on the quay with his sons, watching sadly as the yacht *Victoria and Albert* slowly moved across the North Sea. That night he finally gave way to his suppressed emotions in the first of several long, tender letters to his favourite child. 'I am not of a demonstrative nature, and therefore you can hardly know how dear you have always been to me, and what a void you have left in my heart.'[9]

Though Vicky had not yet come of age she was effectively no longer the responsibility of her parents – much as their letters appeared to overlook the fact. They therefore redoubled their attention on the future King of England. When Bertie reached his seventeenth birthday, he was awarded an annual allowance of £500, mainly for clothing, but with instructions never to 'wear anything extravagant.' In a long and unnecessarily sermonising letter, Prince Albert encouraged him to 'try and emancipate yourself as much as possible from the thraldom of abject dependence on servants', and warned him that 'life is composed of duties, and in the due, punctual and cheerful performance of them the true Christian, true soldier and true gentleman is recognised.'[10] Gibbs resigned his post as tutor, to be replaced by a governor, Colonel Robert Bruce, and a staff of equerries.

Accompanied by Bruce and Teasdale, he was allowed to spend three weeks in Germany with Vicky and Fritz. Desperately homesick and expecting her first child early in the new year, Vicky was as delighted to welcome him for a while as she had Affie in the late summer, and she spared no effort to entertain him. Fritz played his part as the perfect host, and it was at this time that the brothers-in-law forged a close bond which was to survive many a stormy passage ahead in the era of Bismarck's wars.

Bertie returned to Windsor for Christmas, dismaying his parents by talking animatedly about people, parties and balls. Questions about German art and architecture were met with the briefest of answers. Classical culture was never his forte; after an expedition to Rome the following year, he complained about being dragged around the relics of Roman civilisation: 'You look at two mouldering stones and are told it's the temple of something.'[11]

Though Bertie grumbled about the degree of parental supervision to which he was still subjected, his elder sister was hardly less free from their authority. Vicky's letters from her parents were commanding at best, tactless at worst. 'Much as you should avoid every appearance of your new home not being sufficient for you,' Prince Albert told her, 'you must not, on the other hand, give the impression that you wish to discard your country or let it drop.'[12] She must not forget the country of her birth, or what it owed her; there would be nothing in 'these two-fold affections and duties' which would ever clash. It would be a source of pride to all if she was to be known for ever after as 'the English princess', a title her enemies at court were later to give her. Had Albert, the prince who had been regarded by society as something of an outcast because of his foreign birth, ever asked to be called 'the Coburg prince'?

When Vicky became pregnant, the Queen told her it was 'horrid news' which upset them dreadfully, as she felt nothing would come of it. A more incomprehensible remark for a mother to make to her married seventeen-year-old daughter would be hard to imagine. Why was Affie allowed to 'play the sailor' when he came to visit her, instead of improving himself on a tour of the palaces and galleries at Berlin? Why had she not spoken to Colonel Bruce about Bertie's faults? Why must she be 'making too much' of her condition, and exaggerating her physical discomfort 'as you always do'? Vicky had fallen down a set of stairs in the summer, which could not have done her any good. Confused and anxious, she asked Fritz for his advice. He suggested they turn to Stockmar, who was then in Berlin, and ask him to intercede on her behalf. After being consulted Stockmar called on Lord Clarendon, the foreign secretary, and told him that the Queen was behaving extremely badly to her daughter, who was 'worried and frightened to death.' At the same time he wrote in more guarded but no less forthright terms to the prince consort, who took the hint. From then on the letters to Vicky were far less demanding.

By now, the circle of nine children was reduced to seven. With Affie's zeal for everything nautical, it was evident that his future lay in the Royal Navy. In June 1856 he had been taken under the wing of a governor, Lieutenant John Cowell of the Royal Engineers, to superintend his training for the service, and to separate him from Bertie, whose influence Albert believed was harmful. The brothers had shared lessons with Birch and Gibbs, but when the bright and industrious Affie began to imitate Bertie's lazy habits and fits of temper, Albert felt enough was enough.

Affie and Cowell moved briefly into White Lodge, Windsor, and then Alverbank, a large house near Gosport. Here the budding sailor was coached in mathematics and geometry, and was given instruction in seamanship and navigation. In April 1857 he made a brief visit to Geneva to improve his French, and spent some time in Coburg with Ernest and Alexandrine. That autumn at Balmoral the prince consort initiated him into the problems of methodical estate management, something which would stand him in good stead when he eventually succeeded to the duchy of Coburg. For relaxation father and son went shooting and stalking together. As Bertie was still such a disappointment Albert was reassured to some extent by believing that the duchy would be in good hands with this second son who so resembled him in character and interests.

In August 1858 Affie sat his naval entrance examination, and passed with excellent results. After a few days at Balmoral and a short time with Vicky and Fritz in Prussia, Midshipman Prince Alfred joined HMS *Euryalus*, a unit of the Mediterranean Fleet. The

Queen bitterly lamented his going to sea, telling Vicky sadly that it was 'much better to have no children than to have them only to give them up,'[13] while to Albert, the departure of 'the second child lost to our family circle within one year' was 'another great trial'.

Affie sailed home into Portsmouth in February 1860. He had been away from the rest of the family for sixteen months, and much had happened to the rest of them in that time. He, his brothers and sisters had become uncles and aunts in January 1859 with the birth of Vicky's eldest child William, news which caused much excitement at Windsor. Arthur had run around the corridors jubilantly shouting: 'I am an uncle!' while Louise defiantly answered to an order issued to 'the royal children in the schoolroom' that 'we are not royal children, we are uncles and aunts.' Not for some time was it known that in the course of Vicky's prolonged labour, both mother and child had been in such danger that the German doctors were almost prepared to give them up as beyond salvation. Thanks to the single-minded determination of a Scottish doctor sent over specially by the anxious Queen Victoria, both survived, but Prince William entered the world with a permanently damaged left arm.

Bertie had gone to study at the universities of Edinburgh and Oxford, but at the latter he resented not being permitted to reside in the city like an ordinary undergraduate, but instead at Frewen Hall with Bruce and Teasdale. Though he made an effort at his studies and examinations, his parents lamented that he gave too much attention to the pleasures of hunting and rich food, and not nearly enough to his work.

Alice was also on the threshold of maturity. At the age of sixteen, she was beginning to show signs of independence, even stirrings of rebellion against her royal status. As a child she had enjoyed being able to escape the restrictions of her position, finding it tremendous fun to shed family dignity and slip into services at St George's Chapel in ordinary clothes, sitting at the back with her mother's subjects. In the Scottish Highlands she would gladly accompany the Queen, distributing food and clothing to the poorer cottagers. This desire to help those less fortunate then herself persisted throughout her tragically short life. Almost imperceptibly she began to lose confidence in herself, sensitive to criticism, anxious that she was not living up to her parents' expectations, and lacking Vicky's resilience in fighting back against life's problems, failing to see them as a challenge.

It was a trying adolescent phase not helped by her experience with the Prince of Orange, who was chosen by Queen Victoria and Vicky as a possible suitor. Alice was immediately taken by the prospect of becoming Queen of Holland. His initial good behaviour, however, soon turned to rudeness, and gradually it became apparent that he had the makings of an incorrigible womaniser. Alice was left with the dubious consolation of counting her blessings that she had not become betrothed to such a rake after all.

Queen Victoria and Prince Albert had always been impressed by the close bond between Alice and Bertie. There were times during childhood when it seemed she alone could calm him out of his tempers and moods, sharing with him (though she did not like to admit it) a sense of inferiority at being overshadowed by the brilliant Vicky. Even in adolescence she could say things to him, particularly about his behaviour to the rest of the family, that he would have resented from anyone else.

This bond had its parallel in the relations between Affie and Helena. Both had much in common, apart from being physically the toughest as children. Helena was much more level-headed than her more complicated elder sisters, lacking their emotional moments, and therefore far less trouble to the Queen and Albert. Though only fair at art and sewing, and heavy-handed as a piano pupil, she was excellent at mental arithmetic and practical subjects. Like Affie, she revelled in outdoor life, enjoyed long walks and rides, was a good swimmer, and complained crossly that running races against girls was no fun. She had inherited something of her father's fascination with engines and machines, and would spend hours below deck on yachting expeditions at Osborne learning how everything worked. Getting her hands covered in grease never bothered her at all, much as the Queen lamented that dear Lenchen cared far too little about her appearance. The tomboy in the family, she had no use for arguments or quarrels if a bumptious brother tried to tease her. A firm punch on the nose was her solution.

If Helena was the plainest of the sisters, Louise was certainly the prettiest. From childhood she was attractive; even her mother, who never shrank from speaking plainly about the ugliness of most of her brood in turn, could not find fault with her fourth daughter's looks. As a girl she was very lively, if prone to occasional bursts of moodiness. She also outshone all her sisters, with the possible exception of Vicky, in being the most artistic. From the age of three she showed a marked talent for drawing and painting. Executing landscapes and portraits from memory, with a remarkable eye for detail, came easily to her.

Arthur, the born soldier, was in his mother's eyes the least troublesome and most obedient of the nine. 'This Child is dear, *dearer* than any of the others put together, thus *after you* he is the *dearest* and *most precious* object to *me* on *Earth*,'[14] she wrote to the prince consort in October 1858. He had inherited his father's diffidence, and as a boy always found it an effort to meet strangers. As Affie's passion for the navy had always been evident, so it was with Arthur and all things military. Boxes of lead soldiers representing British army regiments were among his earliest toys, and after Vicky's marriage Prussian soldiers were naturally added to these. At the age of five, his favourite Christmas present was a replica of a Guards uniform, complete with bearskin and sword. When staying at Osborne, Prince Albert helped the princes to build a miniature fort in the garden, and this was Arthur's beloved playground for hours on end, as he lay on his stomach behind one of the cannon, planning battles and manoeuvres with his model soldiers. If anybody rivalled his father as a living hero it was his great-uncle Leopold, who had fought against Napoleon Bonaparte. Needless to say, his favourite reading matter consisted of accounts of the Napoleonic and Peninsular wars in which the glorious figure of his late godfather the Duke of Wellington (who died in 1852) loomed large as the mighty victor.

To his mother, the delicate Leopold was 'a very common-looking child' whose deportment was atrocious, but at the same time 'a very clever, amusing but absurd child.' He learned to read quickly and his choice of books was often precocious. At the age of five he wanted to know all about the classical paintings on his father's study wall at Osborne House, and like Louise he showed talent at wielding a brush himself. Music was another source of interest; he enjoyed singing and playing the piano. Yet he longed to join in the rough-and-tumble of the others, and it was galling for him to have to lie on a sofa for days on end to recover from minor childhood accidents. Prince Albert knew how to handle him better than anybody else, refusing to show excessive sympathy, helping him to master the slight speech defect that was a consequence of epilepsy, and always making time to keep his agile mind occupied. When not confined to the sofa he was allowed to ride, take part in amateur theatricals so beloved by the family, and go for walks in the countryside to hunt for flowers and geological specimens – but always under strict supervision.

Beatrice, who was and always remained 'Baby' to her mother well into adult life, was treated more indulgently than her brothers and sisters had ever been. When forbidden certain foods at table, the Queen scolded her half-heartedly with a rejoinder that 'baby mustn't have that.' 'But she likes it, my dear,' Beatrice answered, mimicking her mother's voice to perfection as she helped herself. 'I was very naughty last night,' she announced proudly one day. 'I would not speak to Papa, but it doesn't signify much.'[15]

Queen Victoria realised that much of the zest had gone out of her husband by this time. Overwork, world-weariness and the heartache he had suffered with Vicky's departure for Berlin, combined to sap his energy. She noticed how the tired, worried expression left his face when he watched their beloved youngest child playing, and how happy he was when she crawled across his knees as he played his favourite German airs on the organ.

Family and household alike recorded her more delightful sayings, such as when she refused to be picked up by a lady-in-waiting while convalescent from measles – 'I still have a little Weazle and you might take it.'[16] At the age of three she was an aunt twice over, to Vicky's William and Charlotte (born in July 1860 after a much easier labour than the first). This gave her another excuse to ignore things she did not wish to do. 'I have no time – I must write letters to my niece.'

1860 was destined to be the last year in which the family circle of eleven remained unbroken, albeit widely dispersed. It was also notable in that it marked the start of Bertie's and Affie's careers as widely-travelled royal ambassadors. Throughout her life Queen Victoria never set foot outside Europe, but she was adept at sending the family to various corners of the globe in order that the monarchy should be seen overseas.

The Prince of Wales' efforts at Oxford had not gone unnoticed, and even the pedantic Stockmar wrote to congratulate Queen Victoria and the prince consort on the great improvement in their son after meeting him at Coburg. It was decided, partly as experience and partly as a reward, to despatch him on a tour of Canada and the United States of America. In the course of this, he was to open the St Lawrence Bridge at Montreal, lay a foundation stone for the federal parliament building at Ottawa, and pay a courtesy call on the American president, James Buchanan.

At these functions he acquitted himself with great distinction. At last he could demonstrate that, whatever his shortcomings as a man of learning, he had the charm and social talent that befitted a future King. Although he was instructed to travel incognito, in the States as 'Baron Renfrew' it was too much to hope that the cheering crowds which greeted him everywhere would not acknowledge him as heir to the world's greatest empire. The prince had been unprepared for such adulation, but he enjoyed every moment to the full. For him the highlight was a ball at the New York Academy of Music, to which 3,000 guests had been invited but 5,000 turned up. Shortly before the guest of honour was due to arrive, the floor caved in, but nobody was hurt and the assembled multitudes waited patiently as carpenters and workmen came speedily to the rescue. Bruce wrote censoriously that the prince was 'somewhat persecuted by attentions not in strict accordance with good breeding', but needless to say Bertie did not object. Though his parents were a little too quick to impress upon him that the success of his tour had been due largely to the efforts of Bruce and to the fact that he was their representative, the Queen could not conceal a note of admiration for this previously unsatisfactory eldest son. To Vicky, she wrote that 'he was immensely popular everywhere and really deserves the highest praise, which should be given him all the more as he was never spared any reproof.'[17]

Affie had also worked hard at the social round, many thousand miles away from home. After a few weeks in England in the spring of 1860, during which he passed his midshipman's examination and was prepared for confirmation, he set sail for South Africa. Though still not quite sixteen years old, he coped very well with the itinerary made out for him, be it hunting expeditions in the veldt, releasing the first load of stones for the Table Bay breakwater, or opening the Cape Town public library. He sailed into Portsmouth that November, full of animated accounts of his expeditions, and laden heavily with animal trophies and photographs. The prince consort had engaged a professional photographer to show Affie the rudiments of this infant science so that he should have something to occupy his mind during leisure hours, and enrich the royal photograph albums at the same time. Queen Victoria could not praise him enough: 'He is really such a dear, gifted, handsome child, that it makes one doubly anxious he should have as few failings as mortal man can have.'[18]

All the children except Vicky were together at Windsor that Christmas. Joining them was another guest, Prince Louis of Hesse and the Rhine. He had initially been invited to stay earlier that year. A kindly if rather uninspiring young man, he impressed Queen Victoria and Prince Albert sufficiently for them to be convinced he would make Alice a good husband. He had not yet fallen prey to the temptations of the flesh, and being heir to a relatively minor German state, it seemed unlikely that he – and more importantly Alice – would be required to spend as much time after marriage in Germany as Vicky and Fritz were obliged to. In November 1860 he obtained leave from his regiment in Hesse and returned to Windsor. After prompting, he proposed to Alice and was dutifully accepted. It was arranged that they should be married in January 1862, and Louis stayed with them over Christmas – a chilling experience in every way, for it turned out to be the coldest festive season of the century so far. The Thames was frozen solid, and a freezing white fog hung over Windsor Great Park for days on end.

'How wisely it is ordained that in general we do not know our destiny and end,' Prince Albert wrote to Vicky, informing her of Alice's betrothal, 'but for this, no one would wish to live.'[19] The family's destiny was to give these words an ironic ring within the next twelve months, for 1861 was to be marked by one death after another.

On new year's day, Vicky and Fritz were summoned through the cold dark streets of Potsdam on foot to the deathbed of their uncle King Frederick William IV, who had been little more than a living vegetable for the last four or five years. Fritz's father, now King William I of Prussia, was aged sixty-three and in uncertain health. In his rare moods of optimism the prince consort might have looked forward to the day when he would write proudly to his eldest daughter as Her Majesty Queen Victoria of Prussia.

Later that month Queen Victoria and Prince Albert were distressed by the death of their physician Dr William Baly, killed in a railway accident at Wimbledon, and in February Sir George Couper, the Duchess of Kent's secretary, died after a short illness. 'Grandmama Kent', as the children called her, had been loved and respected by all the family since Albert's tireless peacemaking efforts soon after their marriage, and since the removal of Lehzen and Conroy from the royal household. A warm-hearted old lady, she told her daughter how distressing it was to hear a child cry when scolded. 'Not when you have 8, Mama – that wears off. You could not go through that each time one of the 8 cried!!'[20] was the reply. Her health too was failing, and she died at Frogmore on 16 March, aged seventy-four.

The Queen was shattered at the loss of her mother, and tortured by remorse as she dwelt on the estrangement between them which had so embittered her adolescence. Her grief bordered on derangement, and throughout Europe it was rumoured that she had become insane like her grandfather King George III. In addition to sorting out the Duchess's estate, the prince consort was bowed by the strain of soothing his wife and keeping the ugly rumours of madness from her. She was too distraught to notice how the effort was taking its toll of his tired frame, and with the exception of Alice and Beatrice, the presence of her children became so irksome that for a while she could hardly bear to have them near her. Vicky came over from Germany to comfort her and was told that her voice was too shrill. Bertie angered her because he did not cry for his grandmother, and bossed the younger children around.

By May, the Queen was beginning to recover her spirits. In part this was due to a timely visit from Louis, whose quiet and respectful behaviour contrasted sharply with that of Bertie. His presence, however, had one unhappy effect. Shortly after his arrival he caught measles, which spread to the younger children. Most of them recovered speedily, but for several days frail Leopold was at death's door.

With one family wedding planned, Queen Victoria was anxious to find a suitable princess for Bertie. After his triumphant return across the Atlantic, he had gone very reluctantly to resume studying at Oxford and then Cambridge, prior to a spell of military training at the Curragh in Ireland. To Alice's remark that she would object strongly if anybody was to attempt finding her a marital partner without consulting her, the Queen testily answered that Bertie was incapable of making up his own mind. Photographs of the few eligible European princesses had filled him with dismay, for without exception he found them plain if not downright ugly. However, Vicky had heard nothing but good of the beautiful and charming Princess Alexandra of Denmark. Despite the political differences between Denmark and Germany over administration of the duchies of Schleswig and Holstein, in which British sympathies were largely pro-German, it seemed that she might be a suitable candidate.

Bertie's last night at the Curragh camp was celebrated in appropriate style. A young lady of the town, Nellie Clifden – popularly described as an actress, doubtless a genteel euphemism for a more questionable profession – was smuggled into his bed, and the Hanoverian blood in him was not slow to take advantage of this golden opportunity. From Ireland he came in September to stay with Vicky and Fritz, ostensibly to attend autumn manoeuvres, but in reality to pay a visit to Speyer Cathedral where he could meet Alexandra 'by accident'. After initial nervousness on both sides, the young people made a favourable impression on each other. The eagle-eyed Vicky, pretending to examine frescos with the bishop, noted approvingly that her ruse seemed to be working.

The annual holiday at Balmoral that autumn passed pleasantly enough. Away from Windsor and Buckingham Palace, Queen Victoria became more cheerful, and the Highland air and solitude brought some respite to the exhausted Prince Albert. They had barely returned south again that October before the Queen gave way again to grief at the loss of her mother.

Family worries followed thick and fast. Vicky caught a severe chill at the king of Prussia's coronation, which developed into bronchitis. Anxiety over her son's deformed arm made her worse, and at one point her physician warned the Queen that her life was in danger. At length she recovered, but then Leopold, still weak from measles and renewed bleeding attacks throughout the summer, fell gravely ill. On medical advice he was sent to spend the winter in southern France, under the care of Waterloo veteran, Sir Edward Bowater. In France Sir Edward was taken ill and died soon after they reached Cannes.

The next bad news came from Portugal where Coburgs had married into the reigning Braganza dynasty. Two of King Pedro's brothers, second cousins to Victoria and Albert, were returning home in November after a visit to Windsor, when news came that one had suddenly died of typhoid fever. Five days later King Pedro succumbed to the same disease. Albert had high hopes of the young sovereign with an apparently promising life and reign in front of him, and was shattered by the tragedy. (A third brother followed them to the grave in December.) His resistance was thus already weakened severely by the time he learnt of 'a subject which has caused me the greatest pain I have yet felt in this life.'

On 12 November, he opened a letter from Stockmar. It was rumoured throughout Europe, the baron told him, that the prince of Wales had been having an affair while at the Curragh. In view of his Hanoverian and Coburg heredity, it might have given more cause for alarm if he had not yielded to temptations of the flesh in such an environment, but this dalliance horrified the Queen and her husband. They were so shaken that they could not bring themselves to confide in Vicky (who had probably learnt of it long before they had themselves), merely telling her that there had been bad news but she was not to ask what.

The extra-marital relations in which the late Duke Ernest I and his wife had indulged, and the consequent dissolution of their marriage, had given their sensitive second son an overriding aversion to any form of immorality. Ever since his own wedding, he had tried his utmost to bring his son and heir up to follow his virtuous example, partly because infidelity revolted him, and partly because he and Victoria wished to put the blurred morals of their Hanoverian predecessors firmly behind them as far as the monarchy was concerned. Moreover negotiations with the Danish royal family were at a delicate stage, and they were anxious lest the only princess who seemed a possible bride for Prince Albert Edward might be lost as a result of such scandal. That the Kings of Denmark led private lives hardly above reproach was overlooked.

A searching enquiry revealed that the stories of Bertie's liaison were all too true. At first Albert wrote that he was too heartbroken to see his son, but wanted to protect him as far as possible from the consequences of his behaviour. He must therefore tell Bruce 'even the most trifling circumstance' about what had happened with Nellie Clifden, and would then be forgiven. The prince apologetically confessed that he had yielded to temptation, and the affair was certainly at an end. Albert gave him credit for declining to name the officers responsible, but in forgiving him added that it was vital he should marry early: 'You *must* not, you *dare* not be lost. The consequences for this country, and for the world, would be too dreadful!'[21]

The Prince Consort was already very ill by this time, worries having taken their toll on a constitution undermined by acute rheumatic pains. On 25 November he took a train to Cambridge in order to see his son. They had a long frank talk, and Bertie asked that the 'intimacies' should be kept from his mother. Albert returned to Windsor in a happier frame of mind. Ironically, though, he was even more exhausted than usual, as Bertie had lost their way during the walk and taken his ailing parent further than necessary.

For the next few days Albert doggedly pursued his work, reviewing volunteers at Eton, attending chapel, and writing official papers. His last important task was the redrafting of Lord Palmerston's ill-tempered despatch on the *Trent* vessel, a diplomatic piece of work which helped to mend frayed Anglo-American relations. Yet he could barely touch his food by day or rest by night, and early in December he took to his bed.

'I do not cling to life,' he admitted to his wife in conversation not long before. 'I am sure, if I have a severe illness, I should give up at once, I shall not struggle for life.'[22] The Queen would not accept that he was mortally ill, either from a sense of blind optimism, or (more probably) from an inner desire to act courageously and not give way to misery, knowing how this would distress him. It was perhaps for this latter reason that the doctors hesitated to tell her the worst.

But Alice knew for certain that he did not have the strength to survive. The robust Queen generally enjoyed the best of health, and was impatient of sickness in others. Since Vicky's departure he had come to confide more and more in Alice, and it was to her that he looked instinctively for a sympathetic nurse. As she looked after him, played him his favourite German melodies on the piano, or sat reading aloud to him, the girl in her disappeared and the woman came to life. Her fortitude amazed their doctors and servants. When her feelings became too much for her to suppress, she would tidy his bed and quietly leave for the privacy of her room. On returning, her face would show no sign of the misery she was going through.

In addition to the horror of seeing her beloved father die by inches before her eyes, to her fell the duty of keeping relations and friends informed as to the progress of the illness. When he asked what she had told Vicky, Alice answered that she had said he was very ill. 'You did wrong,' he remarked. 'You should have told her I was dying.'[23] Alice knew that his dearest wish would be for a last sight of his eldest daughter and she entreated Vicky to hurry to England, but she was still very weak herself and the German doctors insisted that her health was not up to such a journey.

The Queen would not hear of Bertie coming to Windsor, maintaining almost hysterically that he had broken his father's heart. On 13 December, therefore, Alice sent him a telegram at Madingley asking him to come immediately. He caught the next train from Cambridge and arrived at the castle at three o'clock the next morning. Albert rallied for a brief while, but it was evident the doctors could do no more. Early in the evening all the children present except Beatrice, and members of the household closest to him, were called in to say farewell. Bertie and Helena joined the sorrowing group who knelt around the bed. Towards half-past nine the distraught Queen was led gently from their vigil by the dean of Windsor who attempted to comfort her, but she was called back by Alice who had recognised the death rattle. At ten minutes to eleven Albert, prince consort, was dead.

Numb with shock, Queen Victoria was taken to her bedroom. After her maids had undressed her, she ran impulsively to Beatrice's room, lifted her from the bed without waking her, wrapped her up in Albert's nightshirt, and carried her to her own room. Alice had her own bed moved into her mother's chamber but the Queen could not sleep until given a sedative.

For the next few nights, the widowed Queen sobbed uncontrollably until she fell asleep from sheer exhaustion. Nobody felt the burden more heavily than Alice, who had tended her father through the distressing last weeks of his life and now had to watch carefully over her mother. Heartbroken herself, grimly forcing back the tears so as not to upset the Queen even more, she shared a common anxiety with the family and doctors that such profound grief might unleash in her the madness which had darkened the twilight years of George III.

'My *life* as a *happy* one is *ended*!' wrote the Queen to King Leopold on 20 December. 'The world is gone for *me*! If I *must live* on (and I will do nothing to make me worse than I am), it is henceforth for our poor fatherless children – for my unhappy country, which has lost *all* in losing him – and in *only* doing what I know and *feel* he would wish . . .'[24]

2

'Every family feeling rent asunder' 1861–72

The funeral of Prince Albert took place at Windsor on 23 December 1861. Queen Victoria did not attend. Initially she had begged to stay close to her husband's body as long as possible, but the doctors pointed out gently that in so doing she risked spreading typhoid fever to other members of the family, and Alice persuaded her to take her nerves to Osborne for a change of scene. Before departing for the Isle of Wight, mother and daughter drove to Frogmore. There they walked around the gardens to chose a place where the royal mausoleum could be built. The Queen intended that she should be laid to rest beside Albert. She was convinced she too would be ready for the mausoleum by the time it was completed.

The Prince of Wales was the chief mourner at St George's Chapel. According to the *Daily Telegraph* correspondent, he 'bore up bravely, but he was evidently suffering profound anguish . . . from first to last not a sob escaped him; but his closely-drawn lips, and from time to time a convulsive twitching of the shoulders, showed how much he was enduring.' His dry-eyed countenance and that of the Crown Prince of Prussia were in contrast to those of ten-year-old Arthur, in black Highland dress, who sobbed as if his heart would break, Duke Ernest and Louis of Hesse, who also wept openly.

Among household and court, even in the government and throughout the country, inquisitive eyes wanted to see who would now be the greatest influence on their widowed monarch. Of her own generation, the only possible mentor was her brother-in-law Ernest, but he had never shown any interest in British politics, and his notorious immorality meant that he was tolerated with reluctance on his rare visits to Windsor. King Leopold and Stockmar, both septuagenarians, were ageing fast and would be dead within the next four years.

Would she take the Prince of Wales into her confidence with regard to matters of state, or even abdicate? Given the customary hostility of Hanoverian sovereigns to their heirs, this seemed unlikely. The violent antipathy to her eldest son, which she had suddenly developed and did not attempt to conceal, made the chance even more remote. When he had begged the Prince Consort at Cambridge not to reveal the precise facts of his experiences at the Curragh to his mother, both had reckoned without her steely determination in prising out from Albert what she termed 'the disgusting details.' 'Much as I pity,' she wrote to Vicky on 27 December 1861, 'I never can or shall look at him without a shudder.'[1]

Deeply penitent, and distressed at having lost his father 'just at a time when I was most in need of his advice and counsel,' Bertie would have left no stone unturned to assist his mother. But it was evident that his presence irritated her beyond measure. One of Prince Albert's closest confidants, Colonel Francis Seymour, tried to act as peacemaker by persuading her that the Prince Consort's 'extraordinary pureness of mind' had caused him to take his eldest son's 'youthful error that very few young men escape' too much to heart. Yet she would not be pacified. The Prince of Wales had broken his father's heart. Behind her unreasonable attitude lay a suspicion that some of her ministers might press for him to take on some of his late father's duties pertaining to government. She was too astute not to realise that Albert had always been regarded as a foreigner, and thus unpopular, with certain of her subjects. Such people who had resented his participation in government might prefer the more outgoing Prince of Wales to assume the mantle of her 'angel'. This she would never countenance.

One of the Prince Consort's last plans had been for the finale to Bertie's education – a journey to Palestine and the Near East, under the watchful eye of Colonel Bruce. Accordingly he was despatched on his tour early in January 1862. While he was away, Lord Palmerston came to call upon the Queen, and discuss the Prince of Wales among other subjects. He must have found it hard to suppress a wry smile when she described him as 'a very good and dutiful son.'

For Alice, there was no such respite from the household of mourning. Suddenly she found herself as temporary regent in all but name. The business of state, to which the Prince Consort had unstintingly dedicated himself and with which Bertie would dearly have loved to assist in any way possible, had to continue as usual. During the dark days when Queen Victoria was in no condition to see her ministers, Alice acted as intermediary. It created a striking parallel with 1837, when the only visible sign of monarchy had been a small feminine figure, clad in black, surrounded by elderly politicians. In later years, Alice was to look back on this time as her Mama's prop and virtual acting head of state, with a sense of wonder that both of them came through the ordeal without losing their reason.

When Prince Louis came to England for the funeral he hardly recognised his betrothed, whom he remembered lovingly as a plump, high-spirited girl of boundless energy. Now he found a careworn, hollow-cheeked young woman, half-resigned to heeding the call of duty and spending the rest of her days with the Queen, trying to fill the vacuum as best she could. Nothing, it seemed, was further from her thoughts than marriage. Nonetheless it had been one of the Prince Consort's wishes, and therefore law to his widow. But she looked at Louis a little more critically than before, commenting on what she saw as 'a lack of refinement' in his character. He must not bring any of his young officer friends into his wife's society, she warned him, for they were sure to be a harmful influence.

As Vicky was still too unwell to heed Alice's telegram of 15 December 1861 that 'Mama wants you so much,' Fritz came instead. Through her tears the Queen told him every detail of her husband's illness and death, and spoke about the effect it would surely have on their children.

Heartbroken as she was by her father's death, Vicky was reasonable enough to appreciate that her mother was wrong in blaming Bertie, and she did her best to act as peacemaker between them. Bertie, she maintained, had merely indulged in a youthful escapade and nothing more. He had only become entangled with Nellie Clifden through a moment of weakness, curiosity and boredom, and never thought that Papa would take this moral lapse so much to heart. The Queen would not be moved; if only Vicky had seen Fritz struck down, get worse day by day and finally die, she wrote back, would she be able to tolerate the sight of the person responsible?

Not until February 1862 was Vicky judged well enough by her doctors to go and visit her mother at Osborne. She was deeply distressed at the misery she found there. 'It is nothing but a great vault,' she wrote sadly to Fritz; 'everything is so different, the old life, the old customs have gone . . .'[2]

Affie, who had been even further away from Windsor Castle than Vicky on that fatal 14 December, was likewise stunned. Father and son had shared a common bond in their love for Coburg, for the boy had discovered on his visits there that he found the same feelings of contentment and tranquillity at the ancestral seat of Rosenau which Albert had experienced at a similar age. On arrival home at Windsor Castle early in 1862 on compassionate leave, he was astonished at the change which had come over their once happy home. He was too young to appreciate fully what his mother was going through, though his own sense of loss was hardly less than hers. At the age of seventeen he was almost an adult, and he resented being treated like a disobedient child every time she reproached him for whistling, laughing or playing his violin. It was useless to argue that he too missed Papa desperately and was not meaning to be heartless. In view of the way in which the Queen had sung his praises only months earlier, and considering the deep affinity which had existed between father and son, it was ironic that Affie's brave attempts to be cheerful should have irked her so much.

None of the elder children was permitted to be cheerful at

home. For the first four, confirmation had been an emotional and solemn ceremony but still something to be celebrated with joy. Lenchen was the first to be denied a table of lavish presents and grand luncheon after being confirmed in April 1862. Nonetheless her commonsense and patience helped her to exercise a stabilising influence in the family. Queen Victoria respected her third daughter's tact, her unwillingness to complain, and never suspected her of making mischief among her brothers and sisters – an accusation which would be levelled at most of the others in time. Though Lenchen was plain and too fond of her food (something she inherited from her Mama), and seemed in danger of becoming too fat to attract a husband, and lacked charm, she could always be trusted. In this she was the opposite of Louise, extremely pretty but at thirteen already showing signs of becoming a rebel, and without the tact to compensate for her capricious behaviour.

Among the younger children, Leopold was affected particularly by his father's death. Now there was nobody in the family who could give him the same encouragement in intellectual pursuits or the same measure of careful sympathy. The Queen was too distraught with grief to control him, and terrified at each new accident which befell him, especially as there was nobody now to assure her convincingly that all would be well. Without his father, he became more defiant and stubborn, regularly bruising himself and being laid up for several days at a time.

On Beatrice the effect was equally pronounced. Not for some weeks did she learn not to ask when Papa was coming home. Gradually the merry, amusing little girl became quiet and withdrawn. Though her laughter did not irritate the Queen, her childish giggle and comical sayings faded away. Deprived of anything but the most guarded contact with Leopold, lest the two of them should find some vigorous game which would result in him bruising himself, she was forced back onto playing with her dolls for company. It was no wonder that she grew up to be extremely shy.

There was to be no break from mourning for Alice's wedding.

The dining room at Osborne was converted into a temporary chapel for the purpose, and it was dominated by Winterhalter's portrait of the parents and five elder children, Albert's hand outstretched as if offering the couple his blessing. Eight months pregnant, Vicky was unable to attend and sent Fritz to represent her. Helena, Louise, Beatrice and Louis's sister Anna acted as bridesmaids. The Duke of Coburg was appointed to give the bride away.

Struggling to restrain her tears, the Queen sat near the altar in an armchair, discreetly screened from the eyes of inquisitive guests by Bertie and Affie standing beside her. Affie sobbed bitterly throughout the service. As the Queen wrote to Vicky next day, the ceremony was more like a funeral than a wedding: 'A dagger is plunged in my bleeding, desolate heart when I hear from (Alice) this morning that she is "proud and happy" to be Louis's wife!'[3]

For the remaining months of 1862, fate decreed that Queen Victoria's eldest children would cause her considerable anxiety for one reason or another. Though she would not have appreciated such a theory at the time, it was fortunate that she was granted little peace and quiet in which to brood continually on her loss. As the ghost of Prince Albert may have reminded her, their children had to come first.

While Alice and Louis departed for their honeymoon at St Clare, a mansion near Ryde, the most pressing concern was that of Bertie's marriage. The Queen's determination to see him leading a pretty bride to the altar, one of the Prince Consort's last wishes, was intensified by rumours that Tsar Alexander was also considering one of the Danish princesses for his eldest son and heir. Realising that there was no time to lose, she made arrangements with King Leopold. These were that she should stay with him at his palace of Laeken in September, ostensibly to visit Coburg as a personal pilgrimage to her husband's childhood home, but in reality to meet Prince and Princess Christian of Denmark and their elder daughters Alix and Dagmar. The Queen was most taken with Alix, whom she found 'lovely, such a beautiful refined profile, and quite ladylike manner.' After a long conversation with the girl's parents, the Queen left for Coburg, while the Danish family went to Ostend.

Later that week Bertie joined them, meeting Alix at Ostend on his way to Brussels. All of them lunched at an hotel together, after which he told Prince and Princess Christian how much he loved their eldest daughter. Next day they drove over to Laeken, where the wily King Leopold relished the prospect of seeing another match in the making. He suggested that all of them should take a walk in the gardens. The young couple were discreetly allowed to lag behind; Bertie proposed and Alix accepted him.

That afternoon he wrote the Queen a long, 'touching and very happy' letter, expressing his delight at being betrothed and his unbounded love for Alix. Fervently, he hoped that 'it may be for her happiness and that I may do my duty towards her.' Ever the dutiful son, he wished that 'our happiness may throw a ray of light on your once so happy and now so desolate home. You may be sure that we shall both strive to be a comfort to you.'[4]

Lady Paget, wife of the British minister in Copenhagen, and one of the persons most responsible for bringing the two of them together, took a faintly cynical look at the proceedings. She recorded that the Prince of Wales had told her he would take a walk in the gardens with Princess Alexandra. In three quarters of an hour he would take her into the grotto, 'and there I will propose, and I hope it will be to everyone's satisfaction.'

Though the engagement helped to mend relations between mother and son, it did little for feelings between England and Germany. Alix's father was next in succession to the Danish throne, and on his accession the smouldering Schleswig-Holstein question would as likely as not result in open controversy. The duchies of Schleswig and Holstein, of which the latter had a large German population, had been placed under Danish rule by the German protocol of 1852. As German nationalist aspirations grew, the people of both duchies were growing increasingly restless. The death of King

Frederick VII of Denmark would invariably bring demands for recognition or self-government to a head. That Britain should as much as hint at a Danish alliance against Germany, by marrying her future king to one of the little country's princesses, was bad enough. But when it became known, probably through the indiscretions of the Duke of Coburg, who described the match coldly as a 'thunder-clap' for Germany, or Baron Stockmar, who was allegedly furious at the news, that Vicky and Fritz had played their part in bringing it about, their standing in Prussia fell accordingly.

The Crown Prince and Princess of Prussia had both been through a testing time, even before they were criticised for their matchmaking. Fritz's reactionary father King William disliked his liberal wife, Queen Augusta, and deeply resented the influence she and the Prince Consort had had on his son and heir. Within a few months of Albert's death, William was faced with a constitutional crisis. The Prussian *Landtag* refused to vote for a series of military reforms on which he had set his heart, and he threatened to abdicate rather than surrender on a point of principle. Fritz was shown a draft of his abdication speech, and was shocked at the thought of succeeding to the throne in such a way. Little did he know that the King had already summoned Otto von Bismarck, former ambassador to the courts of Paris and St Petersburg and widely feared as one of the most inflexible men in Europe. Though the King made a pretence of offering his son the throne, Fritz hesitated, but it would have made no difference if he had accepted. Bismarck, swiftly appointed minister-president of Prussia, soon made his philosophy clear. The great questions of the time, he thundered, would not be solved by speeches and majority decisions, but by blood and iron. A personification of the Prussian character at its most brutal, he stood for the autocratic mien which ran directly counter to everything in which Fritz, Vicky and the Prince Consort had ever believed.

Distressed by the plight of 'our Prussian children', Queen Victoria was able to inform them providentially that Bertie was borrowing the royal yacht *Osborne* for a Mediterranean cruise, while she invited Alix to stay with her in England. It would be polite, she advised, if they joined Bertie on his travels. This would give them a much-needed holiday, and also remove them briefly from the threatening situation in Berlin.

Meanwhile, Affie had just cast another shadow over his Mama's world. After joining his ship again and reaching Malta, he followed the family tradition and had a momentary affair with a girl on the island. In view of the other midshipmen's behaviour, and lack of leisure facilities on the island, it was only to be expected that Affie would have his own little fling. The Queen was shocked by his 'heartless and dishonourable behaviour', and it was left to the ever-diplomatic Vicky to smooth matters over. How could her brother 'play such a silly trick' and 'be so thoughtless as to add to your grief by misbehaviour?' It was evident that Prince Albert's impeccably moral code of living had been something of an aberration. Bertie and Affie had obviously inherited the loose ways of their Coburg grandfather along with the Hanoverian blood.

Affie's indiscretion had come at a most inopportune moment, for the Queen was then having discussions with her government about another grave European matter. The volatile Greeks had just deposed their unpopular King Otto, and appeared determined to choose Prince Alfred for the vacant throne. Under the terms of the 1830 London protocol, members of the ruling families of the protecting powers (Britain, France and Russia) were ineligible to wear the crown of Greece, though the national assembly and people were slow to acknowledge the fact. In November *The Times* announced that 'the choice of Prince Alfred for the Greek throne is regarded as certain,' and at the end of the year he received an overwhelming 95 per cent of votes cast in a plebiscite held by the provisional government to find their next King. Though Alfred was almost unknown in the kingdom, the Greeks assumed that unlimited capital would follow him from Britain, and they would be made a coronation gift of the Ionian islands, and that British ministers would persuade the Turks to add further territory to their boundaries.

Both Prince Alfred and Queen Victoria were disturbed by the idea, for he relished his naval career and it was generally understood that he would succeed his uncle Ernest as Duke of Coburg. They were relieved when the British government made his ineligibility to the throne plain, and the Greeks eventually chose Alix's brother Prince William of Denmark instead.

While Bertie was on his Mediterranean cruise, Queen Victoria requested the presence of her future daughter-in-law at Osborne and Windsor. The Queen was determined to demonstrate that choosing a Danish princess in no way implied British sympathy for Denmark as a nation, and the lengths to which she went in making this clear may have brought relief to German critics, but verged on the insulting as far as the family were concerned. The Prince of Wales, she stipulated, could not visit Copenhagen as it might be construed as a political gesture. She would not admit, except in private, that she thoroughly disliked the Danish royal family, and feared they might have a dangerous influence on her immature son. In vain did Princess Alexandra's parents protest that she was being sent to England 'on approval'. Years later, she was to confess that she had been extremely frightened at the prospect of spending three weeks alone with Queen Victoria, denied the company of so much as a lady-in-waiting of her own choice. Princess Christian was not asked to come, and Prince Christian who escorted her to England was invited to stay for two nights. When he returned to England to fetch her he had to stay at a London hotel, as there was apparently no room at Windsor Castle.

Though thoroughly unnerved by the proceedings, Alix charmed everybody with whom she came into contact. Helena and Leopold had been sent with the party to welcome her to British soil. Smiling gracefully as she and her father stepped ashore from their ship, she took Leopold in her arms and kissed him warmly. From his anxious expression she guessed the little boy had been ill at ease, uncertain what to say to their guest and when to present his bouquet of flowers. It was a spontaneous and totally characteristic gesture which delighted everyone.

Within a few days the Queen was completely captivated by

this attractive, unsophisticated yet serious girl. She was struck by the religious books Alix kept by her bedside, all well-worn with passages carefully underlined. She regularly went to bed at ten each evening, and was exceptionally kind and patient with younger members of the family, the Queen informed Vicky and Bertie in her letters, not without a subtle note of reproach. 'She is so good, so simple, unaffected, frank, bright and cheerful, yet so quiet and gentle, that her presence soothes me.' It was noticed by her cousin Princess Mary of Cambridge that Queen Victoria was seen to smile 'and even laugh cheerfully at times' when Alix was around. There was much merriment when Affie mischievously persuaded Alix to ask his mother one afternoon whether she had enjoyed her forty winks. Any doubt as to the political expediency of a Danish daughter-in-law had obviously been dispelled by her character.

All the same, the Queen was uncompromisingly firm with her. She told the princess that she must put her country and family behind her, and not attempt to influence her husband in any political questions that might arise. 'The German element' had to be maintained in their home, and as if to make this plain she invited Alice and Louis to arrive at Osborne halfway through her stay. In fact Alice needed little persuasion to come. She was apprehensive that the first anniversary of the Prince Consort's death might bring about another period of hysterical grief on her mother's part, and wished to be at hand in order to help comfort her.

However the dreaded 14 December 1862 came and went without any excessive display of misery. As the new year dawned, all royal minds were concentrated on Bertie's wedding. It was planned to take place on 10 March 1863. notwithstanding complaints from senior clergymen about this falling in the middle of Lent. Marriage, they were informed witheringly, was 'a solemn holy act not to be classed with amusements.' For an agonising moment it seemed as if it might be overshadowed by another death in the family, for soon after his return to sea Affie was taken seriously ill, having apparently contracted the typhoid which had carried off his father. Under the care of his governor, his tenacity pulled him through, but he was too weak to travel home from Malta immediately and he had to miss the wedding.

After months of gloom, the country was ready to celebrate in style. There was some annoyance that the ceremony was not to take place in splendour in London, but in the comparative privacy of St George's Chapel at Windsor. But the people of London were determined to welcome Princess Alexandra as she was met by the Prince of Wales at Gravesend, and escorted through cheering crowds and brightly-decorated streets in the capital to Windsor.

One important little act had to be performed before the wedding. Early in the morning of 10 March, Queen Victoria took bride and groom to the mausoleum at Frogmore where her husband's remains had been interred three months previously. They stood before the tomb and she joined their hands together, informing them solemnly that '*He* gives you his blessing.'

Alice's wedding had indeed been more like a funeral, and the Queen was no more inclined to set her mourning aside for her eldest son's marriage. Vicky had written with some excitement of the forthcoming ceremony, only to be asked by her mother how she could possibly think of rejoicing at such a sad occasion. Her ecstasy was 'very incomprehensible', and surely she would miss 'that blessed guardian angel, that one calm great being that led all?'[5]

Nonetheless, all guests royal and non-royal entered warmly into the spirit of the occasion. Despite his initial opposition to the match, Duke Ernest graciously shared with the crown prince of Prussia his duty of supporting the groom. Writing to the Duchess of Manchester afterwards, Lord Clarendon commented that the Prince of Wales in his garter robes 'looked very like a gentleman & more considerable than he is wont to do', while his bride 'made a most favourable impression upon every body but not more so than was deserved for I never saw in any one more grace & dignity & aplomb.'[6]

Five-year-old Beatrice was not one of the bridesmaids, but she was not disappointed. 'I don't like weddings at all,' she told

William Powell Frith, who was commissioned to paint the official portrait of the event. 'I shall never be married. I shall stay with mother.'

Another small child gave a portent of things to come. Four-year-old Prince William of Prussia began what was to be a long career of baiting his English relations unmercifully. On a carriage drive he threw his aunt Beatrice's muff out of the window and addressed his grandmother as 'duck'. Attending the wedding in Highland dress, he became bored during the service and threw the cairngorm from his dirk across the floor. When his uncles Arthur and Leopold scolded him, he bit them in the legs.

Three weeks after the wedding bells pealed, the Queen looked forward with mixed feelings to the birth of a grandchild in her own home. It was thus appropriate that the princess born at Windsor on 5 April should be named Victoria. The Queen was a little jealous, it appeared to those around her, of Alice's condition – that her daughter, not she, was giving birth to another child – but there were compensations in being able to give Alice the benefit of her own experience.

Meanwhile, Louis occupied his time in England by visiting military establishments and industrial cities in the north. His uncle Alexander, whose eldest son Louis would marry the newly-born princess some twenty-one years later, was much impressed by Louis of Hesse's adoption of English ways. He was fond of sherry and horses, read very little, and never wrote at all. What Alexander omitted to add was that in this he was quite unlike the Prince Consort, something which perhaps contributed to his popularity.

When Alice, Louis and baby Victoria returned to Darmstadt in May, the Queen wrote bitterly to King Leopold of her 'loss'. As they had no duties in Germany, and no house to live in, so she mistakenly believed, they ought to stay with her as much as possible. Alice had to tell her tactfully that Darmstadt was her husband's home, and therefore hers as well. He was expected to take his seat in the duchy chamber, and they had to attend official functions and entertainments. Moreover they were planning their own house, and with the subsequent expenses they could not afford to visit England too often. 'A married daughter I must having living with me,' the Queen lamented. Lenchen was approaching a marriageable age. Perhaps somebody could be found for her who would not object to making a permanent home near his mother-in-law . . .

The relatively simple life led by Alice and Louis had its advantages denied to Vicky and Fritz, whose weary years of persecution by Bismarck were just about to begin. In May Bismarck and King William dissolved the *Landtag* after the opposition claimed their right to free speech without interruption from government ministers. Fritz wrote to his father entreating him not to infringe the Prussian constitution, in return for honouring his promise not to oppose his views openly. The King replied that Fritz had broken his promise and now had a chance to make good by distancing himself from the progressive parties. With that he published a decree suppressing the liberty of the press. Fritz was aghast, and wrote to his father twice to protest at such a reactionary measure, but received no reply. At a reception following a garrison parade at Danzig, he made a speech deeply regretting the conflict between government and constitution.

Throughout Europe, liberals warmly applauded the stand he had taken, and Queen Victoria congratulated him; he 'must not shrink from separating himself from all his father's unhappy acts.' King William was furious, and threatened him with removal from the army. Bismarck slyly advised the old monarch against making a martyr of his son, and in the end Fritz was merely ordered to continue his tour without making further speeches. It was a brave gesture on Fritz's part, but one that was never forgiven or forgotten. From now on, he and Vicky were regarded in Prussia as little more than traitors.

To Queen Augusta, Queen Victoria wrote that their children should 'go away and keep aloof from everything,' but to the excitable King she appealed to let Fritz 'decide his own mode of living' and have more freedom. This was more than she wished to do in the case of her own son and heir.

At first the Queen hoped and thought that Alix would reform her son completely, telling Vicky a fortnight after the wedding that 'she quite understands Bertie and shows plenty of character.' Yet she had already noticed that the princess was by no means clever and perhaps not strong-willed enough. Soon disillusion set in; they were becoming 'nothing but two puppets running around for show all day and night.'

London society, leaderless since the Prince Regent's heyday, was just in the process of acquiring another royal figurehead in the shape of his great-nephew. The 'smart set' and the Prince Consort had had no time for each other, and it was to the newly-married Prince of Wales and his pretty wife that society looked for an example in the art of enjoying life to the full. Marlborough House, their London residence, soon became the centre of high life. While the younger children of Queen Victoria were still at home and therefore cocooned in the eternal mourning atmosphere of their mother's homes, Affie quickly gravitated to his brother's domain in London and to Sandringham, the country estate in Norfolk purchased for him. There had been talk of Affie becoming betrothed to Alix if Bertie had turned her down, for he had been fascinated by the Danish princess since first setting eyes on her. Queen Victoria was concerned at his continued infatuation with Alix, and she was certain he did not have the strength of mind or principle of character to stay there regularly without ruining the happiness of all three. But Affie's jealousy of Bertie, such as it was, never became strong enough to destroy their fraternal affection, and Alix likewise was always devoted to Affie.

It was well that the brothers, sisters and their spouses were so attached to each other, for family affection was to be severely tested in the division of national loyalties which arose from the threatening European situation over the next few decades.

Their first taste of family strife came in November 1863, with the death of King Frederick VII of Denmark and the accession of

Alix's father as King Christian IX. Fritz was on his way to join Vicky and the children at Windsor at the time. As expected, King Christian laid claim to the duchies of Schleswig and Holstein. Duke Frederick of Augustenburg, son of Queen Victoria's half-sister Feodora and a friend of Fritz from college days, proclaimed himself head of government of both on the Danish King's death, and in this he was supported by Queen Victoria, Vicky, Fritz, and Queen Augusta of Prussia.

When the Waleses arrived at Windsor, family harmony was shattered. 'The duchies belong to Papa,' Alix declared defiantly, and naturally Bertie sided with her. As providence would have it, Feodora was among the guests present. Support was overwhelmingly on the side of her son, and the tearful, heavily-pregnant Alix revealed a steely side to her character which nobody in England had yet seen. Eventually the harassed Queen Victoria took King Leopold's advice and forbade any further mention of Schleswig and Holstein in her presence.

Vicky and Fritz were in an extremely awkward position. Bismarck and King William intended to annex the duchies for Prussia, although they bided their time and kept the plans secret. In her anxiety for her father, Alix gave birth to her first child two months prematurely; Prince Albert Victor ('Eddy') entered the world on 8 January 1864, just hours after his mother had been watching ice-skating near Frogmore. One week later a combined Prusso-Austrian army marched into Schleswig, with Fritz as one of the senior commanding officers. In England, public opinion and the government were overwhelmingly sympathetic to Denmark, but Queen Victoria was as pro-German as ever, and the nation remained neutral. After a swift campaign Denmark was defeated, and at the resulting peace conference she was called upon to acknowledge Prussia and Austria as rightful rulers of the duchies.

In September 1864 Vicky gave birth to a third son, Sigismund. She had wanted to ask Bertie and Alix to be godparents, but had to accept Queen Victoria's recommendation that the time was not yet ripe for a reconciliation with 'the conquered party.' The Queen was right. Vicky and Fritz met the Waleses in Cologne a few weeks later, and in accordance with royal etiquette Fritz received his brother-in-law in military uniform. Bertie was incensed to see him sporting his war decorations, and wrote angrily of his 'most objectionable ribbon which he received for his *deeds of valour???* against the unhappy Danes'.[7] Privately they could not disagree with this verdict, for Fritz had gone to war on behalf of his country with the greatest reluctance.

On 26 August 1865, the birthday of the Prince Consort, his widow and nine children were together for the first time since Vicky's wedding. This time the scene was Coburg, and the joyless occasion was the unveiling of his statue there. It was made more miserable still by the bitter divisions between them. Vicky and Fritz were uncomfortable about Prussia's role in the Schleswig-Holstein dispute, especially as a treaty had been signed at Gastein two weeks earlier, agreeing to the administration of Schleswig by Prussia and Holstein by Austria – ill-disguised Prussian plunder and a compromise which boded ill for the future. When they attempted to introduce Fritz's uncle Charles, Bertie was outwardly civil but Alix defiantly tossed her head and refused to speak to him.

Yet another bone of fierce contention was to influence the ill-feeling between brothers and sisters. Queen Victoria was determined to have one married daughter living near her, and not 'lost' to a court in Germany. Alix, she lamented, was not dependable, 'and besides she knows *none* of my intimate affairs.' She was not so possessive, fortunately, as to wish to keep Lenchen remaining 'in single blessedness.' Where, therefore, could a tame son-in-law be found?

The gentleman chosen for this somewhat dubious honour was Prince Christian of Schleswig-Holstein-Augustenburg. As a bachelor he had few striking qualities. He was penniless, thirty-four years of age (with a ponderous manner which made him appear much older), balding and not exactly handsome, and he smoked cigars throughout the day. But as a character he was agreeable enough and easygoing. With her characteristic enthusiasm, Vicky pronounced him 'the best creature in the world.' He spoke fluent English, had long been a close friend of

Fritz, and enjoyed playing with the Prussian royal children at their rural retreat of Bornstädt.

Politically, however, he was perhaps best left alone – or treated with care. The younger brother of the dispossessed Duke Frederick, both had been deprived of their army commissions, status and property by Bismarck after the Prusso-Danish war, and henceforth found themselves unwilling enemies of the Prussian establishment and the Danish royal family. All the same, a meeting was arranged between Queen Victoria and Christian. She considered him 'pleasing, gentleman-like, quiet and distinguished.' He had been woefully ill-briefed on the matter, initially believing that she was considering him as a second husband for herself and not as a candidate for her daughter's hand.

When it became known that she was planning a marriage between Lenchen and Christian, she and Vicky at first found themselves alone in their support. Bertie and Alix thought it a 'painful and dreadful' idea. Alice, as supportive of her eldest brother as ever, sided with them as she saw it as an insult to Alix, and she resented Lenchen's being sacrificed to their mother's possessive whims. In addition, she was suspicious of Bismarck's designs on Hesse, and foresaw that such an alliance would cause friction between the family and the court at Berlin. This would do her and Louis no good, and could cause trouble for Vicky and Fritz as well.

Had the matter arisen a couple of years earlier, Alice's words might have carried some weight with her Mama, still grateful to the daughter who had sustained her so unselfishly during the Prince Consort's last weeks and those first bitter months of widowhood. But an unhappy change had come over the relationship between them. Annoyed that neither of her German sons-in-law could be indefinitely by her side at Windsor, Osborne or Balmoral, the Queen had found a faithful male servant in her Highland ghillie John Brown. Far from being asked to stay regularly, Alice and Louis suddenly found themselves simply not invited. Moreover Alice chose to nurse her children herself, a practice which revolted the Queen. She fumed that her daughter was making a cow of herself, and a heifer in the dairy at Balmoral was subsequently named 'Princess Alice'.

'Good Lenchen' did not complain of her role in this most unashamedly-arranged of marriages. She and Christian knew that their prospects were severely limited, and if they turned each other down they would probably regret it. As the Queen wrote to King Leopold in September 1865, three months before his death, she had braved German wrath and risked antagonising the rest of the family in sanctioning Bertie's marriage, and she could not allow their objections to spoil her plans.

Early in 1866, the engagement of Helena and Christian was announced. Bertie and Alix, still smarting, informed the Queen that they felt so strongly about it that they would not attend the wedding. At this Alice, realising that Lenchen was accepting her situation with good grace and was being upset by her brother's ill-feeling, begged Bertie not to 'be the one who cannot sacrifice his own feelings for the welfare of Mother and Sister.' Vicky assured him that the marriage did not mean Mama loved Alix any the less, and Affie told him that they must 'all put a good face on it.' Bertie must try to accept Christian 'for what he is worth personally.' At this united front, Bertie conceded. He was 'most affectionate and kind,' the Queen wrote, 'but Alix is by no means what she ought to be.'[8]

The younger children were beginning to sense the grave political implications of family matrimony. Hearing that the court at Berlin had scoffed at her sister's 'poor match' and that Bismarck had coldly dismissed the 'Anglo-Coburg faction,' Louise was asked by Vicky what Lenchen would like for a wedding present. 'Bismarck's head on a charger,' she suggested.

Already the Queen's prolonged mourning for her husband and seclusion were giving rise to discontent in the country. With extreme reluctance, she opened parliament in person in February 1866 in order to ask for Helena's annuity. Otherwise it was feared that the House of Commons might make its displeasure felt by voting against it. She compared her ordeal to a public execution, professing not to understand why her subjects demanded the sight of 'a poor, broken-hearted widow, nervous and shrinking, dragged in deep mourning, ALONE in STATE as a Show, to be gazed at, without delicacy or feeling.'[9]

Alice tactfully sent her congratulations afterwards, telling her what 'pride and pleasure it would have given darling Papa! – the brave example to others not to shrink from their duty; and it has shown that you felt the intense sympathy which the English people evinced, and still evince, in your great misfortune.'[10] Unfortunately she failed three months later to write to Lenchen on her birthday, and the Queen decided not to invite her and Louis to England for fear of ruining her sister's first months of marriage. She defended her decision to Vicky by saying that Alice had sown 'pernicious seeds' in Louise, and attempted to enlist Affie in her 'cabal' to break their mother's seclusion.

Helena and Christian were married in the private chapel at Windsor on 5 July 1866. Their *pied à terre* had already been chosen – Frogmore, in Windsor Great Park. Six years later they moved to Cumberland Lodge. Both 'looked extremely well' at the wedding, the Queen wrote. Lenchen was 'fortunate indeed, I think, to be able to live in this blessed and peaceful land, safe from all wars and troubles.'[11]

Safety from wars and troubles must have made her elder sisters wish they could change places. Vicky had been so alarmed by Bismarck's manoeuvrings, of which she and Fritz were told nothing, that she had given birth prematurely to her fourth child, a daughter named Victoria. By summer their suspicions were confirmed. Bismarck intended to establish Prussian supremacy in the German confederation by declaring war on Austria and seizing undisputed control of Schleswig and Holstein. They dreaded another conflict, for the family would be divided far more deeply than it had been in the Prusso-Danish war. Supporting the Austrian cause were the Grand Duke of Hesse, and therefore Louis and Alice as well; George, blind King of Hanover, who had succeeded his father King Ernest Augustus in 1851, the last of King George III's sons to die; and Ernest, Duke of Coburg. Louis's brother Prince Henry of Hesse was already commissioned in the Prussian army.

Queen Victoria offered to mediate between both factions, only to be denounced contemptuously by Bismarck on the grounds that she was tying to rob Prussia of her rightful supremacy for purely domestic reasons.

In June the federal army, comprising units from Austria, Hesse and Hanover was mobilised; Coburg remained neutral. Bismarck interpreted this as mobilisation for war. Prussian doctors accompanied their soldiers to the front, and without medical aid or the comfort of her husband, Vicky was forced to watch helplessly as twenty-one-month-old Sigismund died of meningitis. She tried to bury her grief in unremitting hard work, helping to organise hospitals for the wounded.

Alice's knowledge of nursing and human anatomy (another interest which shocked the Queen, protesting that such interests were 'unladylike' and that it was scandalous that men and women should study such a subject in dissecting rooms together) was likewise put to the test. Though she was expecting her third child, she threw herself into the war effort, tearing up sheets to make bandages for the wounded, and begging her mother for spare linen. On 3 July, after a series of victories in smaller battles, the Prussians vanquished the Austrian army on a plain near the town of Königgrätz.

Eight days later Alice gave birth to another daughter, Irene. Her nerves were extremely strained, for the Prussians had celebrated their triumph by invading Hesse, billeting themselves on the unhappy Darmstadt citizens. An irresponsible mob marched on Frankfurt, helping themselves to cab rides, jewellery and food which they charged to the Hesse government account. The little state went bankrupt and the town burgomaster hanged himself in despair.

Even in the aftermath of war Vicky was hardly less distressed than her impoverished sister; 'Who knows whether we may not have to wage a third war in order to keep what we have won?'[12] Though they were all proud of Fritz's part in the victory at Königgrätz, Queen Victoria told Vicky that it had 'been most dearly bought.'

Those of Queen Victoria's children who were still single must have been counting their blessings. It seemed as if matrimony was to be an inevitable cause of ill feeling between brother and sister. The only one who enjoyed a reasonable amount of freedom away from home and the ever-watchful eye of his Mama was Affie. A few months after his promotion to acting lieutenant, he went to study at Bonn, and spent most of his weekends nearby at Darmstadt. Like Bertie, he found the informality of the Hessian court infinitely more comfortable than the heel-clicking militarism of Berlin. He helped Alice with her charity bazaars, and once sold goods at a stall. The Queen was convinced that Alice was corrupting Affie. On the rare occasions that he came home, he was impatient with her servants, and too quick to find fault with the funereal atmosphere which still pervaded Osborne and Windsor.

In 1866 Affie was promoted to the rank of captain, and created Duke of Edinburgh, Earl of Ulster and of Kent. That summer he was appointed to the command of HMS *Galatea*, with orders to take her on a world cruise such as no British prince had yet undertaken. In the eyes of his mother, the purpose was twofold. Firstly, he would continue to fulfil his duties as her representative in more far-flung corners of the British empire, begun during his South African travels in 1860. Secondly, the responsibility and 'separation from his London flatterers' would do him good. Society was turning him into the kind of prince she did not wish him to be. Unlike Bertie, he had a career in the navy to keep him occupied.

Affie had always loved travelling, but it was with mixed feelings that he sailed in *Galatea*. He had already been away from the family a good deal, denied the solace of being with his brothers and sisters at their father's death, and prevented from attendance at Bertie's wedding. However, by June 1867 he and his crew were on their journey to Gibraltar, South America, the remote colony of Tristan da Cunha, and eventually Australia.

The endless round of Australian pomp and ceremony, civic receptions and mediocre concerts soon palled for Affie. Throughout his tour there were ugly demonstrations between

Catholic and Protestant communities, fuelled by Fenian sympathies and inflamed when news reached the continent early in 1868 that three members of the Fenian brotherhood had been executed in Manchester for shooting a policeman. In March Affie attended a picnic in Sydney to raise funds for a sailors' rest home. James O'Farrell, son of an Irish immigrant butcher, found the presence of a British prince a providential target for revenge, and shot him in the back. The bullet was deflected from his spine by heavy leather braces, and he was pronounced out of danger within a few days. But the tour had to be cut short. New Zealand was next on his route, but there had been Fenian demonstrations on South Island and the authorities could not guarantee his safety.

Galatea therefore sailed for home and arrived at Portsmouth in June 1868. Queen Victoria prayed that her son should 'come back an altered being,' but was soon complaining that he had become unbearably conceited, receiving ovations as if he had done something, 'instead of God's mercy having spared his life.'[13] After a few months of seeing his relations in England and Germany, the latter including a meeting with Grand Duchess Marie of Russia, he set sail on a second, more informal cruise, visiting Australia again, New Zealand, India, the far east, and the Falkland Islands, returning home in May 1871.

Though almost six years Affie's junior, Arthur had a limited measure of freedom. Shortly before his father's death Major Elphinstone, a charming man though no intellectual like Birch or Gibbs, had been appointed his tutor. In 1863 he took the prince on a walking tour of North Wales, and next year they went on a more ambitious expedition to Switzerland, following a similar route to that which the youthful Princes Ernest and Albert of Saxe-Coburg had taken as students at Bonn. Arthur thoroughly enjoyed himself on both occasions, and his love of the open air made it evident that he would undoubtedly suit his childhood ambitions to be a soldier.

Already Arthur was aware of a burden on his shoulders. He realised that he was his mother's favourite son, and that after his elder brothers' 'falls', she saw in his innocence a reincarnation of his father's purity. 'I tremble to think of what his pure heart and mind may be exposed,'[14] the Queen wrote to Vicky soon after his confirmation in 1866. He therefore did his best to avoid spending long periods at Balmoral and Windsor with her, knowing that in the family circle he had to be on his best behaviour. It was tempting to contradict her freely as Affie did, or rebel against restraint like Leopold, but he had to suffer in silence.

In July 1866, at the age of sixteen, Arthur went to begin his army training at Woolwich. Knowing that a soldier's life exposed young men to considerable temptation – Bertie's spell at the Curragh had been living proof – the Queen ordered that he should live at the Ranger's House in Greenwich Park, and not at barracks. That, and his essential purity, she was sure, would protect him from sin. As far as history records, he never strayed from the straight and narrow. To have done so, he knew, would have shocked his Mama far more than Bertie's and Affie's transgressions ever did. Thus it was that she would write glowingly of his endless good qualities, all the while to the detriment of his elder brothers with whom she compared him so favourably. The long-suffering Elphinstone was instructed to forbid him to go behind the scenes at theatres or to the races with the Duke of Edinburgh, to make sure he did not wear unbecoming clothes, part his hair in the centre, or put his hands in his pockets. He must keep a daily journal like his mother always did. Such orders made Elphinstone's job an extremely trying one.

In 1869 Arthur was transferred to the 1st Battalion of the Rifle Brigade, then stationed at Montreal. He was greatly impressed with the countryside and the Canadians themselves, whom he found 'a set of fine honest free thinking but loyal Englishmen,' and was exhilarated by being able to take part in action against a band of Fenians who had invaded Canada. After 'a very happy and interesting year,' he rejoined his battalion at Woolwich, which must have seemed very unexciting in comparison.

Leopold's health was a never-ending worry. Like most

children of frail constitution and independent spirit, he was defiant and unruly, chafing at the fuss made of him, only too ready to argue and contradict. From the moment he had shyly greeted Alix on her first visit to England, both had been especially fond of each other. Her hereditary deafness which cut her off increasingly from her husband's circle, and a tendency to lameness exacerbated by rheumatism after the birth of her eldest daughter Louise in February 1867, gave her a special affinity with this young brother-in-law whose short life was to be dogged by physical handicap. Leopold loved playing with his nephews Eddy and Georgie, but inevitably the games became too vigorous and he would suffer again from internal bleeding. For this there was no cure but several days in bed, propped up with pillows, studying art and languages, reading newspapers from cover to cover and discussing them animatedly with anyone who had time to spare.

Leopold, the Queen decided, had inherited his father's brains and inquiring mind. With his love of music, he found much pleasure in playing duets on the piano with her and with Beatrice, or accompanying them as they sang. Unlike his father he was never ill at ease with strangers. As he grew older, the Queen found him invaluable with his fluent conversation for entertaining on state occasions. She gave him the Order of the Garter in 1869, a year earlier than his brothers, as he was 'debarred from every profession and from almost every amusement of his age'; he was the cleverest and most studious of her sons, and the honour would 'give him much pleasure, which he fully deserves.'[15]

As for Bertie, his mother was in two minds. Time, the great healer, had persuaded her that 'Society' had killed her Angel, who could never have lived happily in this wicked world. It was society which had corrupted her elder children, with the exception of Vicky. That Queen Victoria always kept her heir at arm's length and never forgave him for the Prince Consort's death, the verdict of several writers, is immediately disproved by her gracious comments. 'Really dear Bertie is so full of good and amiable qualities,' she wrote to Vicky in 1867, 'that it makes one forget and overlook much that one would wish different.'[16] She always enjoyed his company when the two of them were alone together, and wished she could see him more often; 'I am sure no Heir apparent was so nice and unpretending.'

But she judged him too indiscreet to carry out state duties apart from strictly ceremonial engagements, distrusting his friends in the Marlborough House set and their addiction to such fashionable vices as gambling, racing and smoking. During the Prusso-Danish war he asked, through the foreign secretary Lord Russell, to see cabinet despatches instead of a *precis* from his mother's secretaries. She unhesitatingly forbade any such 'independent communication' between her government and her heir.

Alix she likewise loved but never trusted because of her family connections. Nobody could be 'dearer and nicer' than her daughter-in-law; 'I often think her lot is no easy one; but she is very fond of (Bertie) though not blind.'[17] She allowed people to be too familiar with her, and rose so late in the morning that her poor husband had to breakfast alone on many an occasion. Yet it was always a pleasure, the Queen found, to go on carriage drives with her.

Queen Victoria could be just as ambivalent over her grandchildren. Though she never overcame her repugnance to the process of childbirth, or 'the animal side of nature', she demanded to be present at the births of as many as possible, soothing her daughters or daughters-in-law in labour. The premature arrival of Alix's six children irritated her as she was thus denied attendance at any of them. However she liked to entertain and play with one or other of the Wales grandchildren in their room, but 'one at a time is much the best.'

Young 'Willy' of Prussia always amused her. Her first grandchild, he was a particular favourite as the only one Albert had ever known, and regarded with sympathy because of his deformed arm. She roared with laughter at his comment on a visit to Balmoral that his English relations were *Stumpfnase* (pug-nosed), and treated his 'little tinge of pride' indulgently when he refused to speak a word to an attendant when relegated to a back seat in the pony carriage. Such behaviour from her own infant sons had generally elicited a sharp clip on the ear. When 'Georgie' of Wales was sent under the table at lunch for persistent disobedience, he emerged minutes later without a stitch of clothing. The Queen was overcome with mirth, in contrast to the rest of her company who were quite embarrassed until they saw tears rolling down her cheeks.

Though 'Gangan' loved and was loved by her grandchildren, she viewed the regular increase in their numbers with alternate despondency and a sense of boredom. The birth of Alix's second daughter Victoria in July 1868, her seventh granddaughter and fourteenth grandchild, was 'a very uninteresting thing – for it seems to me to go on like rabbits in Windsor Park!'[18] Alice's irritability and apparent bitterness could be explained in part because she was not strong and 'those large children so quick one after another have tried her very much.' 'Children are a terrible anxiety,' she informed Vicky in 1870, 'and the sorrow they cause is far greater than the pleasure they give. I therefore cannot understand your delight at the constant increase of them!'[19]

To the children, their august mother was no less of an anxiety as the 1860s drew to a close and the fires of British republicanism burned brightly for a time. As Queen Victoria's seclusion persisted, so rumblings of discontent grew louder and accusations about her suspected hoarding of income from the civil list became more outspoken. When she remonstrated with Bertie about his 'inconvenient friends', he answered candidly (admittedly in a letter from Egypt, several thousand safe miles away) that she might spend more time in London as her people could not bear seeing Buckingham Palace perpetually unoccupied. She retorted that the noise of London was bad for her nerves, only to be told that 'we live in radical times, and the more the *People see the Sovereign* the better it is for the *People* and the *Country*.'[20]

Alice's equally tactful rejoinders to her mother had no more effect. Henry Ponsonby, equerry to the Queen and her private secretary from 1870 to his death in 1895, reported to his wife that he had a very grave conversation with the princess 'who takes the gloomiest possible view of all the talk, even abroad, about the Queen's retirement and not even seeing much of or talking to her children.'[21]

But the Prince of Wales' way of life was partly responsible for the crown's unpopularity. As his mother had feared, his acquaintances were bound to lead him into trouble sooner or later. In February 1870 Sir Charles Mordaunt filed for divorce from his wife, citing two of the Prince's friends, Lord Cole and Sir Frederick Johnstone, as co-respondents. A counter-petition regarding her insanity was filed, and she confessed to having 'done wrong' with the Prince of Wales and others. He was subpoenaed as a witness, and twelve of his letters to Lady Mordaunt were read out in court. They were perfectly innocuous, and his emphatic denial of adultery when questioned in the witness box even brought forth a brief round of applause at the proceedings. However, it emerged during his evidence and that of her servants that he had repeatedly called on her during her husband's absence, and had been left undisturbed with her on many an occasion. Queen Victoria never doubted her son's innocence for a moment, and stood loyally by him, but she was distressed at 'his intimate acquaintance with a young married woman being publicly proclaimed,' and he admitted to being shaken by the experience. In March he was booed loudly as he entered his box at the theatre, and three months later he received a frosty reception as he drove up the course at Ascot.

In July 1870 Europe was once more witness to a battlefield. France was provoked by Bismarck's artful scheming into declaring war on Prussia, who promptly rallied all Germany to her side. The Princess of Wales, who had been deeply hurt by the Mordaunt affair and had gone to visit her parents at Copenhagen, hoped fervently that Prussia would be soundly defeated. Though her husband could not share her views for the sake of his two eldest sisters, he was indiscreet enough to tell the Austrian ambassador in London, Count Apponyi, that he believed Prussia would be taught a lesson at last. His remarks were reported widely and he had to add defensively that 'as all our relations are in Germany, it is not likely that I should go against them,' but there were many in Prussia who never forgave or forgot. The war was swift and conclusive. Barely six weeks after the commencement of hostilities, Emperor Napoleon surrendered and a republic was proclaimed in Paris. Throughout Britain many radicals saw this as an example to be followed, and there was a virtual epidemic of 'republican clubs' throughout the cities.

'Bertie must envy Fritz who has such a trying but useful life, wrote Vicky. Under the circumstances it was a less than wise remark, but once again she and Alice were feeling the strain of war. Fritz had left his family immediately after the christening of his third daughter Sophie to take command of the Prussian Third Army, while Louis had been appointed to head the Hessian division.

Believing the odds to be fearfully against them, Vicky took charge of nursing operations at Homburg. Wounded soldiers, German and French, were resigned to their doom as they were brought in to die on filthy floors of makeshift huts, and her obvious concern for their plight deeply touched them. The crowded little shacks where men were dumped and left unattended in their dirty uniforms for hours at a time revolted her, and she paid for a number of inexpensive purpose-built hospitals out of her own pocket. The walls were to be painted in cheerful colours, and each ward was to have its own bathroom and drainage. It was only a short time before this hard-working, energetic little figure was too popular with patients for the liking of others. A band of lady-helpers, led by Countess Bismarck, dressed in their best clothes, could not conceal their disgust at *Die Engländerin*'s eagerness to share her duties with 'low-class' women nurses. Her patience worn thin by anxiety and fatigue, she politely but firmly dismissed them, finding them more trouble than they were worth. An unguarded comment on the doctors as 'mischievous, stupid old things,' and rumours that her sympathies were really on the side of the French, resulted in her recall to Berlin by King William.

At Darmstadt, Alice set up a medical depot in the grand ducal palace. Politically at least she was in a more favourable position than her sister at Berlin. Nobody questioned her German loyalties at this time. Yet no sooner was her fear of French invasion of Hesse over, than a new distress came upon her. She was grieved at the fate of the deposed Emperor and Empress, from whom she and her family had known nothing but kindness. However, her quietly efficient work for the sick and dying men on either side brought nothing but praise in Hesse, where she acquired a well-deserved reputation of Florence Nightingale proportions. She spared herself nothing. On learning that a man she had just helped to lift on a stretcher was dying of smallpox and highly contagious, she shrugged it off as an occupational hazard.

Her devotion was all the more remarkable as she was expecting another child. After her doctor came into contact with dangerous fever and dared not treat her for fear of passing on the infection, Queen Victoria sent out one of her physicians from England. On 6 October, Alice gave birth prematurely to a second son, named Frederick William ('Frittie') after the Crown Prince of Prussia. As she lay exhausted in her bed, it seemed the only sound she could hear regularly outside her window was the beat of muffled drums as another officer or soldier was escorted on his last journey. Her doctors insisted that she take an indefinite period of leave, and she went to stay with Vicky at Berlin. Wisely, the two of them did not reveal to their mother that Vicky acted as wet-nurse to baby Frittie, Alice being too weak.

They were overjoyed to see each other again, and found their mutual company a comfort while their husbands were away, but they were deeply upset about the 'shocking means' used to bring about the unity of Germany. What would Papa have thought of this war, they asked themselves.

In England, Helena was facing a different dilemma. To the Duchess of Sutherland, she confided her husband's distress at the war. He was anxious to play his part in helping to fight for Germany, but the ministers thought it better for him not to go. 'I need not tell you my *gratitude* not to see him go,' she wrote, 'though I should have encouraged him to go had it been possible,'[22] Yet she was able to work on behalf of the London committee for aid to the sick and wounded.

In January 1871, the German empire was proclaimed at Versailles. King William of Prussia was raised to the title of German Emperor (in preference to the style 'Emperor of Germany' which would have been unacceptable to the other German Kings and heads of state), and Fritz and Vicky Their Imperial Highnesses. The distinction was not lost on Queen Victoria, who realised with more than a touch of jealousy that her eldest daughter could soon find herself an Empress while her Mama was a mere Queen.

It was against this troubled European background that Princess Louise became engaged. The Queen's forecast at her birth that this daughter might 'turn out something peculiar' had in a sense been fulfilled. At the age of eighteen her talents as a painter and sculptress were evident, but so were her feelings of inferiority. 'She is very odd,' the Queen told Vicky, 'dreadfully contradictory, very indiscreet and, from that, making mischief very frequently.'[23] The incorrigible girl was given to making embarrassing remarks to the effect that 'Mama was not too unwell to open Parliament, only unwilling.' But it was unlikely that there would be any problem in finding a husband for any princess as attractive as her.

In May 1868 the Danish press had reported that she was to be engaged to Crown Prince Frederick of Denmark, this being followed by a speedy denial in *The Times*. Vicky felt sorry for this young sister whose boredom and frustration with her mother's gloomy life was beginning to have an adverse effect on her. She invited Louise to Berlin, not without an eye to pairing her off with some eligible Prussian prince. In the ballrooms of the German palaces this lovely princess attracted the attention of many a young man with her vivacious manner, cheerful conversation and above all her sparkling appearance. Yet they were made uneasy by her self-assured manner and air of independence. She was diplomatic enough to conceal her feelings, but she found their arrogance and chauvinistic rudeness to women utterly repugnant. Moreover, they had no sense of humour whatsoever. When she told them mischievously that she had retained her incognito of 'Lady Louise Kent' at home after travelling abroad with her mother (who had used the title countess of Kent for herself) in order to make gentle fun of her, they took it very seriously. The experience convinced her that she would never marry a foreigner – least of all a Prussian.

Both Vicky and Louise were interested in the issue of women's rights, and corresponded with the social reformer Josephine Butler. 'I do take great interest in the happiness and well-being of women,' Louise assured her in 1869, 'and long to do everything that I can do to promote all efforts in that direction.'[24] There was never the slightest chance that she could be moulded into an obedient Prussian *hausfrau.*

Vicky could do something for Louise, however. She persuaded Queen Victoria to let her make use of her skills by joining a painting course at the National Art Training School of Kensington (now the Royal College of Art), founded by Prince Albert from profits made after the great exhibition. Papa, Vicky tactfully pointed out, would have greatly approved of one of his daughters reaping the benefits of his work in this way. In the course of her studies Louise met the sculptress Mary Thornycroft, at that time making busts of the royal family, who encouraged her in her work and introduced her to the sculptor Edgar Boehm. Louise revelled in her freedom, for now she realised that at art school she could be accepted for her talent alone, instead of being treated with fawning deference as the Queen's daughter. Later she was elected to the honorary fellowship of the Royal Society of Painters and Etchers. Admittedly her taste and style in art were very conservative. She admired the Pre-Raphaelites and became a close friend of some of them, as well as of more academic painters like Sir Lawrence Alma-Tadema, but more avant-garde artists like the Impressionists meant as little to her as did the more abstract work of Auguste Rodin.

Queen Victoria, a skilled watercolourist herself, took great pleasure in her daughter's achievements, and the two of them drew much closer as a result. On Louise's twentieth birthday, the Queen wrote that: 'She is (and who would some years ago have thought it?) a clever, dear girl with a fine strong character, unselfish and affectionate.'[25]

Louise's art was one matter; but what about her marriage? Vicky still hoped that she could arrange a match between her sister and Fritz's cousin Albrecht, but neither Louise nor the Queen 'would ever hear of the Prussian marriage, which must be considered at an end.' The artistic princess would not be swayed from her intention of staying in Britain. On 3 October 1870 the Marquess of Lorne, heir to the Duke of Argyll, proposed to her on a walk at Balmoral and she accepted him. John Douglas Sutherland Lorne, a Liberal member of parliament,* was a poetic, literary-minded man who shared many interests with Louise, walking in the Highlands being one of them. She was so set on marrying him that she threatened to enter a nunnery if her wishes were thwarted.

In Britain the news was received well, even though the Queen was hardly justified in calling it the most popular act of her reign. Thanks to Bismarck, Germany's reputation had sunk very low indeed, and it would have done nothing for the monarchy's precarious standing had another German match been announced, especially so soon after the defeat of France. As was to be expected, Berlin's attitude was one of contempt. Vicky was initially cool on the matter, though she realised in her heart of hearts that her sister was far too independent of mind to be happy with a Prussian. Queen (shortly to be Empress) Augusta, once such a close friend of Queen Victoria, was silenced

---

* He represented Argyllshire, 1868–78; later sat for Manchester South as a Unionist, 1895–1900.

with the blunt remark that 'Princes of small German houses are very unpopular here.' Lorne himself took it all with good humour: 'My ancestors were Kings when the Hohenzollerns were *parvenus*.'

Vicky was not the only one of the family who disapproved. Bertie objected, mainly on political grounds. His sister's marriage to a member of parliament, he suggested, might give rise to the belief that the crown was laying itself open to a charge of alignment with party politics. Besides, would there not be problems in assigning the correct rank to husband and wife?

The Queen brushed his objections aside without hesitation. She made it abundantly clear that the Germany of 1870 had changed much for the worse since her husband's time. In 1862 she had yearned for everything German and instructed Vicky to 'Germanise' Bertie as much as possible, as she particularly wished 'that element' to be retained in her family. 'Times have much changed,' she wrote to him in November 1869, when he voiced support for the Prussian marriage; 'great foreign alliances are looked on as causes of trouble and anxiety, and are of no good. What could be more painful than the position in which our family were placed during the wars with Denmark, and between Prussia and Austria? Every family feeling was rent asunder, and we were powerless . . . In beloved Papa's life-time this was totally different, and besides Prussia had not swallowed everything up.'[26] Where Louise's position was concerned, this posed no difficulty. Moreover the marriage would (so the Queen hoped) infuse 'new and healthy blood' into the royal line, and strengthen the throne morally as well as physically.

Henry Ponsonby shared the Prince of Wales's anxieties about the position of a princess being a subject's wife. No such marriage had been given official recognition since the wedding of King Henry VII's daughter Mary to the Duke of Suffolk in 1515. Louise felt these difficulties herself, particularly with regard to her servants. She would have footmen, she told Ponsonby. 'Footmen, mind. I don't want an absurd man in a kilt following me about everywhere.' Queen Victoria would not have appreciated this cutting remark against her favoured John Brown.

Even the Queen had misgivings about her daughter's new status. When the Duke of Argyll suggested that she could be 'Lady Lorne' except in her mother's house, she worried lest Louise might lose the H.R.H. from her name altogether.

The five months which elapsed between engagement and wedding were to be difficult ones. Shortly before the court was due to leave Balmoral for Windsor, Louise took to her room with a rheumatic knee. Henry Ponsonby thought the princess was exaggerating her complaint because she did not want to return to the vicinity of London while the Waleses were so hostile about her marriage. However, as in the case of Lenchen's marriage, Bertie soon relented, and he was present with the family on 21 March 1871 when Louise and Lorne were married at Windsor. The groom, attired in the uniform of the Argyll and Bute volunteers, entered the chapel to strains of *The Campbells are coming*, and the Queen gave her daughter away.

The year 1871 may have opened with a popular royal wedding, but for the royal family it was to be a critical year which almost ended in tragedy.

Two weeks after Louise and Lorne waved goodbye to their wedding guests as they left for their honeymoon in Florence, the Princess of Wales gave birth to a third son. Unlike the other young Waleses, this baby did not thrive. Hurriedly christened Alexander John Charles Albert, he lived a mere twenty-four hours. The parents grieved bitterly for this child which had barely lived at all, tears rolling down the Prince of Wales's cheeks as he placed the tiny body into a coffin and arranged the satin pall and white flowers on top. Queen Victoria felt deeply for them and offered to come to Sandringham at once, but Bertie gently declined. His wife, he told her, needed peace and quiet. The princess added to this her hope that the Queen's first visit to their house should be an occasion of joy, not sorrow. All of them would soon recall this remark with a certain irony.

During the summer Vicky and Fritz came to Osborne and Balmoral on holiday. Their arrival so soon after the Franco-

Prussian war did not pass without press criticism, but the Queen was anxious to restore family harmony. The longer a meeting on friendly ground was delayed, she believed, the more difficult it would be to smooth over misunderstandings and bring about a reconciliation between them and Bertie and Alix. At last Fritz had a chance to confide in them his utmost suspicion of Bismarck, and his fear that one day the imperial chancellor might declare war on England.

There was another subject of conversation, once Mama was out of earshot – her seclusion. Louise's wedding had done nothing to stem the tide of English republicanism. At Balmoral Vicky, Bertie, Alice and their spouses decided with regret that only one course of action was possible. As the eldest and most literate of her children and inveterate family peacemaker, Vicky would have to compose a carefully-phrased letter, signed by all the family, lamenting that 'our adored Mama and our Sovereign' seemed unconscious of the dangers to the monarchy, and urging her to show herself more.

Fortunately the letter was never sent. Just as it was ready to sign, Bertie heard that the Queen was unwell, and he advised that it should not be sent until the new year, if at all. What might have been an irretrievably damaging rupture to already uncertain family harmony passed into oblivion. Queen Victoria was too perceptive not to realise that something of the kind was afoot, and vented her anger on a government minister, Lord Hatherley. Overwork and worry, she told him angrily, had killed her beloved husband and several members of her governments, past and present. Unless her ministers supported her, she could not go on but would have to give up her burden to younger hands. 'Perhaps then those discontented people may regret that they broke her down when she might still have been of use.'

The Queen's physical sufferings began in mid-August with a sore throat. Within days she was bedridden with a combination of gout, neuralgia and an agonising abscess on the arm. Never had she felt so terrible since an attack of typhoid at the age of sixteen. Her servant had to lift her from couch to bed, feed her like a baby and even help her to blow her nose. By the end of the month Dr Jenner warned Ponsonby that he feared at one point she might have only a day to live. Lady Churchill suggested that her children should be sent for, only to be told sardonically by Sir Thomas Biddulph, Master of the Household, that 'that would have killed her at once!'

At length she recovered, though it was not until the first week of November that she was strong enough to attend church again. Ironically, it was a further spell of family unpleasantness which seemed to hasten her recovery by awakening the fighting spirit in her – a succession of 'Brown rows'.

John Brown had started his career as the Prince Consort's Highland ghillie, and was now the Queen's personal servant. His honest and blunt outspoken manner amused her, surrounded as she was by relations, household staff and obsequious ministers who were generally afraid of her. On one memorable occasion he silenced Gladstone with a curt 'You've said enough.' He helped her onto her ponies, lifted her into the carriage when rheumatism made walking painful, saw that she was wrapped up properly in bad weather, and checked that there was whisky in her picnic hampers instead of 'old woman's tea'. When her illness was at its most acute, she could not bear to be with anybody for long except Brown and 'baby Beatrice' (now fourteen), the only people whom she maintained really understood her.

The elder children loathed Brown and his unashamed rudeness. It embarrassed them to see him dancing reels with the Queen at the ghillies' ball at Balmoral each autumn, ordering everybody around, and they were ashamed that she should allow herself to become the subject of scurrilous gossip which made less respectful elements among her subjects refer to her as 'Mrs Brown'. Vicky was sharply reprimanded after her eldest daughter Caroline refused to shake hands with him; 'Mama says I ought not to be too familiar with servants.' Affie had quarrelled with him at a ball that summer, and after Brown complained that the Duke of Edinburgh was persistently snubbing him, the Queen ordered Ponsonby to arrange a reconciliation. Affie agreed as long as Ponsonby was present as a witness; when he saw a man on board ship it was always in the presence of an officer. The Queen was furious; Balmoral was not a ship 'and I won't have naval discipline introduced here.'[27]

During her illness, Queen Victoria lost two stone in weight. Family and household were astonished by the change in her manner and appearance, but this did not stop attacks on her from the outside world reaching a new height. On 6 November Sir Charles Dilke, radical Liberal member for Chelsea, delivered a widely-reported speech at Newcastle inciting his audience to depose her forthwith and set up a republic. The excitement and anger at this had barely died down when a telegram arrived from Sandringham. The Prince of Wales had had a feverish attack. Next day, the Queen heard, it was 'mild typhoid'.

Alice, that most experienced of royal nurses, chanced to be staying at Sandringham at the time, and she did more to help see her brother through his illness than anyone else. She was very efficient in her methods, but Alix's lady-in-waiting, Lady Macclesfield, found her unbearably domineering, and her dismissal of providence ('there is no Providence, no nothing') as 'such rubbish' verging on heresy. She was 'the most awful story-teller . . . meddling, jealous and mischief-making.'

Though she had so wished Queen Victoria's first visit to Sandringham to be a happy one, Alix sent sorrowfully for her and she arrived on 29 November. The house was soon packed with argumentative relations. Affie and Arthur were there, incurring the wrath of others by going skating on the lake, or suggesting optimistically that Bertie ought to be well enough in a couple of days to come shooting with them. Leopold arrived longing to comfort Alix, 'whom he idolises'. Louise had to share a bed with Beatrice after being ejected from her room, when the Duke of Cambridge detected a smell which he thought was bad sanitation. It turned out to be a gas leak.

The Queen still took her daily walk in the grounds, notwithstanding snow and slush. But she did not dare to leave the house for more than half an hour a day. She spent much of her time sitting anxiously behind a screen, watching her son as he laughed and sang in his delirium, believing himself to be King already, making suggestions which made everyone's hair stand on end, and hurling pillows around the room. Alix sat distraught by his side, creeping away occasionally to fall asleep from exhaustion. The strain so exacerbated her deafness that it was almost impossible to wake her from her slumbers. Servants who tried to keep her from the sickroom in order to prevent her from hearing her husband's obscenities and more intimate revelations need not have bothered.

Lady Macclesfield complained bitterly that the house was swarming with people. Nobody could keep things quiet; 'the way in which they all squabble and wrangle and abuse each other destroys one's peace.'[28] Queen Victoria did her best to rule the roost with a rod of iron. Ponsonby was amused by her regular sentry duty at the bedroom door to prevent visitors from entering, and her decision as to who should leave Sandringham and when.

One day he and Haig, the Duke of Edinburgh's equerry, were going into the garden when they were nearly knocked down by a stampede of royalties, headed by the Duke of Cambridge. They thought there was a mad bull on the rampage, until the least breathless of them cried out, 'The Queen! The Queen!' Everybody dashed into the house and waited behind the door until the small plump figure dressed in black had hobbled past. When the princes had gone, Ponsonby and Haig could hardly contain their laughter.[29]

On 13 December, with the ominous tenth anniversary of Prince Albert's death on everyone's mind, the crisis was at hand. The Queen and Alix turned to one another in tears, saying, 'There can be no hope.'[30]

That evening, however, the doctors reported signs of modest improvement in their patient's condition. Dr Gull was cautious in his judgement, stressing that hardly anyone had been known to recover from such a grave attack of typhoid. On 14 December Bertie was reported to be exhausted but sleeping peacefully and quite lucid when awake. Affie claimed a little boastfully that he had saved his brother's life by recommending the addition of pale ale to his diet. It was a quiet Christmas at Sandringham and Windsor, whence the Queen returned once he was out of danger.

Thankful as she was that her son had been spared, Queen Victoria could not deny herself the thought that if her husband had had the same treatment, he might have survived. She could have added that her son had far more will to live.

When the press and public praised Alice for having nursed him back to health, their mother objected. Alice had rightly received the credit for her devotion during the Prince Consort's final illness. Now, she decided, it was the wife's turn. To Mrs Gladstone, she said that the Princess of Wales had done the nursing. Apparently 'people imagined it was his sister.'

The government chose to mark the heir's recovery by a public service of thanksgiving at St Paul's on 27 February 1872. The Queen disliked any idea of 'public religious displays,' but was moved deeply by her subjects' affection – 'Such touching affection and loyalty cannot be seen anywhere I think.' Two days later a Fenian agitator chose his moment to threaten Her Majesty with an unloaded pistol, only to be disarmed and seen off by Prince Arthur and John Brown. This was followed by Dilke's demand in parliament that a committee should be formed to examine the Queen's expenditure. He received short shrift from his colleagues. Republicanism had indeed been dealt a heavy blow from which, unlike the typhoid victim of Sandringham, it did not recover.

3

'Fresh blood' 1872–86

The ten years following the Prince Consort's death had been an eventful, often traumatic time for the family. Marriage, conflicting loyalties between warring European territories, and Queen Victoria's obstinate seclusion had all strained fraternal ties, but in most cases they had the happy result of bringing mother, sons and daughters closer than ever.

Superficially, however, nothing had changed. Queen Victoria allowed herself to be taken in by Bertie's tears at the sight of his childhood wheelbarrow at the Swiss Cottage on his first visit to Osborne after recovering from typhoid. But her fervent hope that he was a reformed character did not last long. By early summer, she intimated that he was 'going about' too much. 'What can I do, if you go about so little?' he retorted despairingly.

Gladstone braved the wrath of his sovereign by proposing a new role for the Prince of Wales. He and the princess, it was thought, might reside in Ireland for four or five months of the year, where he could undertake some form of administrative business, to be mutually agreed. 'The nature of his duties would afford an admirable opportunity for giving the Prince the advantage of a political training which, from no fault of his own, he can have hardly be said hitherto to have enjoyed.'[1] And if Her Majesty was to decide that she was no longer capable of performing 'the social and visible functions of the Monarchy,' could she not invite the prince and princess to reside at Buckingham Palace in her absence for two or three months annually, and perform them on her behalf?

Such proposals, worthy though they might be, were instantly dismissed. The Irish plan was doomed; Ireland, the Queen informed Gladstone coldly, was the least loyal of her dominions, it would mean exile for the prince and do his health much harm, and he was not of sufficiently independent character to stand against the pressures that would be exerted on him to lean towards one political party or the other. In short, the emerald isle was 'in no fit state to be experimented upon.' As for the Buckingham Palace suggestion, the 'fashionable set' had already exercised a most harmful influence on her heir and his wife. It would never do to encourage them still further. Experience was no prerequisite, she went on, for a successful monarch. She could never take the slightest interest in public affairs before her accession to the throne, though in fairness she might have added that the struggles with her mother and Conroy, when she was a girl in her teens, made her position hardly comparable with that of a man of thirty with five children.

By the end of 1872 the Prince of Wales had been thrown back on to a life of frustrating unemployment, relieved of necessity by the distractions of his city and society friends. Early the next year his secretary Sir Francis Knollys asked Lord Rosebery to lend his London home as a convenient rendezvous at which the Prince of Wales and the Duke of Edinburgh could meet their so-called actress friends. Rosebery declined, but other contemporaries were only too eager to accommodate the heir and his brother.

On 22 April 1872 Vicky gave birth to her eighth child, a daughter named Margaret. Six years earlier, while expecting her fourth baby, she had written to Fritz that, despite the pain and discomfort, 'one is never so happy as when one is pregnant & during the first weeks after the birth of a child!' Her feelings had not changed by 1868, after the birth of a sixth; 'All the pain of labour is nothing compared to the happiness of having such a dear little creature to hold & to nurse oneself'.[2] She felt she owed Germany another son, though this time she felt she had enough children and did not intend to go through another confinement; 'what one has to endure is too wretched'.[3]

Beatrice was privileged to be invited to act as one of the sponsors of her new baby niece. It was one of the few excitements of a hopelessly over-protected life. In her mother's estimation she was 'an unusually dear, gentle child, very quiet, always contented and with the most remarkable even temper.' The unfortunate child was given no chance to be anything else. Dancing partners were limited to her brothers, and at meals she dared not discuss any subject but the weather without an imploring look at her mother. Guests and members of the household who were unguarded enough to mention such words as 'marriage', 'engagement' and 'wedding' could expect to receive a message from Her Majesty afterwards that these were not fit subjects to be brought up at table in the presence of Princess Beatrice.

Yet there were persistent rumours that Queen Victoria was seriously considering marriage for Beatrice with a bachelor prince whose looks were as dashing as his political status was controversial – Louis, Prince Imperial, only son of Napoleon and Eugenie.

The exiled family at Chislehurst, Kent, had no firmer friends than the Queen and her children. After Napoleon's death they became even closer, and the Queen was a great admirer of the young soldier prince. From the day he and Beatrice were seen chatting at a military review in Bushey Park, speculation was rife that the Queen would find a way around the political and religious differences and eventually announce an engagement between the two. It only came to an end with the prince's death in action during the Zulu war in 1879.

There were still problems between Alice and Helena, caused mainly by finance and jealousy. Helena and Christian, now parents of two sons and two daughters, led a placid existence unruffled by political complications of the kind which had made her sisters' German marriages unhappy. He was appointed Ranger of Windsor Park, hardly the most arduous of tasks. His work was limited to such mundane duties as culling the frog population at – inevitably – Frogmore, which he did by consulting a naturalist who recommended introducing more ducks onto the pond. One morning when they were staying at Osborne and the Queen was not in the best of tempers, she looked out of the window and saw Christian pottering about aimlessly in the garden. Immediately she sent a servant to give him a message that he must occupy himself with something or go for a ride. Regardless of the fact that the poor man had precious little to do, it irritated her to see him so idle.

Helena occupied her time by endless good works, such as founding and becoming patron of the National School of Needlework in Sloane Street, and opening charity bazaars. In this she was following the example set by Alice in Darmstadt. At committee meetings for her various benevolent institutions, she exercised an authority as befitted the Queen's daughter. 'So we all agree on that point, don't we?' she would say, adding with barely a pause for breath: 'Therefore let us pass on.'

At chapel in Windsor Park she could be an embarrassment. During a national dock strike the Archbishop of Canterbury composed a prayer of intercession, to be read in every church, that the dispute might be settled. She picked up the relevant leaflet from her pew, examined it carefully through her glasses, and put it down with an extremely penetrating whisper: 'That prayer won't settle any strike.'[4]

Though Helena looked up to her sister and sympathised with her privations, the latter envied the comparative affluence of the couple at Windsor Park. The Queen complained regularly of Alice's cutting remarks. She could barely afford holidays for herself and her growing brood of children. Invitations to England were rare, and when they did occur there was generally unpleasantness. When dining at Osborne one night Alice dropped unsubtle hints about requiring a horse, quiet enough for herself but sufficiently strong to act as a charger for Louis. The Queen changed the conversation swiftly to their beef and cutlets.

In April 1872 Alice celebrated her twenty-ninth birthday, but the physical and mental strain she had suffered throughout her adult life had aged her well beyond her years. Like her father, she was unequal to the burdens she took upon herself.

Already she was a prey to neuralgia, rheumatism and severe headaches. Not only did she lack Vicky's resilience, but more importantly she was denied the happy marriage of her elder sister. Louis was kind and apparently faithful to her, but cared more for the parade ground than for domestic comforts. His idea of normal daily routine was to rise at six in the morning, and drill his soldiers for three solid hours. For leisure he enjoyed going shooting, but Alice's attempts to interest him in things cultural or intellectual fell on barren ground.

As a result she turned elsewhere for suitably challenging company, in particular to the controversial theologian David Strauss. His *Life of Jesus*, published in 1835, explored a theory that while the story of Christ was based on historical fact, the supernatural element was mythical. He was bitterly reviled in orthodox Christian circles, but Vicky was interested in his work 'to rid the purely historical and credible from all earlier and later embellishments.' When he moved to Darmstadt, Alice invited him to the palace frequently and found his conversation fascinating. She had often questioned the essential doctrines of Christianity as a young girl, and was glad to find somebody with whom she could discuss such matters rationally. Throughout Germany Alice became extremely unpopular, especially after she persuaded Strauss to dedicate a volume of his lectures to her. Princess Louis of Hesse, the Empress Augusta angrily told her friends, was a complete atheist.

Vicky had already known the grief of losing a young son, and the same tragedy was about to overtake Alice. Her elder son Ernest, born in 1868, was healthy enough, but Frittie was haemophilic. At the age of two he cut his ear, and bled until his hair and neck were matted with blood. The grim necessity of watching and restraining the playful boy was not to last long. In May 1873 she was in bed when her sons came to wish her good morning. They started playing together, and Frittie fell out of the window, landing on a stone terrace twenty feet below. He was picked up unconscious and bleeding, and by evening he was dead. 'Why can't we all die together?' wept

Ernest, filled with remorse at the thought he might have been responsible in part for his brother's accident.

Alice never recovered from the shock. To her mother, she wrote pathetically some three months later that she still could not bear to play on the piano 'where little hands were nearly always thrust when I wanted to play.' Not even the birth of her youngest child May, born the following year, could assuage her grief. From this time her letters betrayed a weary resignation, almost a longing for the inevitable end.

Despite Queen Victoria's objections, Leopold chose to go up to Oxford, largely to escape from his over-protected home life. He studied art, science and modern languages at Christ Church, and was granted an honorary degree in November 1872. For the first time in his life he could lead a comparatively normal existence, associating freely with contemporary graduates and men of letters such as John Ruskin, Benjamin Jowett and Charles Dodgson (Lewis Carroll). He built up a comprehensive library including these and other authors of the day, and collected ceramics and works of art relating to the Stuart period. Visits to concerts, the opera and theatre were another joy, and he would count the composers Charles Gounod and Arthur Sullivan among his friends.

It was ironic that he should be enjoying better health than usual when he had an unpleasant reminder of mortality in the shape of Frittie's death. To Alice, he wrote sadly 'that it is perhaps better that this dear child has been spared all the trials and possible miseries of a life of ill health like mine.'[5]

Alice saw little of her husband, but she was cheered by regular visits from Affie. He was always happy in the company of his sister and her Hessian relations, who in turn found him 'frank and jovial.' Already he had been instrumental in helping Alexander's son Louis to join the British navy. Shortly after his return from the second cruise of *Galatea* in May 1871, Affie told his mother that he intended to meet Tsar Alexander II of Russia with a view to asking him for the hand of his daughter Grand Duchess Marie.

To Queen Victoria, the idea of a Romanov daughter-in-law would be rather a mixed blessing. Ever since the Crimean war Russia had been a traditional enemy of England, who was suspicious of her intentions over the Black Sea and central Asia, and regarded her imperial dynasty as 'false and arrogant'. Moreover, if one of her sons married a princess or Grand Duchess belonging to the Greek Orthodox church, would there not be an endless procession of priests in and out of Clarence House, his London residence? But she had long since accepted that finding him a wife would be difficult. As long as he could choose someone to suit and please him, she would not mind who it was; the choice was becoming so limited that 'I think we must get over the difficulties concerning religion.' She was assured that the Greek church, unlike the Roman Catholic church, did not refuse to acknowledge any creed other than their own, and the foreign secretary Lord Granville advised her that a Russian Grand Duchess would be more suitable than an English subject, a Catholic, or a daughter of the dispossessed King of Hanover.

The courtship was a trying one for all parties concerned. The Tsarina seemed reluctant to part with her beloved daughter, and made the excuse that she was too young to contemplate matrimony; the Tsar was not opposed in principle to a union between their families, but the English court would have to wait a year for 'any definitive decision,' which would however not be binding; and rumours reached England that the Grand Duchess had had an affair with one Russian officer, plus regular correspondence with another. Her parents were therefore keen to marry her off as soon as possible. Though mortified by what seemed an eternity of shilly-shallying, Affie was prepared to be patient. Instead of appreciating the depth of his feelings for Marie and his willingness to wait, Queen Victoria snorted that he had no pride or dignity, only 'plenty of false pride when it ought not to be there.' As for the Romanovs themselves, she was disgusted at what she felt was their 'shabby treatment' of her family.

At length patience brought its own reward. On 11 July 1873 at Jugenheim, Affie asked for Marie's hand and she accepted him. But still the Queen could not accept the situation with good grace. Her initial reaction was astonishment 'at the great rapidity with which the matter has been settled and announced.' To Vicky, she announced simply: 'The murder is out!' Would Marie be able to alter her future husband's 'hard, selfish, uncertain character'?

She would, of course, have to see Marie before the wedding took place. As she could not be expected to travel to the continent for anything resembling official business, either the tsar or tsarina would have to bring their daughter to England. The tsar's reaction to this was brief and to the point; Queen Victoria was a 'silly old fool.' The Tsarina offered to meet her halfway at Cologne, a suggestion the Queen dismissed as 'simply impertinent.' Alice bravely tried to persuade her mother to concede, only to be told witheringly that her Mama was not going to have her own daughter telling her what she should do. She, the 'Doyenne of Sovereigns,' had been on the throne nearly twenty years more than the Tsar. Grumpily she resigned herself to waiting for the day when the Duchess of Edinburgh would step on English soil for the first time.

Affie and Marie were married at St Petersburg on 23 January 1874 at a double ceremony – the first service according to the Greek Orthodox church, the second according to the rites of the Church of England. It was a unique marriage among Queen Victoria's children in being the only one she did not attend. By way of compensation she selected Arthur Stanley, Dean of Westminster, to perform the English service, and commanded Lady Augusta to report back to her in the fullest detail. Among the other guests were Bertie, Alix (whose sister Dagmar was married to the Tsarevich), Affie's governor Sir John Cowell, Arthur and his governor Sir Howard Elphinstone. Representing the German courts were Vicky, Fritz and Duke Ernest of Coburg.

The bride and bridegroom arrived at Windsor on a sunny day in March. Queen Victoria had at last repented of her persistently churlish attitude, and welcomed her second daughter-in-law whom she found pleasantly unaffected and civil. True, she was not in the least bit pretty or graceful (and would become more plain and dowdy as the years passed, making it obvious that she cared nothing for her appearance), but she spoke faultless English, and was not in the least afraid of her husband.

Sadly, the Grand Duchess's first good impressions proved to be misleading. Queen Victoria's anxieties about having a member of the 'false and arrogant' Romanov dynasty in her family were soon justified. Marie and her father informed the Queen that she was to be known as Her Imperial Highness, 'as in all civilised countries.' The not-yet-imperial Queen retorted indignantly that she did not mind whether her daughter-in-law was called Imperial or not, as long as Royal came first. Then it was debated which title should come first – Grand Duchess of Russia, or Duchess of Edinburgh? Feeling out of her depth on the matter, the Queen referred it to Ponsonby, who was amused by the fuss and quoted Dr Johnson to his wife: 'Who comes first, a louse or a flea?'

Next there was an argument about Marie's position at court. It irked her that as an emperor's daughter she was not granted right of precedence over the princess of Wales, daughter of the King of a comparatively humble country like Denmark. The tsar agreed gallantly with Queen Victoria that Princess Alexandra should indeed precede her, but asked for his daughter to take precedence over her other sister-in-law. This the Queen would not countenance, but Marie exacted her own subtle revenge. At her first drawing room in England she took malicious pleasure in flaunting her splendid jewellery. The princesses could not hide their jealousy, while the Queen looked at the pearls and diamonds in icy silence. It was as well that the Duchess of Edinburgh soon had further preoccupations. By Christmas there was a family of three at Clarence House, for on 15 October she gave birth to a son, named Alfred after his father.

Alone among his brothers, Arthur was still the only one who never vexed his Mama, apart from the occasional concession to fashion – 'unbecoming' hair or 'dreadful' collars. Vicky had him to stay early in 1872, and she compared him favourably with the less cultivated Prussian officers and soldiers. Fritz took him shooting, both of them showed him the little farm at Bornstädt, and he went to a *soirée* given by the 1st Guards regiment. He was still a little shy, and this diffidence protected him from Fritz's licentious relations, who evidently knew better than to try and find him the Berlin equivalent of a Nellie Clifden. After his return to England, Vicky praised her 'good and amiable brother,' who had 'gained friends and admirers everywhere, winning all hearts by his charm of manner and civility.' Among these friends and admirers was the eleven-year-old Princess Louise, daughter of Fritz's drunken brutal cousin Frederick Charles. As yet she was too young to think of marriage, but Vicky was devoted to the girl's mistreated mother, Marianne, and she could not but hope that a match between her and her brother might take place one day.

Meanwhile Arthur persevered conscientiously with his military career. In 1873 he was attached to the staff of an infantry brigade at Aldershot, and during manoeuvres there he was promoted to brigade-major. His room in one of the lower huts of his battalion headquarters was so small, he wrote, 'that I could lie in bed and open the window and poke the fire.' According to his colonel, the prince worked like a slave; 'his General told me that no poor man in the army working for his advancement could work harder than he does or do his duty better.' In May 1874 he was created Duke of Connaught and Strathearn and Earl of Sussex.

As the years passed, Vicky valued the love of her husband, mother, brothers and sisters all the more. The estrangement of her eldest son Willy was becoming more evident. Whether his deformed arm was more responsible for the shaping of his unstable character than the flattery of courtiers and Prussian relatives, one cannot say. What is certain is that during his adolescence the relationship with his parents became progressively worse. Bismarck was much to blame for helping to turn him against them, but nobody was more responsible than his grandmother the Empress Augusta. As a future King of Prussia and now a German Emperor of the future, she petted and indulged him shamefully. In order to curry favour, she had told him that his mother could not bear to nurse him as a baby because his crippled arm was repugnant to her – a cruel lie if ever there was one. The most affectionate of mothers, the only reason Vicky had not nursed him, Charlotte or Henry, her three eldest, was because Prussian court etiquette forbade her to do so. Not until the birth of her fourth child, Victoria, was she allowed some say in the matter. In consequence she was always to enjoy a closer relationship with her younger five, those whom she was permitted to bring up as she pleased.

When the ex-Emperor Napoleon died in exile in Chislehurst in January 1873, Vicky was thoroughly upset. She could not help but compare the happiness she had found at the glittering Parisian court as a girl of fourteen, with Napoleon's pathetic downfall and disease-ridden last years. Willy could not understand her emotional outbursts, for he recalled that she had been similarly reduced to tears when his father had gone to fight the infidel whose death she now mourned. Puzzled, he took the matter to his tutor Georg Hinzpeter, who chose his words with care and led the boy to believe that his mother was indulging in treason by lamenting the death of Germany's enemy.

It would have been much better for all involved if only Willy had been able to talk to his father. Like Bertie, Fritz had been saddened by his inability to enjoy a happy relationship with his father, and he had hoped to try and establish harmony with his own children from the start. In the days when Prussia was just a kingdom, father and son had spent many a happy hour lazing on the floor in their palace at Potsdam, turning the pages of richly-illustrated German medieval histories. But Bismarck had cunningly elected to send Fritz on every empty representative mission possible, in order to keep him away from his family. The less Prince William saw of his father, the more he would look upon him as a stranger as he grew up. This would make him more amenable to the influence of Bismarck and less to that of his father, and at the same time foster the damaging impression that Crown Prince Frederick William was a weak ineffectual father, dominated completely by his English wife.

In 1874 Willy was sent to the *Gymnasium* (grammar school) at Cassel for three years, an almost revolutionary proposal which astounded the court. The idea had been suggested by Hinzpeter, but he put it to Vicky in such a way that she soon believed it to be of her making. Like the tutor, she felt that it would prevent 'that terrible Prussian pride' from ensnaring her son. He must not grow up with the idea that he was of 'different flesh and blood from the poor, the peasants and working classes and servants.' She became so enthusiastic that she accepted all responsibility, and had a furious row with the emperor as a result.

Willy's education at this most forward-thinking of German schools was not an unqualified success. His fellow-pupils looked up to their eventual ruler and flattered him endlessly. He had gone there with misgivings about the liberal notions of his parents, and the history lessons served to reinforce his faith in Bismarck's policies of blood and iron which had created the German empire. Between them, the school and Hinzpeter had encouraged him to speak out without hesitation. The consequences for his parents, if not for country and continent, were to be disastrous.

Though still largely unemployed in an official capacity, Bertie was given several opportunities to exercise his diplomatic skills at home and abroad. In November 1874 he and Alix paid an official visit to Birmingham. The city had a reputation for radicalism and the Lord Mayor, Joseph Chamberlain, was a noted republican. Yet the prince's tact and the princess's charm won him over completely, and he surprised the public by acknowledging in his address at dinner that the throne was truly recognised and 'respected as the symbol of settled government.' 'Radical Joe' was soon to be no friend of the republican movement. Both he and the former firebrand Dilke would be welcome as regular guests at Marlborough House before long.

In October 1875 Bertie set out on a seven-month state visit to India. Queen Victoria was initially against such a long separation from his family, but at length she was persuaded to give it her approval, though she supported him in not allowing the indignant Alix to accompany him and the party. They were extravagantly entertained by Indian heads of state, and generously showered with jewels and trophies.

Yet it was not all a life of merrymaking and big-game hunting. The Prince of Wales was angered by the arrogance of English civilian and military officers. Like his mother, his views on racial prejudice were remarkably ahead of their time. He wrote to the Queen to deplore widespread 'brutality and contempt' shown to the Indian population, and the British governors in India were accordingly instructed to put their house in order. During his homeward journey he was irritated by learning from the newspapers that an act had been passed creating Queen Victoria Empress of India. Both she and Disraeli apologised gracefully for the oversight.

Soon after returning from India, Bertie accepted the presidency of the British section of an international exhibition to be opened in Paris in May 1878. It was no mere honorary position, for he did much to organise Britain's role in the display. Two days after the exhibition opened, he attended a banquet at which he proposed the health of the French president, Marshal MacMahon, after the Queen's health was toasted. It was the first time he had publicly honoured the head of the republican government, and he declared that the *entente cordiale* between both countries was not likely to change. The British ambassador in Paris informed Lord Salisbury, the foreign secretary, that the Prince of Wales's visit and general behaviour had made England extremely popular in France. His talents as an ambassador had already been recognised, and they would have no little effect on his role – indeed Britain's role – in Europe during the next thirty years.

In September 1875 Queen Victoria and Beatrice visited Louise and Lord Lorne at their country seat, Inveraray Castle. The few days passed pleasantly enough for some but not for others. According to Ponsonby, it was a trying time for the Argylls, who found Her Majesty behaving just as if she was at her own home. She considered herself as paying a visit to her daughter, and rarely saw anybody else, 'the rest of the family being merely accidental.'

Those who had foreseen problems in the Queen's daughter marrying a subject would have had their fears realised. Louise did not let slip the opportunity of pouring out her troubles to Mama. Her rooms were not good enough, she could not dine alone when she wished, and the Campbell ladies did not treat her with due respect. As Ponsonby remarked, it was unjust of her to make such a fuss. After all, she had married into a ducal family, and it was up to her to live with them as one of the family: 'It is absurd talking of two dinners in a private house'. The mild-mannered Marquis of Lorne apparently supported her in all her complaints and thought that his father should do more for her.

The general opinion was that Louise was not merely restless, she was an active mischief-maker. Inveraray, once such a happy home for the Argylls, Ponsonby continued, had been turned into 'a perfect pandemonium' by her presence, and her departure with Lorne for a winter in the south always caused sighs of relief all round. Others suspected that she was getting bored with her husband, and the shackles of marriage were not for her. Queen Victoria's hopes that the union would have infused 'fresh blood' from Scotland into her family came to nothing, for Louise was unable to have children. In later life she told a lady-in-waiting that she had received about 150 letters from well-meaning members of the public suggesting remedies for her predicament, but 'none of them were any good.'

Though the years after the Franco-Prussian war were relatively free of armed conflict in Europe on the scale of those that had divided Queen Victoria's family between 1864 and 1871, there were several war scares that made them wonder whether they would ever live to see another year of unclouded peace.

France's unexpectedly quick recovery from defeat, and payment of her indemnity eighteen months earlier than stipulated in the peace treaty, was followed by reorganisation of the Prussian army. Rumours of an Austro-Italian-French coalition swept the continent, and Vicky came to dread the possibility of seeing her husband go off to war again – perhaps even against England.

Soon afterwards the threat to peace came from the Balkans. As *The Times* had warned on his marriage, the Duke of Edinburgh 'would be in a singular position if war suddenly broke out' with Russia. When the Ottoman provinces of Bosnia and Herzegovina rose in revolt against oppressive Turkish rule, unrest spread and in April 1877 Russia declared war on Turkey. Affie was in command of HMS *Sultan*, attached to the Mediterranean fleet, required to be close to Constantinople in order to protect the lives and property of British subjects in the area.

Within a year the Turks were forced to surrender and sue for peace. The treaty of San Stefano, signed in March 1878, justified Europe's worst fears in seeing substantial Russian territorial gains. For weeks the possibility of war between Russia and Britain hung in the balance. A well-intentioned but tactless act of Affie suddenly brought home to them all the painful division of family allegiances.

Among his officers on board *Sultan* was Prince Louis of Battenberg, whose younger brother Alexander ('Sandro') was aide-de-camp to the Russian commander-in-chief, Tsar Alexander II's brother Grand Duke Nicholas. When Louis heard from the German ambassador and his wife that Sandro was in Constantinople, he was determined to see him, and Affie granted him permission to go ashore. The brothers were overjoyed to see each other safe and sound, and Louis invited Sandro on board *Sultan*. Later they went on board the flagship together, and then to *Temeraire*, a modern battleship equipped with several new devices. The commander-in-chief, Vice-Admiral Phipps-Hornby, was embarrassed at having a foreign officer on board one of his ships at such a delicate time, although Sandro had taken care to appear in German (not Russian) uniform, and he hesitated to interfere with a fraternal union of this nature. However, as Prince

Alexander was an officer he had to be accorded certain privileges, such as being invited to watch a demonstration of fleet exercises, and dined on board the flagship. The brothers later went ashore and visited Russian army headquarters, where they were received cordially by Grand Duke Nicholas and shown round the camp where several Turkish soldiers were imprisoned and captured armaments kept.

When informed of their activities the British ambassador at Constantinople was aghast, fearing that peace negotiations would be jeopardised by the entertaining of a Russian officer on board a British ship and made a party to confidential information. In order to prevent sovereign and admiralty from hearing vague rumours from unofficial sources, he cabled to London. Queen Victoria's fury knew no bounds, for Affie's behaviour, well-intentioned though it was, had come perilously close to treason. She wrote angrily to him that he had been *most injudicious and imprudent* . . . I own I should hardly believe you *capable* of such imprudence and want of (to say the least) *discretion'.*[6] He had undoubtedly injured the prospects of both Louis and himself. *Sultan* was due to return to England for maintenance, and as her captain was duty-bound to return with her, the Duke of Edinburgh would have to be posted elsewhere without delay, and perhaps even forfeit his leave. At Darmstadt Alice had heard that he could not show his face in England after such careless pro-Russian behaviour, and even his favourite sister Helena wrote to her to confess how ashamed she was of him.

At length the Queen was persuaded – not least by Bertie – that no harm had been done, and the British ambassador's telegram had been exaggerated. Sandro had not been shown confidential equipment or naval secrets. Louis of Battenberg was so upset by the storm that he had seriously considered resigning from the navy, but he received a somewhat grudging apology from the admiralty and a warm welcome at Marlborough House from Bertie. By early summer Affie had been forgiven as well, but only after threatening to demand a court of enquiry in order to clear his name.

One small dilemma remained. After Affie had spent the summer at Coburg, to be with Marie who presented him with a third daughter, Alexandra, in September, he wanted to return home. Peace had been declared and confirmed by the congress of Berlin in June, and there was no prospect of active service to detain him at Malta. But Queen Victoria did not wish to have him back, partly as she thought it too soon after the *Sultan* affair and partly because she regarded him as a bad influence on Arthur.

Just in time (for Affie was threatening to resign his commission if not allowed to return home, or alternatively given something constructive to do), a solution was found. Disraeli, who as prime minister had handled the statesmen of Europe so well at the Berlin congress, decided to appoint the Marquis of Lorne governor-general of Canada. It would be flattering to the Canadians, he believed, to have the Queen's son-in-law and daughter living amongst them.

The appointment was not received with unqualified approval. Lady Dufferin, wife of a recent ex-governor of the dominion, told Ponsonby that Lorne was terribly vague in his conception of the duties of his new office, and his administrative capabilities still had to be developed. Admittedly he had sat as member for Argyllshire for ten years and served as secretary to his father, Secretary of State for India. But it was the general opinion that he fulfilled his parliamentary duties gracefully rather than actively. As for Princess Louise, was there not a danger that she would treat the Canadians condescendingly? Her behaviour to her in-laws had left something to be desired.

At least Lorne made himself popular in government circles by solving what Disraeli and the admiralty wearily referred to as 'this Duke of Edinburgh business.' He suggested that in view of his wife's royal status, it would be appropriate for them to land at Halifax from one of Her Majesty's ships. HMS *Black Prince*, to which Affie had been transferred when *Sultan* returned to Portsmouth for refitting, was chosen to make the Atlantic crossing which would take the new governor-general and his wife to Canada.

Affie was not the only son to displease his Mama that year. Leopold misbehaved as well, though on a lesser scale. Since leaving Oxford he had chafed even more at his sheltered home existence. Although now in his early twenties, he was still sent to his room when amateur theatricals or dancing took place, in case the excitement proved too much for him.

After some hesitation, the Queen allowed him to go and visit Italy. Though she feared that 'cold churches & galleries, & visiting frivolous parties' might have an adverse effect on his health, she gave her consent, and he left at the end of February 1878. Having visited Paris, Nice, Naples and Vesuvius, he had reached Lake Como by May, and from there wrote to his mother, informing her that he did not intend to return home for the spring visit to Balmoral. This 'shameful heartless letter' was shown by an indignant sovereign to most of the family, as well as Disraeli and Ponsonby, who told his wife with some admiration that the errant prince 'was firm against coming to Balmoral and protested against the Queen regulating his every movement – but he was respectful and dutiful in expression.'[7] A lady-in-waiting at Balmoral had recently said that when people were temporarily unhappy they sometimes killed themselves, to which Ponsonby irreverently observed that 'suicide might be common here.' The Queen begged Vicky, then staying in England, to suggest to her brother that he should stay instead at Buckingham Palace, 'in his room upstairs,' if he really had such an extraordinary aversion to her beloved Highland home. On no account was he to attend Ascot or Epsom, or even go to Bertie and Alix at Marlborough House 'and amuse himself as he likes.'

Leopold did none of these things. He was reluctantly given permission to spend three or four days in Paris. Having arrived there, he coolly informed the Queen that he intended to stay there for a fortnight. She objected strongly to his prolonged presence in 'that sinful city,' apart from which he was bound to fall ill again. But he proved her wrong by returning unscathed. He had won his point by proving that he did not need to be cossetted all the time, and earned a measure of respect for standing up to her. From now on, she was prepared to acknowledge that he could be trusted to travel abroad without injuring himself.

Arthur had also done something which did not win the Queen's wholehearted approval. In March 1878 he announced his engagement to Princess Louise of Prussia. Arthur was so good, she told Vicky, that there was no need for him to get married at all. Moreover, she particularly disliked the girl's father (and in this she was not alone), and the Prussian royal family, with a few honourable exceptions, were so proud and overbearing. But if Louise was so unhappy at home and fond of England, 'I shall become reconciled to it.' When she met 'Louischen' for the first time, she was immediately impressed. The eighteen-year-old princess was 'a dear sweet girl of the most amiable and charming character,' and she knew that 'dear Arthur could not have chosen more wisely.'[8] It was significant of her acceptance of the match, and indeed of her increasingly liberal attitude towards prevailing customs, that she was 'a little surprised' but no more when Arthur and Louise drove down to Frogmore alone. She could not understand that engaged couples thought nothing of being stared at or laughed at as they appeared in public together without a chaperone. Young people were getting 'very American' in their habits, she thought disapprovingly. The wedding, she insisted, would certainly have to take place in England, and the Prussian court proved amenable to this.

The months leading up to the Connaught wedding should, therefore, have been a happy time for the family. Instead they were destined to be overshadowed by tragedy in Darmstadt.

In June 1877 Louis had succeeded to the Grand Duchy of Hesse and the Rhine. Alice was now therefore Grand Duchess and *Landesmutter* (mother of the country). It proved an insupportable burden for her, already worn out by years of personal sorrow and unremitting overwork. Since her wedding in 1862 Hesse had seen the flowering of many organisations for the improvement of health services and education, all owing their existence to the tireless efforts of Alice. In addition to maintaining these, she now had to assist her husband with additional duties of administration and the ceremonial round. Too much, she said wearily, was being demanded of her. Moreover, she had become bitterly disillusioned with her kind but dull husband. In October 1876 she admitted in a long letter to Louis how disappointing her life in Darmstadt had been. She would have been perfectly happy living in a cottage, she said; 'if I had been able to share my intellectual interests, and intellectual aspirations with a husband whose strong, protective love would have guided me round the rocks strewn in my way by my own nature, outward circumstances, and the excesses of my own opinions.' So many times she had tried to talk to him about more serious matters, but 'we have developed separately – away from each other; and that is why I feel that true companionship is an impossibility for us – because our thoughts will never meet.'[9]

Even her mother, with whom she had had her differences, was not always much of a comfort. About a year later, she wrote an undated letter to Louis referring to some correspondence with her Mama, 'so unfair that it makes me cry with anger . . . I wish I were dead – and it probably will not be too long before I give Mama that pleasure.'[10]

Ironically it was Queen Victoria who recognized that her frail, exhausted daughter was badly in need of a complete rest. She therefore paid for the family to come and spend a holiday in Eastbourne in the summer of 1878. Yet Alice, who was judged by the royal household to have become increasingly German, could not and would not relax. She spent her time in a ceaseless routine of visiting hospitals and charity organisations. She opened a bazaar for the building fund of All Saints Church, inspected the Christ Church schools and gave away prizes at the college. But she could not hide her intense weariness of spirit. Before going north to Balmoral, she wrote apologetically to her mother that: 'I don't think you quite know how far from well I am, and how absurdly wanting in strength . . . I am good for next to nothing and I fear I shan't be able to come to dinner the first evenings. I hope you won't mind. I have never in my life been like this before. I live on my sofa and see no one . . .'[11]

By a cruel stroke of fate, a pleasure steamer named *Princess Alice* was sunk on the Thames near Woolwich one Sunday afternoon while she was still in Britain. Over six hundred, many of them children, were drowned. Alice was one of the first to send a message of heartfelt sympathy to the bereaved, and a contribution to the relief fund. The disaster was an ironic forerunner of what was shortly to happen.

On 8 November, soon after the family's return to Darmstadt, fifteen-year-old Victoria took to her bed with a fever later diagnosed as diphtheria. The rest of their children (except Elizabeth, hurriedly sent to stay with relations) and their father caught it in turn; the youngest, four-year-old May, died on the 16th, by which time Ernest was at death's door.

After going through the heartbreaking ordeal of a virtually secret funeral, Alice steeled herself to break the news to her convalescent daughters and husband, but at first she dared not tell Ernest. He kept asking after her, sending her little notes, and then a book. Eventually she could keep it from him no longer, but told him his little sister was in heaven. The effect on him was even worse that she had feared. He sobbed so bitterly that in an outburst of emotion she forgot her doctor's instruction. Trying to comfort him, she kissed him on the forehead. In the immortal words of Disraeli when he addressed the House of Lords later that month, it was 'the kiss of death.'

On 8 December the Queen received a telegram with the dreaded news that her daughter had diphtheria. 'She will never have the strength to get over it,' she remarked sadly. She sent Dr Jenner to Darmstadt, but there was nothing he could do beyond helping Alice's doctors to make her last unhappy days as comfortable as possible. In her weakened state, she stood no chance of survival. Early on the morning of the dreaded 14 December, she fell into her last peaceful sleep.

That the princess 'who behaved so admirably during her dear father's illness . . . should be called back to her father on this very anniversary, seems almost incredible, and most mysterious!'[12] wrote the Queen. Perhaps she suffered a twinge of remorse. It was no less ironic that the first of Queen Victoria's nine children to die had been the one least understood by her mother, the one who had suffered so much from parental criticism and insensitivity, and the one who had needed security and physical and mental comfort so badly – something she had never found in marriage.

'It often tormented me to see her so frail, so white,' Vicky wrote with tears in her eyes, 'though it only added additional charm and grace to her dear person and seemed to envelop her with something sad and touching that always drew me to her all the more.'[13] She and Fritz desperately wanted to attend the funeral on 17 December, but the German Emperor forbade them to go for fear of infection. Instead the Prince of Wales, together with Princes Christian and Leopold, travelled from England for the ceremony. The haggard, bowed figure of Bertie, who had told his mother with a heavy heart that 'it is the good who are always taken' was almost unrecognisable to guests so familiar with the genial man usually so full of life and laughter. At Alice's memorial service held at Windsor the same day, it was on Alix's arm that the Queen leaned. Alix it was who gave her mother-in-law unstinting comfort and sympathy during the next few days of mourning, and the experience marked a new phase in the affection between the women. From then on, Queen Victoria had barely a word of criticism to utter against her.

Alice was never forgotten by the people of Germany and England whose lot she had worked so unsparingly to improve. In Hesse the hospitals and schools she had established continued to flourish under those to whom she had set such a fine example, and in Eastbourne a Princess Alice Hospital was opened in her memory in 1883.

Helena paid a touching tribute to the memory of her sister by writing a foreword to an edition of Alice's letters to Queen Victoria, published in 1884, prefaced with a biographical sketch by Dr Karl Sell, a clergyman from Darmstadt. The book was so popular that a revised edition was issued the next year, in which

Sell's text was replaced by a 'Memoir of Princess Alice by her sister Princess Christian.' Such efforts evidently gave Helena a taste for literary work. A couple of years later, after researching in the Berlin royal library, she translated and wrote an introduction to an edition of the memoirs of the margravine of Bayreuth, sister of Frederick the Great, and of the margravine's correspondence with Voltaire.

As soon as the doctors felt it safe for them to travel, Louis and their motherless children were invited to England by the Queen. They came in January 1879 and stayed for two months. Before their departure, she asked their English governess to send her daily reports on their progress and education. Their aunt Helena was to go to Darmstadt each year to see them, and they were to spend part of every holiday with the 'Christians'. It was suspected that the Queen considered a marriage between Louis and Beatrice, so that the children would have a mother again. At the time it was against the law for a widower to marry his deceased wife's sister. A bill permitting such an alliance was privately supported by Queen Victoria and the Prince of Wales, and reached the statute book in 1896, by which time the surviving Hesse children were all married and Louis had been laid to rest beside Alice.

Court mourning was suspended for the marriage of Arthur and Louise, to take place on 13 March 1879. Rumour had it that Queen Victoria did not wish their wedding to be delayed, because her son had become terribly absent-minded. He had fallen out of a window, onto the head of a policeman, though neither gentleman was hurt so much as startled. A few days beforehand, she informed Elphinstone that Arthur was extremely worried and tired. He needed dosing, 'for he is yellow and green'.

All Queen Victoria's children as adults frequently gave the impression of absent-mindedness. Their nephews and nieces noticed that they would become aware of a youngster in their presence, start a conversation with him or her and then wander off, leaving a rather dismayed child. Members of the household found that Beatrice in particular had an odd habit of not appearing to listen to them, or else talking to somebody else while they were speaking, but she still took everything in: 'your story is reproduced afterwards correctly.'

The wedding took place at Windsor. Queen Victoria wore a long white veil and court train for the first time since her widowhood. Arthur cut a dashing figure in his Rifle Brigade uniform, ablaze with British and Prussian orders and looking almost as magnificent as his bride's escorts, her father in a scarlet general's tunic (hence his nickname, the 'Red Prince'), and Fritz in his white Cuirassier's uniform. Despite her shy disposition, Louise was 'too happy to be self-conscious,' bowing radiantly to the assembled company as they walked up the aisle.

Only her boorish father seemed unwilling to enter into the spirit of the occasion. He was rude to most of his in-laws in turn, complained peevishly that his daughter's rooms at their first married home, Bagshot Park in Surrey, were too small, and told the Queen that he had hoped his previous visit to England was to have been his last. It would have been a source of satisfaction all round if only it had. Six years later cancer, possibly aggravated by heavy drinking, silenced him for good.

Soon after his marriage the Duke of Connaught became president of the Surrey football association. One day he was strolling across a field near his home when he came across two teams of lads playing the game with a rather tattered ball and coats to mark the goalposts. They were having an argument about the rules, and seeing him coming (but without recognising him), they asked him to referee. He gladly agreed, and after watching them a few minutes showed them some passes. 'Are you a footballer, Guv'nor?' asked one. He replied, smiling, that he was a soldier. 'What a waste!' was the retort. 'When you might 'ave played 'alf-back!'

It was frequently a source of disappointment to the locals that Arthur did not wear his uniform when at home. Youngsters would peep through the park railings, hoping in vain that they might catch sight of him attired in full military dress. 'I suppose he only puts it on for the Duchess to see in the evening,'[14] one disgruntled watcher observed after seeing him emerge yet again looking the perfect country squire.

When unrest broke out in Egypt in 1882, Arthur, now promoted to major-general, was placed in command of the 1st Guards Brigade, serving on the expedition under Sir Garnet Wolseley. He had a narrow escape from death in action when a shell burst between himself and another officer, and after the battle of Tel-el-Kebir in September, at which the Egyptian nationalist army was crushed, Wolseley wrote to Queen Victoria that 'on all sides I hear loud praises of the cool courage displayed when under extremely heavy fire,' by the Duke. It was agreed that Arthur took more care of his men than most of the other generals serving under Wolseley. At the same time he insisted on the use of his military, not royal, rank in connection with his army duties. A senior colonel who persisted in addressing him as 'your Royal Highness' was told sharply that 'on the parade ground I am "sir" and nothing else.'

Vicky and Fritz had stayed with Bertie and Alix at Marlborough House when they came to England for Arthur's wedding. They had just spent a trying few months, for in June 1878 Emperor William had almost fallen victim to an attempt on his life. A socialist agitator had shot and severely wounded him while on a carriage drive in Berlin, and for six months Fritz was regent of Prussia – a temporary appointment which, thanks to the machinations of Bismarck, ensured that all power stayed firmly out of the Crown Prince's grasp. On relinquishing the hollow regency after his aged father's astonishing recovery to full health, he received nothing more than a formal letter of thanks. Just before their return to Berlin after Arthur's wedding, Vicky wrote dejectedly to Queen Victoria thanking her for her kindness, the recollection of which would cheer her once back 'in a milieu which wants no common strength of mind not to be utterly depressed and become bitter.'[15]

Still grieving for Alice, Vicky's share of tragedy that winter was not yet over. After coming home again, she and Fritz were watching their younger children rehearsing a pantomime one afternoon when Waldemar complained of a sore throat. This youngest son had an irrepressible sense of humour and love of animals which was not shared by everyone. He had given Queen Victoria the fright of her life on a visit to England by deliberately letting Bob, his pet crocodile, loose in her study one evening. Yet for all his fondness of practical jokes, he was a delicate, undersized child. The diphtheria which had killed his aunt and cousin was diagnosed, and on 27 March, six weeks after his eleventh birthday, he too died.

Vicky was never the same after the loss of Waldemar. Not even the birth of a first grandchild (and Queen Victoria's first great-grandchild), Charlotte's daughter Feodora, born on 12 May, could alleviate the misery of her and Fritz. It said volumes for the prejudice of Orthodox Protestants in Germany, recalling how scandalised they had been by the view of Strauss and his royal supporters, that a Prussian minister of their persuasion told his congregation that he hoped the prince's death was a trial sent by God to humiliate his mother's hardened heart.

The new life Louise and Lorne had found for themselves in Canada, several thousand miles away from the Queen's all-pervading presence, was initially a success. They held court at Rideau Hall, Ottawa, overlooking the St Lawrence River. Louise was pleased by the recreational facilities – curling and tobogganing in the park, skating rinks and tennis courts in the grounds, and a large tent for garden suppers in the summer. As a hostess, she combined something of the English court's stiffness with an informality which shocked the less broadminded French Canadians. The press were soon to criticise her for employing masters of deportment to teach the people the correct courtly graces and backwards walk, and Catholic clergymen raised disapproving eyebrows at the suggestion that ladies should wear low evening dresses at Government House. Louise laughed that she could not care less if they came in blankets. At receptions, she wrote home proudly, there was 'no hand-shaking, no kissing and no feathers.' She raised no objection when several of the gentlemen became tipsy after a new year state ball. Like her mother, she was not censorious about occasional drunkenness. After having witnessed John Brown at Balmoral year after year, the men at Ottawa must have seemed comparatively decorous.

In her spare time Louise amused herself by writing an operetta, redecorating the interior of Rideau Hall, writing and illustrating an article on Canada for the English press, and going fishing. But after a while she became bored. Like Vicky and Alice, at receptions she was often seen to monopolise in conversation people she found interesting, not caring that others were being neglected. One observer who knew the family well said that Louise was even more shy than Vicky and, though very likeable as a person, lacked her eldest sister's charm of manner. Pleading ill-health, the lack of refined society and aesthetic opportunities in Canada, not to mention the 'impossible winters,' she returned home for a holiday.

Suitably refreshed, she went back to Canada after a few weeks and joined her husband on a tour of the wild west, made partly across prairie trails in wagons with relays of horses. The adventure inspired them both in different ways. Lorne wrote a long epic poem about their travels, while Louise was fired with enthusiasm by Canada's possibilities as a developing nation. She wrote home asking for Leopold to join them. All three travelled around Canada and then made a brief visit into the United States. In New York one newspaper published an effusive article about their royal guests, headed *VIC'S CHICKS* in bold type. Leopold had a terrier bitch who rejoiced in the irreverent name of Vic (had the heifer Princess Alice been thus neatly avenged?), and when he sent the article back to England his mother was not amused. 'How odd of them to mention your dog,'[16] she remarked.

For a time Louise found a mission in Canada for which she was well suited – encouragement of the arts. In 1880 a Royal Canadian Academy of Art was founded, and Lorne nominated the academicians. Each of these was called upon to donate a painting which would form the nucleus of a Dominion Gallery. During their travels in the west, they met an expedition from the

Smithsonian Institute collecting Indian relics on Canadian soil. This encouraged them to call a meeting of scholars and scientists to organise a Canadian Royal Society.

In February 1880, they had an accident on their horse-drawn sleigh while driving to a reception. The vehicle overturned, but while Lorne escaped with only minor injury, Louise fell on her head, suffered severe concussion, a badly cut ear, and straining of the muscles and sinews of her neck. Badly shaken and in great pain, she took a prolonged period of convalescence in Bermuda, England and then Europe – so prolonged, in fact, that it was said she had used her injuries as an excuse to get away indefinitely from her unsuccessful marriage. According to Ponsonby, Louise had been away from Canada so much that she was judged a failure there. As for husband and wife, both were happier without each other.

Louise regularly craved independence. So did Leopold, and after standing up firmly to his mother by snubbing Balmoral in favour of Paris he had finally won some measure of freedom. His interest in education resulted in invitations to preside over various committees and open colleges. Among causes dear to his heart were increased facilities for technical education, support for the Royal Institution for the Deaf and Dumb, and the establishment of a national conservatoire of music. Both Disraeli and Gladstone wrote to congratulate him on his speeches.

Leopold and Affie were both very musical, and they shared a common friend in the composer Arthur Sullivan. He persuaded them to support the cause of more free tuition for young students in music, and they made regular speeches on the subject. In December 1881, both brothers and the brother-in-law Christian were present at a meeting at the Manchester Athenaeum to promote the establishment of a Royal College of Music. While Affie took the chair, Leopold gave the address, in which he traced the history of music in England from medieval times to the present day. Affie, it is said, sometimes augmented his addresses with solos on the violin, although his prowess on the fiddle was disputed by several who knew his performances with the bow rather better than they wished to. One lady was proudly shown both his violin bows; he explained to her that he used one for solo work and another when playing in orchestras. She was tempted to remark what a pity it was he did not possess a third one for playing his instrument in tune.

Affie and Marie did not make a popular couple. He was frequently away from England, and thus not so well-known as his brothers. Those who met him occasionally found him touchy, reserved, a bore, and too fond of the bottle for his own good. In an age of heavy drinking, it was said the Duke of Edinburgh was a heavy drinker, particularly towards the end of his life when sorrow overwhelmed him. In fact, Affie was by far the most shy of the brothers. To those who knew him well, such as Sullivan, he was a valued friend with a wealth of interests, as well-informed on flora and fauna as on details of all the ships in his squadrons.

He was also responsible for inaugurating what would become one of the royal family's most priceless assets. Since boyhood he had collected postage stamps, and in 1890 he attended the inaugural ceremony of the Philatelic Society in his capacity as first honorary president, opening their first exhibition. Shortly before his death he sold his collection to Bertie, who presented it to his equally philatelically-minded son George.

As for Marie, she was too proud of her Russian ancestry to wish herself popular in England. She had always disliked her husband's country, and after the anti-Russian fervour of 1877–78 her contempt for the English hardened into lasting resentment. She absented herself from court as much as possible as she was not granted precedence over her sisters-in-law – mere princesses. Much would have been forgiven Marie by the English if she had possessed something of the Princess of Wales's charm or beauty, but fate had seen fit to bestow neither upon her. She was ungainly, unfeminine, and wore clothes that were as unbecoming as her physical appearance. Ironically her four daughters, who all despaired of their dowdy Mama, were all extremely attractive and high-spirited youngsters, whereas the three Wales girls, 'their royal shynesses,' were plain and lethargic creatures. Only the youngest, Maud, took at all after their mother in looks and energy.

Marie was cordially disliked by most of her in-laws apart from Leopold. His interest in education and the arts made him a man after her own heart. Yet his impish sense of humour proved almost too much for her on one occasion. Staying at Clarence House, he appeared at breakfast in the morning with a handkerchief over his mouth. He had lost a tooth, he explained. She was alarmed at this, and asked him to take the garment away from his face, to reveal a large hole in his gums. Having extracted his share of sympathy from her, he roared with laughter. The cavity was black sticking-plaster and the stains on his handkerchief red paint.

Yet Leopold longed to be given some more constructive activity. One evening at Balmoral, after a game of billiards with the Liberal member of parliament John Bright, he told his equerry that if not given something useful to do he would stand for parliament as an 'extreme radical.' Nobody took him seriously, for he was known to be a committed Tory, but it was recognised that he was too intelligent for his talents to be wasted in mere representative duties and idleness. He approached Disraeli, who was not alone in detecting the young man's resemblance to his late father, and felt that he might be able to take the Prince Consort's place as a confidential assistant. Such a course of action, the wily prime minister knew, could reduce the work imposed on him by constant attendance on the sovereign and at the same time provide the prince with suitable employment.

Leopold was accordingly appointed to help the Queen with her private correspondence and despatches, with special emphasis on foreign affairs, and was given a key to cabinet papers. Bertie was understandably indignant that his brother should be allowed access to state secrets denied to him, heir to the throne, and it said much for his magnanimity that relations between them were not soured.

The ill-feeling between the courts of Berlin and St James since Helena had married Christian in 1866 was shortly to be laid to rest. Prince William of Prussia had fallen for his cousin Elizabeth of Hesse, Alice's second daughter, but she disliked him and had already lost her heart to Grand Duke Serge of Russia, younger brother of the Duchess of Edinburgh. Willy's next choice was Princess Augusta of Schleswig-Holstein, 'Dona' to the family. She was the daughter of the dispossessed Duke Frederick, niece of Christian and Helena, and granddaughter of Queen Victoria's half-sister Feodora.

Vicky and Fritz welcomed their engagement when it was announced in February 1880. They felt that an alliance with their dynasty was an atonement for past wrongs; they admired Willy for his determination to marry Dona in the face of disapproval from Berlin; and they hoped that marriage would soften him after a life at Bonn university and the barracks had turned his head. It was left to Queen Victoria to sound a note of warning. Ella, a girl of character, would have been a restraining influence on her cousin; could the same be said of 'gentle and amiable and sweet' Dona?

The Queen did not have to wait long to be proved right. With Dona's blind adulation Willy's vanity reached epic proportions, as he proved on a visit to England in the autumn. While staying with Christian and Helena at Cumberland Lodge, he visited the Waleses at Marlborough House and accepted their invitation to stay and celebrate Bertie's birthday a few days later. Without any warning, he left the day before the birthday and returned to Cumberland Lodge. Bertie was privately thankful that his nephew had departed, for he saw that the tiresome boy was turning out to be an equally tiresome young man, but Helena and Christian found his behaviour rather embarrassing.

Barely two weeks after Willy's marriage at Berlin on 27 February 1881, St Petersburg became the scene of a thoroughly macabre family reunion. On his return from a military review, Tsar Alexander II fell victim to an assassin's bomb. Affie and Marie immediately hurried to the capital to attend the funeral.

The new Tsar and Tsarina, Alexander III and Marie, were perpetually haunted by the memory of their father's mutilated yet still semi-conscious body being brought back to the palace through snowy streets stained with the blood of soldiers killed in an attack earlier that day. Stringent police precautions made the Romanovs and their guests virtual prisoners in the Winter Palace, and the only place where they could exercise was a narrow courtyard which the English guests thought even worse than a London East End slum.

Affie cabled to Bertie that they all wished for the presence of himself and Alix. Though Queen Victoria hesitated to risk the life of her heir and his wife on such a hazardous mission, her ministers believed that their presence could help to bring about a closer understanding between both imperial powers. From Germany came Fritz, sent by his unfeeling father and Bismarck who shrugged off the warning letters he and Vicky had received, telling him that he too would be killed if he went to Russia. The obsequies passed off without incident, but several ingenious conspiracies and devices were discovered by the police before the gathering left Russia. There were rumours of mines underneath the church and torpedoes embedded in the frozen river Neva.

In May 1881 Leopold was created Duke of Albany (a title that had lapsed since the death of the childless Frederick, Duke of York and Albany, in 1827), Earl of Clarence and Baron Arklow. Now aged twenty-eight, he was earnestly looking for a bride. It was suggested that Frances Maynard, the beautiful seventeen-year-old stepdaughter of the Earl of Rosslyn, might be suitable. At their first meeting, however, she fell in love with Leopold's equerry Lord Francis Brooke, heir to the Earl of Warwick, and married him instead. (Later she became a mistress of Bertie's, but fell from favour after becoming a passionate socialist). Leopold was best man at the wedding, by which time he was engaged to Princess Helen of Waldeck-Pyrmont, sister of Queen Emma of the Netherlands. They were married on 27 April 1882 at Windsor, the groom having just recovered from an attack of severe bruising after slipping on some orange peel at a hotel on the French Riviera. The Queen gave them the Claremont estate in Surrey as a wedding present.

The bride was a princess of considerable character, and almost alone among the Queen's children-in-law was totally unafraid of her. Whenever she had a problem she would not write or send messages to her through an intermediary, like her children did, but insisted on confronting her face to face. Queen Victoria could not but respect this young woman who had the courage to stand up to her, but Ponsonby recorded one evening that she conspicuously did not appear at the Queen's table but dined alone with her husband. The interview beforehand, he surmised, must have been a lively one.

When their first child was born on 25 February 1883, the Queen found it hard to believe that her frail son had lived long enough to present her with another granddaughter. When she first set eyes on the baby, named Alice, Leopold was recovering from a bad knee on one sofa, Helen resting on another. Queen Victoria had also injured her leg, 'and when I came as a third helpless creature, it had quite a ludicrous effect.'[17]

Much as he loved Claremont, Leopold still thirsted for regular employment independent of his mother. When the governor-generalship of Canada fell vacant on the expiry of Lord Lorne's five-year term of office, he applied for the post. After being advised that the Fenian movement was particularly active there – and perhaps also in view of the fact that Lorne's appointment had not been a very successful one – the Queen asked Gladstone to veto his candidacy. A few months later he tried for the governorship of Victoria, Australia, undaunted by the memory of his brother Affie's narrow escape from an assassin's bullet at Sydney in 1868, but this was rejected on similar grounds.

As foretold all too often, Leopold was not to live to a great age. The weather in February and March 1884 was particularly harsh, with biting east winds by day and heavy frost at night. On medical advice he was sent to Cannes, leaving behind him Helen who was expecting a second child in the summer. In the hotel one afternoon he slipped on the tiled floor at the foot of a staircase, and hit his knee hard against the bottom step. For anybody else, the result would probably not have been serious, but in his case it proved fatal, and despite prompt medical attention, he died two days later, on 28 March. The hotel staff thought that his fall had been the result of a momentary lapse in consciousness, and initially epilepsy was though to be the cause of death. Official certificates from London and Cannes did not give any, but a slow haemorrhage was probably responsible.

Although grieved at his loss, Queen Victoria could only be thankful that he had survived a precarious childhood, through a succession of trials and sufferings, to make a happy marriage. 'For him we must not repine,' she wrote to Vicky the following day; '. . . there was such a restless longing for what he could not have.'[18] In spite of ill health he had made small but perceptible contributions to the standing of education and the arts of his day, thus pursuing a role similar (if on a lesser scale) to that which the Prince Consort had undertaken. There was a pleasing irony in that Queen Victoria's shortest-lived child was father to the princess who ultimately attained what was at the time a record age for a member of the British royal family. Alice, later Countess of Athlone, died in January 1981, within two months of what would have been her ninety-eighth birthday.

Almost alone among Queen Victoria's children, the marriage of Leopold and Helen had not been criticised by dissenting voices at home or abroad. Vicky's betrothal had come under fire from *The Times*, who wished 'some better fate' for her than being wedded to a prince from pro-Russian Prussia during the Crimean war. The Berlin court had scoffed at 'poor matches' of most of her brothers and sisters, or alternately protested at being insulted by a Danish bride or a Scottish groom. The weddings of Affie and Arthur had been received with less than rapturous approval in England.

Yet nobody was prepared for the fury which confronted Queen Victoria's eager sanctioning of Battenberg alliances with members of her family. The morganatic marriage in 1851 of Prince Alexander of Hesse to Countess Julie Hauke, lady-in-waiting to the Tsarina, had produced a daughter and four sons. Louis, the eldest son, married his cousin Victoria, Alice's eldest daughter, at Darmstadt on 30 April 1884. Scornful remarks were made in Berlin about the Battenbergs' humble origins, but the Queen had grown used to these ritual complaints and she was a warm admirer of the handsome Louis. The court at Darmstadt, a sad and quiet one for some five years, was suddenly overwhelmed by a host of royalties from Europe.

Though only four weeks had elapsed since Leopold's death, the Queen hoped it might bring some comfort into their lives. Instead it was almost overshadowed by the unwelcome news that her widowed son-in-law had found consolation with a Polish divorcee of dubious reputation, Alexandrine von Kolemine. Grand Duke Louis's children liked her and were glad that their lonely father had found love again. For once the usually observant Queen noticed nothing, but when he married her in a secret ceremony a few hours after his daughter's wedding, the remaining guests were panic-stricken. The news gradually filtered out, and Lady Ely, one of the Queen's ladies, was asked to tell her sovereign. With icy calm, the Queen sent for Bertie and gave him the unenviable task of informing 'la Kolemine' that the marriage must be declared null and void.

The indignant German Empress immediately recalled Vicky and Fritz to Berlin, for this short-lived liaison had been the last straw. She was already irritated by the Victoria-Louis match, by Ella of Hesse's betrothal to Grand Duke Serge of Russia (she had hoped for one of her Baden grandsons to marry the princess). But another *mésalliance* had incensed her most of all.

Sandro, who with his brother Louis and Affie had been at the centre of the *Sultan* affair, was elected sovereign prince of Bulgaria in 1879. While his liberal uncle and champion Tsar Alexander II reigned in Russia, Sandro had a powerful patron, but the Tsar's assassination brought the suspicious reactionary Tsar Alexander III to the imperial throne. The new Tsar never liked Sandro, and resented his refusal to rule Bulgaria as a mere satellite state of St Petersburg. His throne was therefore beginning to look increasingly insecure by 1883, the year he went on a tour of Europe. At Potsdam he was presented to Vicky and Fritz, and this handsome young eligible bachelor was soon seen as a candidate for the hand of Princess Victoria ('Moretta') of Prussia. Whether the two were really in love, or whether Sandro was merely looking hastily for an attractive consort to provide him with sons and make his position as sovereign prince more secure, has been argued endlessly.

Vicky was extremely keen on the match, and after a visit to Balmoral, Sandro found further champions in Queen Victoria and Bertie. Fritz disapproved, perhaps because he thought a Battenberg prince not good enough for a Hohenzollern princess (as did his parents), or maybe because he was anxious to avoid unpleasantness and another family row. Bismarck and Emperor William were not only opposed to it on dynastic grounds. They were convinced it was part of a scheme, supported if not originated by Queen Victoria, to alienate Germany from Russia.

Before the matter was resolved one way or the other, Battenberg brother number three fell in love. This was Henry ('Liko'), a twenty-five-year-old officer with the Prussian household cavalry at Potsdam.

Beatrice had celebrated her twenty-seventh birthday a fortnight before attending the wedding of her niece Victoria at Darmstadt. It seemed she was doomed to live out her childhood promise that she would never get married. Therefore it was a shock to her mother when she announced nervously, soon after their return to England, that she was in love – with Prince Henry of Battenberg. Finding it impossible to believe at first, the Queen then told herself that it was an infatuation that would never have happened if Beatrice had not just lost her brother Leopold. Or had those dreadful scenes at Darmstadt been responsible? She prayed fervently that this youngest daughter would be spared to her, protected from the horrors of marriage.

But Beatrice proved that she also had a will of her own. For weeks, mother and daughter communicated merely by means of written notes passed between them at the breakfast table.

At length the Queen relented, thanks in no small measure to Vicky's tactful persuasion. Surely Mama recalled how dearest Papa always wanted his children to be happy; how lonely she, Mama, had been before she met and married Papa, with no friends of her own age; and there was nobody of Beatrice's age now that Leopold was gone. The Queen conceded that Beatrice could marry Liko after all if that was what she wanted, but on condition that he retire from the Prussian army; she should continue to be her mother's unofficial private secretary and confidante; and that both of them should live with her in England. Liko, the Queen admitted to Vicky, had completely won her heart, but still the prospect of her 'precious Baby's marrying at all' was a great trial; 'I hope and pray there may be no results! That would aggravate everything and besides make me terribly anxious.'[19]

As expected, there was hostility from Berlin, where Vicky found herself alone in her excitement at Beatrice's forthcoming marriage. What did Fritz mean, the Queen asked coldly, by saying that Liko was not of the blood – 'a little like about animals?' How dare Willy and Dona, 'poor little insignificant princess' who was of hardly more noble birth than the Battenbergs, be so impertinent and insolent? How could the Empress Augusta object, when the father of her son-in-law was the son of 'a very bad woman'? Fresh blood had to be infused into the family occasionally, or the race would degenerate morally and physically. In any case, 'if the Queen of England thinks a person good enough for her daughter what have other people got to say?'[20] They had plenty to say, but she would not be deterred, though she thought it extremely unkind of Fritz to write to Arthur, in order to try and use his influence to prevent the Queen from making Liko a Royal Highness.

Beatrice and Liko were married at St Mildred's Church, Whippingham, on 23 July 1885. It was the first time that a sovereign's daughter had wed in a parish church. Liko's white military uniform, on which the Queen insisted despite asking him to give up his soldiering career, made him look oddly out of place in a village setting, and Alix mischievously dubbed him 'Beatrice's Lohengrin.' Though it was the ninth occasion she had stood beside a child on his or her way to the altar, Queen Victoria wrote (forgetting in her excitement that she had not been at Affie's wedding), 'I think I never felt more deeply than I did on this occasion, though full of confidence.'[21] In fact she had less reason to experience any heartache as she gave her daughter away, for she was not losing a child but indeed gaining a son.

At least one observer was unimpressed by the spectacle of the royal family as they attended this wedding. The reporter of the weekly journal, *Truth*, admittedly an organ which had little reverence for the crown, noted that the Queen looked 'exceedingly cross' and tapped her foot 'in a very ominous way' during the Archbishop of Canterbury's lengthy address; the Prince of Wales was 'fidgety', the Grand Duke of Hesse looked 'old and haggard', the Duke of Edinburgh 'even more sour and supercilious than usual', and the Duchess's 'sullen expression which [had] become habitual . . . appeared to be accentuated for the occasion.' Princess Louise, the report continued, 'looked well but has a very flighty manner', while Lord Lorne, in tartans, 'certainly looked very common'. Only Prince George of Wales received any praise; though 'a very ordinary looking lad . . . [he] apparently has more go about him than his brother.'[22]

Liko brought back an air of happiness to the Queen's domestic life such as she had not known since the Prince Consort's death. Once more there was a man in the family, one who was not terrified of her, and one with whom she could make light-hearted conversation and laugh at meals. She gave him a yacht in which he could make pleasure cruises as far afield as the Mediterranean, and a bicycle which he mastered with ease. He was more fortunate in this than the Duke of Connaught, who was given command of a bicycle regiment, and learned to cycle in order to make a fitting impression on his men – only to fall off in an undignified heap the first time he attempted to return the salute of an NCO from his saddle.

Liko took the lead in helping to revive the *tableaux vivants* which Prince Albert had so loved helping his small children to prepare for their mother's amusement. He shared the roles with Louise and Lorne, who outwardly maintained the facade of a happy marriage for the Queen's sake, though it was recognised that they were heading for eventual separation, the widowed Duchess of Albany, and ladies and gentlemen from the household. Queen Victoria looked forward to these performances with almost childish enthusiasm, though she stipulated that she must be permitted to act as censor. For example, it would never do for the Marchioness of Lorne, even if playing the part of a villainess in a French comedy, to be reproved as 'a degraded woman' by an assistant under-secretary.

At the same time, it was not for members of the audience – be they ever so exalted – to chatter and make endless conversation during recitals. Beatrice, normally so placid, was once moved to tell her Mama sternly to be quiet. The Queen disarmingly hid her face in her hands like a naughty child, promising 'I will be good! I will be good!'

It said much for Liko's powers of persuasion that he prevailed upon his mother-in-law to relax her attitude on smoking. Prince Christian had only been permitted to indulge in this anti-social vice in a small cubbyhole at Osborne which was reached by crossing the servants' quarters and an open yard. Now, thanks to Liko, they could also use a more conveniently situated, well-furnished sitting room for the purpose. Even so there was no relaxation of the rules at Windsor. Only the billiard room was available for smoking and only after eleven o'clock each evening. Here Affie tended to occupy one of the best chairs and hold forth endlessly about himself. In consequence Liko gave up smoking for a while, finding his naval brother-in-law's conversation more than he could stand.

Christmas 1885 at Osborne was the happiest that any of the family could remember for a quarter of a century. Beatrice and Liko were allotted a suite in the new wing. Helen of Albany and her children, plus the Connaughts and their family, were there to share the festivities – presents on the tables, party games, theatrical performances, and beech logs burning brightly in the polished steel grate of the Queen's sitting room.

'Papa always wanted his children to be happy,' Vicky had often said wistfully. The ghost of the Prince Consort must have looked on with wholehearted approval this time.

Despite Queen Victoria's initial fears, there were shortly to be 'results' of the marriage. On 23 November 1886, Beatrice gave birth to a son Alexander, soon known as 'Drino'. For the time being, Liko's happiness was apparently complete. The Battenbergs generally craved adventure, but the quiet domestic world of Prince Henry was safe if dull compared to the misfortunes of brother Sandro. Early one morning in August 1886, a gang of drunken officers had broken into the palace at Sofia, seized the sovereign prince and forced him at gunpoint to sign a deed of abdication. In December the prematurely aged, weary prince arrived in England and received a welcome at Windsor from the Queen almost unparalleled since she had beheld her cousin Albert forty-seven years before. 'Sandro reminds me of Papa,' Louise remarked to her mother. He still hoped to marry Princess Victoria of Prussia, he told them; but their ill-fated engagement did not cast the only shadow that threatened to fall across the triumph of Queen Victoria's approaching jubilee celebrations.

4

Victorian Sunset 1887–1901

The Prince of Wales set the tone for the memorable year of 1887. On new year's day he presented Queen Victoria with a jubilee inkstand, in the shape of an imperial crown which opened to reveal her portrait inside the lid. 'Very pretty and useful' was her verdict. Throughout all the activities and preparations for the festivities in June – rehearsals for the thanksgiving service, examination and despatch of jubilee coins and medals, lists of guests, remission of sentences for convicts throughout the empire – Bertie was 'very kind and helpful.' Without his constant support, zeal for organisation, and shouldering of the burden of entertaining guests from all corners of the globe, she admitted, she would never have managed. Inevitably, there were some tiresome problems to be surmounted. Why, she asked crossly, could a private soldier obtain leave as a mere formality while it required a special bill in parliament to secure the arrival of the Duke of Connaught, now lieutenant-governor of Bombay and commander-in-chief in the Bombay presidency, home from India for the occasion?

Yet Arthur's passage back was only a minor inconvenience. Far worse was the unfolding of a personal tragedy in Germany. During a visit to Italy with his family the previous autumn, Fritz had caught a severe chill. He could not shake off his cold or an uncomfortable hoarseness that winter, and early in the new year De Wegner decided to seek specialist advice. In March Professor Gerhardt, lecturer in medicine at Berlin university, examined the Crown Prince and discovered a small swelling on the lower portion of the left vocal cord. This, he assured the patient and Vicky, could soon be cured with simple albeit painful treatment. After unsuccessful attempts at removal of the growth and cauterisation, Gerhardt sent him for a cure at Ems. Fritz felt so much better on his return to Berlin that he believed himself completely cured. It was an unpleasant shock when he was examined again and told that the swelling was larger than before. By the time Gerhardt had decided to seek another opinion, Fritz suspected that something was seriously wrong with him. When the third specialist consulted, Dr Bergmann, recommended splitting the larynx in order to remove the swelling, Vicky was horrified. At this Bismarck intervened, insisting that no operation of such gravity could take place without consent of the Crown Prince and the Emperor. After a consultation involving three more doctors, it was decided to call in a specialist from outside Germany. Any operation, it was understood, might well prove fatal. Even if the Crown Prince survived, he would almost certainly lose his voice as a result. It would vindicate the cause of German science if a foreign doctor was left to take the crucial decisions, and therefore the blame if and when anything went wrong.

For political reasons, it was inadvisable to choose a specialist from Austria or France. The name of Dr Morell Mackenzie, a Scotsman based in Harley Street, appeared the most obvious. He was a proven expert on diseases of the nose and throat, spoke fluent German, and already knew Gerhardt. Above all, he was British. What a triumph it would be for the anti-English faction at court if a fellow-countryman of their unpopular Crown Princess could be held responsible for the death of their Crown Prince.

At the German doctors' request, Vicky cabled for Queen Victoria to send Mackenzie at once. This she did, adding a private caveat that the Scot was clever but 'greedy and grasping about money and tries to make a profit out of his attendance.'

Mackenzie arrived in Berlin on 20 May, and after consulting his colleagues he examined Fritz's throat. He removed a small portion of the swelling and passed it to Professor Virchow, at the Berlin institute of pathology, for diagnosis. It was deemed too small, and on request he removed a larger sample two days later. At this stage the arguments began. Gerhardt insisted that

Mackenzie had injured the healthy right vocal cord and made it bleed. The German doctors maintained that the only course was for them to operate immediately. Mackenzie told them that if they did, the Crown Prince would certainly die.

Vicky and Fritz had set their hearts on being in London for the jubilee. Between them and Mackenzie, they decided that they should all go to England, and Fritz could attend the celebrations while undergoing treatment as a private patient in the doctor's surgery. There was criticism in Berlin. What if the ninety-year-old Emperor, becoming progressively weaker after a series of fainting fits, should die while his heir was abroad? What if the heir should have a relapse and be too ill to return home? Gerhardt said that either event was perfectly possible, but he and his colleagues – apart from two, Dr Wegner and the younger Dr Landgraf, who it was agreed should be part of the suite going to England – did not begrudge the absence of their imperial patient, which would free them from responsibility and place the burden firmly on Mackenzie.

Although more desperately worried than she dared to admit, Vicky put a brave face on events. 'One cannot be kept a prisoner here,' she said, 'or be prevented from following a useful course by the fear of what might happen.'

Their immediate destination in London was a hotel at Norwood, within comfortable reach of the metropolis, but a satisfactory distance from midsummer heat and dust. After a few days of peace and quiet there, they moved to Buckingham Palace on 18 June so Fritz could have a couple of days' complete rest before the procession to Westminster Abbey.

On 20 June, the fiftieth anniversary of her accession (or, as she humbly recalled, the day fifty years ago on which her dear Uncle William died), Queen Victoria came from Windsor to Buckingham Palace and was hostess at a luncheon party to visiting royalties from Europe and the east. In the evening there was a large family dinner party. 'The day has come,' she wrote in her diary that evening, exhausted, 'and I am alone, though surrounded by many dear children.'[1]

For Prince Albert, had he lived, it would certainly have been a proud day. In that sense she was alone, but all surviving seven children and their spouses were there, plus the widowed Grand Duke Louis of Hesse (who had quickly been forgiven his liaison with Madame Kolemine) and the Duchess of Albany. It seemed appropriate that Bertie's younger brothers had travelled back with their families from outposts of their mother's empire. Affie, now a rear-admiral and commander-in-chief of the Mediterranean fleet, had come back from his base at Malta. Arthur had likewise obtained leave from India with little difficulty.

The climax of the jubilee was the procession to Westminster Abbey and the thanksgiving service on 21 June. Vast crowds lining the route were rewarded by seeing almost every member of their sovereign's family passing by. In ten carriages sat her daughters, daughters-in-law, granddaughters, granddaughters-in-law and their ladies. They were followed by her sons, five sons-in-law, nine grandsons and grandsons-in-law, all mounted on chargers and attired in glittering uniforms. The Prince of Wales was resplendent in the scarlet tunic and plumed helmet of a British field-marshal, while his elder son Prince Albert Victor was in the blue and gold of the 10th Hussars, and Prince George in naval lieutenant's uniform. It was agreed by family and public alike that the German Crown Prince, in his cuirassier uniform and silver helmet surmounted with the imperial eagle, was the most magnificent of all. Towering above his relations on either side, he looked, it was said, like 'one of the legendary heroes embodied in the creations of Wagner.' His health was still a closely-guarded secret.

At the end of the service (which included a *Te Deum* and chorale composed by the Prince Consort), the family filed past Queen Victoria to pay her homage as she sat on the coronation chair. The men bowed and kissed her hand; the women curtsied and were tenderly embraced. But the most spontaneous gesture was that shown to Fritz, who happened to be standing by her chair as she stepped down and was embraced with deep affection.

At the palace the Queen presented jubilee brooches to all the princesses present, and tie-pins to the princes. After a delayed luncheon she watched a march past by the naval guard of honour, and attended a present-giving ceremony in the ballroom. Resting on her sofa later, she opened scores of congratulatory telegrams, assisted by her daughters and Liko.

The following day continued in similar fashion. A large luncheon party was held at the palace, the family gathering later immortalised in a painting by the Danish artist Lauritz Tuxen. There was a presentation of jubilee medals to the kings and princes, and a garden fete for 26,000 schoolchildren at Hyde Park, where every young guest was given a commemorative mug. At Windsor a statue of the Queen by Sir Edgar Boehm was unveiled, and a torchlight procession of Eton boys entered the castle quadrangle singing college songs. Almost a month of reviews, receptions and garden parties followed. Always impervious to cold, Queen Victoria abhorred heat, and was relieved to bid farewell to the midsummer temperature and bustle of London as she returned to Osborne on 19 July. Even there, a large block of ice was vital at the centre of her dinner table each evening to keep the air cool.

Vicky and Fritz stayed with the Queen for the rest of the jubilee summer, and he appeared to be improving, free from the pressures and intrigues of Berlin. Yet it was impossible to relax completely. Affie's eldest daughter Marie, who played with them as they sat on the beach near Osborne, later recalled with a strange lack of understanding that her uncle Fritz was very jolly as he pretended to bombard her and her sisters with sand and dry seaweed, 'yet one somehow felt he was condescending.' Her aunt's forced gaiety was equally apparent; 'her smile had something of sunshine in it when the weather is not really warm.'[2]

In August they all went north to Scotland. Vicky and Fritz stayed at Braemar, driving daily the few miles to Balmoral where the Queen and Beatrice, expecting a second child in the autumn, were resting from their exertions in the south. Fritz's voice improved, and the Highland air made him feel much better. The Queen was relieved at his apparent progress. She did not know that Dr Mark Hovell, a senior surgeon at the throat hospital and perhaps the most capable (but regrettably the least assertive) doctor involved of all, had examined Fritz and was certain the growth was malignant.

Yet Mackenzie was confident of eventual recovery, and rash enough to say so. Fritz was similarly optimistic and deeply grateful, and anxious that his mother-in-law should make some acknowledgement of his work. On 7 September, therefore, the Queen invited Mackenzie to lunch at Balmoral, knighting him afterwards at an improvised ceremony in the drawing-room. She still had her misgivings and doubted his suitability, but to refuse Fritz's request was tantamount to telling him he was doomed. After laying down the sword she asked Mackenzie searching questions about her son-in-law's illness. It disturbed her that he could tell her so little.

It was not only the Queen who was uneasy. In Berlin, the court was asking when Crown Prince Frederick William was going to come home. The conservatives resented his indefinite presence in England under the care of a doctor whose diagnosis was believed to be wrong; the liberals feared that Prince William was gaining too much influence in state affairs during his father's absence. But as Vicky retorted, it would be 'madness' to jeopardise her husband's chances of recovery by returning too hastily.

As summer turned into autumn the Scottish weather became cold and damp, and Mackenzie stressed the need to avoid Berlin over winter. Early in September, the entourage headed for Toblach in the Austrian Tyrol, then Venice and later Baveno in Italy.

At Balmoral the jubilee celebrations were not yet over. On 6 October Bertie unveiled a statue of Queen Victoria at a ceremony attended not only by the Queen, Beatrice and Liko, but also by ex-Empress Eugenie, plus tenants and workers from the

Balmoral and Abergeldie estates. Later that week he had lunch privately with his mother, who noted in her journal tenderly that he had not stayed alone with her in Scotland for nearly twenty years; 'he is so kind and affectionate that it is a pleasure to be a little quietly together.'[3]

On 24 October Beatrice gave birth to a daughter, the first royal child to be born in Scotland since 1600 when the future King Charles I had entered the world. The cottagers were delighted at this news, and even more so when they heard that the christening was also to be on Deeside. Eugenie was invited to be one of the sponsors for the princess, whose chosen names were Victoria Eugenia Julia Eua – but the rector misread the handwritten documents and the last name became Ena instead. It was a cheerful Christmas at Osborne that year, with two Battenberg infants in the house. At Whippingham school the Battenbergs and Lornes were on the platform to hand out presents.

Meanwhile at Villa Zirio, San Remo, on the Italian coast near the French border, festivities were anything but cheerful. Vicky and Fritz had moved there to its temperate climate at the beginning of November. Within a week of their arrival, Fritz had ominous new swellings on his throat, and he found it an effort to sit up. Mackenzie was summoned, and after examining his patient he no longer talked lightheartedly of a cure. He had to admit that the disease was almost certainly cancer.

In Berlin, once the news had reached them, the calumnies against their Crown Princess increased a hundredfold. She had so set her heart on becoming Empress, it was said openly, that she had kept the gravity of her husband's illness a secret, afraid lest he would be passed over in favour of their eldest son. She had refused to listen to German doctors, obstinately preferring to summon one from England. Both of them had given him falsely optimistic hopes about his condition, and to satisfy her own whims, she had dragged him to London where he exhausted himself in her mother's jubilee procession. Furthermore she and Mackenzie had conspired to distrust his German colleagues, thus preventing an operation on the sick man while such a step might have saved his life. One of their servants had spread malicious rumours that the Crown Princess and her chamberlain, Count Seckendorff, were lovers; she had prevented the operation so that her husband could live just long enough to leave her with an imperial dowry and the count, whom she would therefore marry as soon as she could afterwards. Mackenzie likewise came in for vicious slanders. Some whispered that he was Jewish (anti-Semitism was rife in Berlin, and official circles had been shocked when Vicky gladly accepted the honorary chairmanship of an orphanage for Jewish girls); others said that he too was the lover of the Crown Princess.

Willy was still smarting from his experience at the jubilee. After entertaining false hopes that he and Dona would be representing Prussia instead of his father, he was insulted at finding that not only did his parents go after all, but also everyone was more interested in his father's health than in him. He had been only too happy to return to his flatterers at Berlin, who sent him to San Remo in order to bring his father back to Germany for an operation. Worn down by weeks of anxiety, harassed by the quarrelling doctors, the sight of her son trying to order them around was more than Vicky could tolerate. In her own words, she 'pitched into him . . . with considerable violence,' and threatened to see that he was forbidden from the villa in future. Chastened, he explained apologetically that he had been sent as the Emperor's representative, and he was merely obeying orders. Apologising for losing her temper, she told him that she bore no grudge, but she would not brook any interference.

The only pleasure that Vicky and Fritz knew for the next four months was the company of friends and more welcome relations. Bertie, Affie and Louise were among those who came to try and raise their drooping spirits, play backgammon and chess with the invalid and soothe his wife every time she broke down under the sheer weight of misery of their ordeal.

On the morning of 9 March 1888 Fritz was walking in the grounds of the villa when he was handed a telegram addressed to His Majesty Emperor Frederick William. His long reign as Crown Prince was over, but in circumstances pathetically different from those which he and his family had envisaged. After choosing the title Frederick III, one of his first actions was to send Queen Victoria a telegram expressing his desire for a 'close and lasting relationship between our two nations.' Two days later, the new Emperor and Empress entered Berlin in a swirling snowstorm.

Bertie represented Queen Victoria at the Emperor William's funeral, a ceremony Fritz had to be persuaded by doctors not to attend because of the extreme cold. A few days later the Queen announced her intention of coming to see her stricken son-in-law at Berlin. At this the Bismarcks and their cronies were furious, believing that she would use her visit to sanction openly the engagement between her granddaughter and the ex-Prince of Bulgaria. Unknown to all but a few confidantes, Queen Victoria had revised her opinions and decided against the match. He could never marry her granddaughter while Crown Prince William was so hostile towards him, and Liko for one wondered whether Sandro had really been in love with her; he suspected that Vicky had pushed him into it and felt honour-bound to proceed with the marriage once it was permitted. Moreover, since living in Darmstadt as a private citizen, Sandro had fallen in love with an opera singer, Johanna Loisinger.

On the morning of 24 April, the royal train drew into the station at Berlin. Queen Victoria, Beatrice and Liko went straight to the sickbed at the Charlottenburg Palace. As Vicky ruefully remarked, it was the first time that she and Fritz had had Mama under their own roof as a guest. The Queen sat beside the bed, holding Fritz's hand and talking cheerfully about the family, while he wrote at intervals on his pad and passed it to her. She did not tell him of the romance between Sandro and Johanna, as he had given his blessing to the marriage between him and Victoria in a letter to Willy left with his will. Only when she was alone with Vicky did the Queen tell her; Vicky reproached herself bitterly for giving her daughter false hopes, but she had begun to appreciate that eventual marriage in the face of such overwhelming odds was unlikely to be for the best.

Despite gloomy predictions from her prime minster Lord Salisbury that Her Majesty would be exposed to fierce anti-English demonstrations in the streets, the people of Berlin could not cheer her loudly enough. Whenever Vicky took her seat in the carriage beside her mother, there were equally hearty cries of 'Long live the Empress!' No further proof was needed that Vicky was much-loved by the people into whose nation she had married; it was merely the arch-conservative circles at court and society who hated and feared her, and had done their best to blacken her name. Bismarck had been quite patronising about Queen Victoria before her arrival, but etiquette required him to request an audience with the Queen and the prospect had visibly unnerved him, much to Ponsonby's amusement. The meeting lasted an hour, and was restricted to uncontroversial matters such as Crown Prince William's 'inexperience'; the chancellor's and Queen's only other meeting, at Versailles in 1855; and an assurance that the chancellor was not contemplating the 'cruelty' of a regency for the ailing Emperor. At the end he emerged from it mopping his brow in relief, exclaiming with admiration that 'one could do business with her!'

One month later, on 24 May (the Queen's birthday), royalty attended the wedding of Vicky's and Fritz's second son Henry to his cousin Irene of Hesse at the Charlottenburg chapel. A shallow and easily-led youth, Henry had sided with his elder brother and sister against their parents at first, but Irene (unlike Dona) was a princess of some character whose steadying influence had made him much more amenable to his English relations. Fritz's gallant effort in attending his son's wedding in full uniform won the admiration of all but the most cold-hearted guests present. Bismarck's son Herbert had the bad taste to remark afterwards to Bertie that a sovereign who could not take part in debates should not be allowed to reign. It took the normally affable prince all his self-control to resist an overpowering temptation to throw the younger Bismarck bodily out of the room.

At the beginning of June, the court moved to the Neue Palais at Potsdam, which Fritz asked should be renamed Friedrichskron in his memory. Here he had been born and here, overlooking the garden he and Vicky had so lovingly built soon after their marriage, he wished to die. On 15 June the family gathered in the sickroom, Willy and Dona with their large suite ordering the servants around as if they owned the place already. During the morning Fritz slipped in and out of consciousness, and shortly after eleven o'clock his last struggle was over. 'I must stumble on my way alone!' the grieving widow wrote to her mother that evening. 'I shall disappear as much from the world as possible and certainly not push myself forward anywhere!'[4]

As if the tragedy of her husband's slow death, and the demise of all their hopes for the future, was not enough, Vicky was subjected to an astonishing if not totally unexpected campaign of persecution in Germany. While her husband lay dying their eldest son had placed a secret guard around the palace, so that nobody could leave without a permit. He had intended to prevent the removal of private correspondence, knowing it would not show him in a particularly good light. Fortunately Vicky and Fritz had had the foresight to place it in safe custody already, at Windsor and at the British embassy in Berlin. The German doctors published an angry self-defence and provoked Mackenzie into publishing his retaliatory diatribe *The Fatal Illness of Frederick the Noble*, a book which alienated his support in Britain. Some of Fritz's Franco-Prussian war diaries were published in a German journal that autumn to prove that he had been more responsible for unification of the German empire than the vacillating Bismarck, resulting in a savage witch-hunt against several of Fritz's friends.

Queen Victoria readily admitted that Vicky's tragedy was far worse than hers in 1861. For some years, she had regarded her imperial daughter as 'too high and mighty,' too grand and too intellectual for comfort. With Fritz's death, all was changed. Mother and daughter had a common bond in their widowhood, but at least Albert had not left his wife to face a torrent of abuse after his death that was to be the lot of the eldest daughter for whom they had entertained such high hopes.

Vicky knew where the blame lay with regard to her son's attitude towards her. Two weeks into her widowhood, she wrote to her mother explaining that she closed her eyes and ears to the official world, as it was 'the only way not feel the profoundest irritation with William. I am only too ready to make all allowances for him, when I think of the deplorable friends he has had, & of all the nonsense with which his head has been so systematically stuffed!!'[5] Painfully aware of the tension between mother and son, Queen Victoria wrote asking Emperor William II 'to bear with poor Mama if she is sometimes irritated and excited. She does not mean it so; think what months of agony and suspense with broken and sleepless nights she had gone through . . .'[6] She went on to add that she trusted he would observe a decent interval of mourning for his father before paying any visits to other sovereigns – and his grandmother would surely be the first to whom he would pay his respects in person. The Emperor, however, had no such intentions. He had a duty, he answered, to show himself and assert his powers. To him there seemed nothing incongruous in paying a state visit to Russia within a month of his father's death.

Alix had never forgiven the Germans for their copious insults to Denmark, but she had been fond of and respected Fritz and Vicky. It took little persuasion on the Queen's part to ask her if she would accompany Bertie to the funeral. Once at the sad ceremony he forgot his usual discretion, so angry was he with his nephew. Not content with echoing the general opinion that 'William the Great needs to learn that he is living in the nineteenth century and not in the Middle Ages,' he asked Herbert Bismarck rather unwisely if it was true that the late Emperor Frederick had mentioned anything about Germany making concessions to other European countries by returning Alsace-Lorraine to France, Schleswig to Denmark and Hanover to the Duke of Cumberland, who had recently married the Princess of Wales's youngest sister Thyra. When he heard this, William loudly declared that he would not tolerate such an insult to his father's memory. Considering he had readily tolerated a host of other insults aimed at the same target, this was rich indeed.

In September Bertie was due to join Emperor Francis Joseph of Austria at manoeuvres, and go shooting afterwards with Crown Prince Rudolf. Emperor William waited till his uncle had arrived in Vienna, then ostentatiously announced his own imminent arrival, stating that no other royal guest should be present at the Habsburg court while he was there. It was left to the embarrassed British ambassador in Vienna to tell the Prince of Wales that he would have to leave the city forthwith. Bertie had no option but to take advantage of a hasty offer of hospitality from the King of Roumania for a few days. But within twenty-four hours Vienna was buzzing with the news that the German emperor had threatened to cancel his visit unless the Prince of Wales was asked to depart immediately.

Queen Victoria was incensed at this insult to her son and heir. Her grandson's wish to be treated as 'His Imperial Majesty' in private as well as public was '*perfect madness!*' His excuse that the Prince of Wales had treated him as a nephew and not as an emperor was 'too *vulgar* and absurd, as well as untrue, almost *to be believed*.' If he had such intentions, he had better never come to England again; 'The Queen will not swallow this affront.'[7]

Bertie was so angry and upset by his nephew's behaviour that, in a moment of weakness which he soon regretted, he tried to prevent Vicky from coming to England later that year. Queen Victoria soon put him in his place – it would 'only encourage the Emperor and the Bismarcks still more against us'. What Vicky and her three youngest daughters, her *Kleeblatt* or trio as she called them, needed was a good rest away from the poisonous atmosphere of Germany. The Queen sent the royal yacht to meet them at Flushing and welcomed them personally on landing, an honour indeed, as she generally never went further to meet her guests than the front door of Windsor Castle. On 19 November Vicky arrived dressed in black from head to foot, trembling with grief.

She spent her forty-eighth birthday quietly at Windsor, seeing nobody but her immediate family. The present tables were loaded with parcels and flowers, and the Queen gave her a generous contribution towards a mausoleum for Fritz. Yet even in her childhood home, she was not free from news of further persecution directed against her friends in Germany. Only a few days later Sir Robert Morier, then British ambassador in Rome, was accused of treachery. During the Franco-Prussian war, it was said, he had betrayed military secrets learned from the Crown Princess and her sister Princess Louis of Hesse to French commanders, resulting in an ambush and heavy losses of German soldiers. Herbert Bismarck had been among the wounded, and this was his father's means of revenge. The Prince of Wales was also a friend of Morier. Infuriated at this smear against him and his two favourite sisters, he and Queen Victoria demanded an official apology. However Sir Edward Malet, British ambassador in Berlin, was slow to respond; Lord Salisbury had never liked Morier; and though the London press was forthright in its condemnation of the Bismarcks' outrageous slander and the campaign of vilification against the late Emperor, Dowager Empress and their associates, no apology was received.

Vicky and her daughters returned to Germany in February 1889, their nerves healed to some extent by the peace of England and by the family's solicitude. Vicky had even taken the news of Sandro's marriage with relative calm, assured by her mother that his marriage with Johanna Loisinger was the best thing that could have happened to him. He had taken the title of Count Hartenau and applied for a commission in the Austrian army. But his health and nerves, like those of other Bismarckian victims, were ruined by his recent experiences. Prince Alexander of Hesse had died on 15 December 1888, six months to the day after Fritz; within five years Sandro, Morier and Mackenzie were all dead.

The Queen's fondness for her first grandchild, and the only one Prince Albert had ever known and doted on, soon reasserted itself. Salisbury was anxious that relations with Germany should not be soured beyond repair, and the Emperor was invited to

Osborne for Cowes week in August 1889. Vicky hoped it might make him more amenable to her, and though the Queen and Bertie were still waiting for him to apologise for his behaviour at Vienna the previous year, Lord Salisbury pointed out rather cravenly that England was the only European country which had not yet received the Emperor. Reluctantly but with some hope that she might be able to influence him for the good, Queen Victoria received him at Osborne on 2 August. One thing uncle and Emperor shared apart from their ancestry was a passion for uniforms. The Emperor, recently appointed an honorary admiral of the fleet, could not contain his excitement at wearing the same uniform as St Vincent and Nelson; 'it is enough to make one quite giddy.'[8]

Bertie found his enthusiasm disturbing. One reason Willy wanted to visit Cowes (and he was honest enough to admit as much) was so he could inspect English naval equipment. Already boasting about his 'expert' knowledge of guns and armaments, he declared that one day the German fleet would excel that of England. After returning to Germany, he thanked the Queen profusely for her hospitality, adding that he would now take an interest in her fleet 'as if it were my own, and with keenest sympathy shall I watch every phase of its further development . . .'[9] Many a British admiral and naval commander would soon rue the day.

A week earlier, on 27 July 1889, Bertie and Alix had acquired a son-in-law. Their eldest daughter Louise, like the aunt after whom she was named, had fallen in love with a Scotsman who had sat as a Liberal in the house of commons* before inheriting his father's peerage. The Earl of Fife, whom the Queen rather reluctantly created a Duke on his marriage, was a man after the Prince of Wales's own heart; he was rich and he enjoyed racing. The Queen warmly approved of him, although others found him as coarse and foul-mouthed as Queen Victoria's

---

* He represented Nairn and Elgin, 1874–79.

other Highland hero, the late John Brown, and being eighteen years his wife's senior, he looked far older than the eternally youthful Princess of Wales.

At a Balmoral servants' ball, Fife suggested to Queen Victoria that they should dance a reel together. After momentary hesitation the Queen disappeared, returning some minutes later in a shorter skirt. The two of them 'chose the kind of reel usually danced by sweethearts . . . and danced in rather an improper way.'[10] Nobody dared to tell Her Majesty that she had made herself look rather ridiculous.

Vicky's third daughter Sophie was engaged to Constantine, Crown Prince of the Hellenes. 'The royal mob', as Queen Victoria termed them, descended on Athens for the wedding on 27 October 1889, Vicky and Bertie among them. Vicky's heart still ached for Moretta, who had learnt that it was her father's dying wish to see her and Sandro happily married. For a while she refused to speak to Emperor William, blaming him bitterly for ruining her life and Sandro's by scaring him off. Determined to marry the first eligible man who asked her, she became engaged in June 1890 to the kindly but unprepossessing Prince Adolf of Schaumburg-Lippe, and they were married at Homburg the following November.

All but one of Vicky's children, Margaret ('Mossy'), were now married. By contrast, only one of Bertie's brood had walked up the aisle. Both his sons were in their twenties, and the elder generation were beginning to seek brides for them, in particular for Eddy.

Eddy had always been a problem child. A chronically slow-witted and possibly dyslexic child (one tutor said in despair that he barely knew the meaning of the words 'to read'), he grew up a listless and dissipated young man, with most of his father's faults but none of his strength of character. Though he enjoyed army life more than a spell at Cambridge, his superior officers could find nothing positive to say about him. There were dark rumours about his secret double life, and his more than passing connections with the Whitechapel ('Jack the Ripper') murders and the Cleveland Street homosexual brothel scandals. 'Kind dear

Eddy,' as his adoring sisters and mother called him, could by no stretch of the imagination be regarded as a promising future King. Ironically his brother George, to whom he was devoted, was a lively and intelligent if not over-clever young man.

Efforts were made to interest him in two of his German cousins in turn. Alix of Hesse turned him down; 'She refuses the greatest position there is,' wrote Queen Victoria sadly. Mossy of Prussia was also regarded as a possible wife for him, but in their case the lack of romantic attachment was mutual. By the time he was created Duke of Clarence and Avondale in May 1890, it was clear that dissipation was beginning to undermine the sickly young man's health. His lack of success in finding a wife had seemingly done him little if any harm, for he fell in and out of love with remarkable ease.

The next recipient of his affections was the doubly ineligible Princess Helene d'Orleans, daughter of the pretender to the French throne and a Roman Catholic. Staunchly anti-German since the Prusso-Danish war and implacably opposed to the idea of a Hessian or Hohenzollern daughter-in-law, Alix unwisely encouraged the young lovers, and while staying with the Fifes that August at Mar Lodge, they became unofficially engaged. The Queen had not been asked for her consent beforehand; considering that she had quailed at the thought of a Grand Duchess from the Greek Orthodox church for her second son, and in view of her dislike of immoral frivolous republican France, it was astonishing that she gave the couple her blessing. Helene was prepared to change her religion and become a Protestant, but neither her father nor the pope would countenance her leaving the Roman Catholic church. While these difficulties still remained unsolved, Eddy lost his heart to Lady Sybil St Clair Erskine and was secretly writing her passionate letters. Alix could have spared herself many a sleepless night worrying that her lovesick boy was yearning for his French sweetheart if only she had known.

It was ironic that Albert Edward, Prince of Wales, should view his son with the same sense of despondency and impatience with which the Prince Consort had regarded him some forty years earlier. Eddy knew what a disappointment he was; he admitted to being afraid of his father, and unhappy that he was not 'up to' what was expected of him. To compound the irony, Bertie's plans to send his troublesome son on a tour of the colonies out of harm's way had to be shelved while his attention was diverted by two public scandals in which his name figured prominently.

In September 1890 the Prince of Wales went to stay with the shipowner Arthur Wilson at Tranby Croft, near Doncaster, for the St Leger race meeting. Each evening the guests played the very popular but illegal game of baccarat. On the first occasion Arthur Wilson's son, also called Arthur, noticed that Sir William Gordon-Cumming was deliberately cheating by varying the size of his stake after looking at his cards. Shocked, Wilson alerted his parents after the game was over. In turn they quietly told the remaining guests, and Gordon-Cumming's cheating was thus carefully observed when they played again the following evening. Next morning he was formally accused. Panic-stricken, he asked to discuss it with the Prince of Wales, who told him there was no point in denying the charge. He agreed to sign a pledge never to play cards for money again, to which the other players (including the heir to the throne himself) added their signatures as witnesses, and leave the house next day as the price of their silence.

Everyone hoped that would be the end of the business, but early in the new year details of it found their way into London society gossip. In January 1891 the Prince of Wales was informed that Gordon-Cumming, still protesting his innocence, intended to bring a civil action against his accusers in order to clear his name.

Bertie and Knollys tried in vain to have Gordon-Cumming brought before a board of army inquiry or an inquiry held by the Guards Club Committee. As in the Mordaunt case, Queen Victoria gave her son full support. She recognised that he had only become involved in order to help his friends, and her anger was reserved for those who had asked him to sign the document;

her only condition was that he should promise her never to play baccarat again. The Princess of Wales also judged her husband to be more sinned against than sinning. As usual, she wrote to Prince George, that his father 'through his good nature was dragged into it and made to suffer, for trying to save with the others together this worthless creature, who since then had behaved *too abominably* to them all.'[11]

But the 'worthless' baronet and his advisers, convinced of his innocence, persisted in bringing the matter to court. Proceedings lasted from 1 to 9 June 1891, and there was nothing to prevent the Prince of Wales from being called as a witness. To a casual observer, it might almost have seemed that the heir to the throne was on trial. The Solicitor-General, Sir Edward Clarke, who represented Gordon-Cumming, was unnecessarily offensive, suggesting that it was not the first time honourable men had been known 'to sacrifice themselves to support a tottering throne or prop a falling dynasty.' The prince had put himself in the wrong on two counts, by encouraging the playing of an illegal game and by ignoring article 41 of Queen's Army Regulations, which stipulated that all serving officers (Field-Marshal HRH The Prince of Wales included) should order any fellow-officers accused of dishonourable conduct to refer his case directly to his commanding officer.

For a short time, the monarchy's standing in the country fell close to the depths it had known at the height of the republican agitation twenty years before. The Queen found it 'a fearful humiliation to see the future King of this country dragged (and for the second time) through the dirt . . .'[12] The jury returned a verdict against Gordon-Cumming, who was expelled forthwith from the army, his clubs and society. But Bertie was angrily abused, and opinion was prevalent that the baronet had been victimised as a guest condemned on the evidence of his hosts, and the prince's gambling habits were censured. In parliament, radicals reminded the government that a grant had recently been made to the Prince of Wales's children and asked if this had been used, or even voted, to meet their father's gambling debts. The church declared that the sole result of half a century's prayers for the heir to the throne was one public scandal after another. Despite joint urging from Queen Victoria, the Archbishop of Canterbury and *The Times*, he would not be pressurised into any hypocritical denunciation of gambling and betting. He told the archbishop privately that his first experience of playing cards for money had been at the home of Bishop Wilberforce, and horse racing was a sport enjoyed by many of the British people. His fondness for country house parties continued unabated, though he never returned to Tranby Croft.

Even before the court case was over, Bertie found himself involved in another humiliating issue.

Throughout his married life, his name had been linked, with varying degrees of discretion, with several married female companions and mistresses. Among them were the 'Jersey Lily' Lillie Langtry (also a close friend of Prince Leopold, who had hung her picture on his wall until it was removed by his disapproving mother), actress Sarah Bernhardt, and the American millionaire's daughter Miss Chamberlayne. Alix, whose male ancestors had not been uniformly noted for unimpeachable morality, tolerated most of them, and extended the hand of friendship to several. One she had never liked, though, was the attractive but spoilt and unscrupulous Frances Brooke. She had had an affair not only with the prince but also with Lord Charles Beresford, an old friend of Bertie and Affie. When the liaison with Beresford ended and he returned penitently to his wife, Frances wrote him a presumptuous letter of reproach verging on hysteria, accusing him of infidelity and desertion. Beresford had authorised his wife to open all his post in his absence – he was away for much of the time on active naval service – and it therefore fell into her hands. She deposited it with her solicitor George Lewis, threatening to prosecute Lady Brooke for libel if she persisted in making a nuisance of herself. Lewis informed her and she went straight to his office, demanding it back on the grounds that she wrote and therefore owned the offending epistle. He refused, saying it was legally the property of the person to whom it was written.

In desperation she turned to the Prince of Wales, as a mutual friend, and asked him to use his influence. After his involvement with the Mordaunt case, and in a similar quarrel concerning Lord and Lady Aylesford and Lord Blandford in 1876, he should have been more prudent, but it was not in his chivalrous nature to stand by while his friends were in trouble. He went to see Lewis, who allowed him to read the letter. Commenting that it was the most shocking he had ever read, he asked the solicitor to destroy it, only to be told that this could not be done without the consent of Lady Beresford. By way of a compromise, she asked for its return and sent it to her brother-in-law for safe keeping.

As a punishment for not cooperating, Lady Beresford found herself ostracised by Bertie and the rest of society. She complained bitterly to Lord Salisbury that he had taken up the cause of 'an abandoned woman' against that of 'a blameless wife.' In January 1890, before returning to sea, Lord Beresford called on his old friend, charged him with needless interference and coming close to wrecking their marriage, and promising to exact reparation or revenge. Refusing to be intimidated, Bertie intensified the social boycott of Lady Beresford, and eighteen months later in despair she put her London house up for sale, telling her friends that she planned to move abroad rather than stay at home and face further humiliation.

This coincided with the Tranby Croft case. Knowing how vulnerable the Prince of Wales now was, Lord Beresford threatened to publish all the squalid details of their argument in the press, and asked his wife to inform Lord Salisbury of his intention. The prime minister intervened with greatest reluctance, but he persuaded them not to make the affair public. Unfortunately he was unable to prevent the circulation of three copies of a leaflet by Lady Beresford's sister, Mrs Gerald Paget, telling the whole story from her point of view. These copies were circulated among society in London and in America, and the business certainly did not remain secret for long.

Alix had spent several weeks with her parents in Denmark. After her worries about Eddy, and the anxiety over the Tranby

Croft storm, the bad publicity about this new indiscretion of her husband proved too much for even her patience. Although expected back in England on 13 October, she changed her plans and went to Livadia in the Crimea, where the Tsar and Tsarina were about to celebrate their silver wedding.

Misfortunes followed thick and fast. For the first time since his marriage, Bertie spent his birthday apart from his wife, and in a Sandringham which had been considerably damaged by fire a few days before. Three days after his birthday, George fell seriously ill with typhoid fever. Alix came hurrying home from Russia, her impatience with her husband forgotten in this shared anxiety. Not for another three weeks was their second son declared out of danger.

On the very same day, Eddy became engaged at last to an eligible princess. He should either go on a colonial tour, a combined colonial and European tour, or else marry the highly suitable Princess May of Teck. The daughter of Princess Mary of Cambridge and the Duke of Teck, she came from a royal line noted for its eccentricity, but despite her antecedents she was evidently a young woman of commendable stability and strength of character. These she would certainly need, in addition to her powerful sense of duty, if she was to become the Duchess of Clarence. As planned, Eddy met her while they were staying at Luton Hoo near Bedford, fell in love with her, and on 3 December he proposed. The wedding was fixed for 27 February 1892.

Over Christmas, the Beresford affair was finally settled. A week of diplomacy, culminating in a formal exchange of letters (drafted by Lord Salisbury) between the Prince and Lord Beresford, and the temporary exclusion from court of Lady Brooke, laid the scandal to rest. In March 1892 she was eventually given back the letter which had precipitated so much trouble.

The royal mood over the festive season was, therefore, one of relief that so much was behind them. As Bertie wrote to Vicky on 30 December 1891, he could not regret that the unhappy year was about to end, as during it he had 'experienced many worries and annoyances which ought to last me a long time.'

But at least he had George's recovery and Eddy's engagement to be thankful for, and also the birth of a first grandchild on 17 May, the Duchess of Fife's daughter.

Yet 1892 had barely begun before another family tragedy unfolded. On 4 January Princess May and her parents went to Sandringham to celebrate Eddy's twenty-eighth birthday. A serious epidemic of influenza was raging at the time, and at Sandringham both Knollys and Princess Victoria of Wales were laid low by the virus just after Christmas. On the day before his birthday, Eddy took to his bed with a fever. Next morning he came downstairs to receive his presents, but felt so wretched that he returned to bed straight afterwards. The following day the doctor pronounced him to be seriously ill with inflammation of the lungs. The family were buoyed up with hope that he would recover, as his father had done from typhoid some twenty winters before, but in vain. On 13 January, the doctors advised sadly that nothing could be done. In despair Alix turned to them and said 'Can you do *nothing* more to save him?' The look in her eyes, May later wrote, was the most heart-rending she had ever seen. The next day, the ever-dreaded 14th, Eddy died.

His parents were heartbroken. Eddy had been lethargic and totally unfitted for the reins of kingship, but to his family he had always been amenable and affectionate. Moreover the tragedy had occurred at a time when his future appeared to be settled. Though May had recognised what a formidable task lay ahead of her, she might just have been the making of him. Their engagement had been one of the few consolations at the end of a singularly unhappy year for the Waleses. Alix, according to her husband and mother-in-law, 'though bearing up wonderfully, (did) nothing but cry.' 'It is hard,' wrote Bertie sorrowfully to Queen Victoria, 'that poor little May should virtually become a widow before she is a wife.'[13]

Despite Alix's wish that he should be laid to rest beside his baby brother Alexander John, Bertie insisted with a heavy heart that the burial had to be at Windsor. He sobbed throughout the ceremony, a business made more unhappy still by another family disagreement. Alix wanted the service to be private, and she was indignant to find that her three sisters-in-law (Vicky was the only one absent, being in Germany at the time) had come from Osborne, apparently sent by the Queen. To make matters worse, when they tried to leave the chapel afterwards, the door of their pew was temporarily jammed. Later Ponsonby was ordered to take the matter up with Bertie, who told his equerry testily to inform those at Osborne that 'the harem of Princesses' was not locked into the pew. None of them had anyway been wanted at the funeral, as the Princess of Wales had particularly requested privacy. If Princess Beatrice (evidently the most offended) was annoyed, 'she must get over it – as she likes!'[14]

The tragedy had brought Bertie and Alix as close as they had ever been, but their relations with the rest of the family suffered. While Alix was readily forgiven her tears and moodiness, as late as June Queen Victoria was writing with asperity to Vicky that 'poor Bertie's' nature was not one 'made to bear sorrow, or a life without amusement and excitement – he gets bitter and irritable.' When Gladstone became prime minister for the fourth and last time in August 1892, he told his family that there was only one solution to the royal problem; the Queen should abdicate in favour of her son. Far from this being considered – and such a suggestion would have come ill from her least-liked prime minister – she continued to exclude him from her confidence in a manner he found needlessly galling. Despondently he told Knollys that there was no point in his staying on at Cowes or Osborne, as he was not the slightest use to the Queen. She listened more to the Duke of Connaught than to him.

During Bertie's temporary retirement from public life, Affie came from Devonport (where he was serving three years as commander-in-chief) to London in order to deputise for him as the Queen's representative at various levees and functions.

Sadly there was to be a rift between the brothers. George was created Duke of York in May 1892, mainly to give him some confidence in himself. He had still been convalescent from typhoid when his brother died, and he was overwhelmed by the loss; apart from which, he had to give up the naval career he loved, in order to prepare himself for eventual succession to the throne. Both Affie and Queen Victoria hoped he might become engaged to Affie's eldest daughter Marie – to the Queen 'it was the dream of Affie's life.' The cousins had been extremely fond of each other since their days together on Malta when Affie was in command of the Mediterranean fleet and George had served under him as a junior lieutenant. Certainly the Duke of Edinburgh could not have wished a better husband for his daughter than the industrious, naval-minded, stamp-collecting nephew with whom he had so much in common. But the anti-English Duchess was determined that no child of hers should marry an Englishman. She made Marie write George a stiffly-worded note to the effect that he must not think there was anything more between them than friendship, and then contrived to bring about her engagement to the pleasant but weak-minded Crown Prince Ferdinand of Roumania.

Affie was displeased with his wife, and more angry still when Bertie accused him of snubbing George. For a while relations between them were strained, but at length Bertie appreciated how he had wronged him. Nobody could have been more pleased at this turn of events than Alix. Much as she liked Affie, she had never been friends with his wife, and thought her daughter 'a perfect baby,' as well as much too German.

However, the year 1892 ended on a happier note. Bertie had received, albeit at irregular intervals, edited reports of cabinet meetings which were sent to the Queen. Towards the end of the year the foreign secretary Lord Rosebery sent him the gold key which had been made for the Prince Consort, and used by him to open foreign office despatch boxes. For the next few years, except when he was abroad, he was kept as well-informed about official foreign business as the Queen. Informal conversations with Rosebery, ambassadors and others, helped him to supplement the documents he read.

At about the same time, he accepted an invitation from Gladstone to become a member of a royal commission on the aged poor. This pleased him all the more because Lord Salisbury had rejected his offer the previous year to serve on a potentially controversial inquiry into the relations between employers and the working class. The new royal commission addressed itself to the problems of persons rendered destitute by age. For once Bertie had found a subject concerning the welfare of his mother's subjects to which he could make a genuine contribution. A fellow-commissioner James Stuart, radical Liberal member for parliament for Hoxton, remarked that the prince asked very good questions. He thought at first that he had been prompted to them, but found out that they were of his own initiative, and proved he had a considerable grasp of his subject. The commission's report was, as had been expected, a controversial one in terms of party politics. The prince signed a statement to the effect that he was obliged to observe strict political neutrality, and it was not until the next century that state pensions were provided for by act of parliament.

By this time the Duke of York's matrimonial future had been happily settled. Most of the royal family, including the Queen, his parents and the Duke and Duchess of Teck, favoured the idea that he should marry Princess May. Among most of them was the feeling that it would prove to be a happier match for her than one with the listless Eddy. There was already a precedent for such a union, for Alix's sister Dagmar's marriage to the future Tsar Alexander III had been very successful; Dagmar had initially been betrothed to Alexander's tubercular elder brother Nicholas, whose deathbed wish was that she would marry 'Sasha' instead.

In the spring of 1893 George and May were staying at Sheen Lodge. His sister Louise suggested that he should take May into the garden and show her the frogs. Neither of them had evinced any interest in amphibians before, but the Duchess of Fife's suggestion had the required effect. He proposed to her, and the wedding took place on 6 July in the chapel at St James's. Perhaps it crossed the minds of Bertie and Affie that it had all been for the best; might Marie of Edinburgh not have been a shade too theatrical to make the down-to-earth Duke of York a good wife?

There was no little confusion before and after the ceremony when the groom was asked whether he had come to London on business or just for the wedding, while the Tsarevich Nicholas was congratulated on having found himself such a wonderful wife. The cousins bore a striking physical resemblance to each other. Contemporary photographs reveal only slight differences in eyes and height, Nicholas being a little taller; several of the family were hard-pressed to tell them apart.

There was only one cloud on the horizon of that otherwise happy summer of 1893 – the German Emperor's behaviour. 'The boss of Cowes', as Bertie privately dubbed his nephew, had so enjoyed his first visit to the regatta that he made a point of returning year after year in his imperial yacht *Hohenzollern*. When Bertie in a moment of friendship (which he later had reason to regret) made him a member of the Royal Yacht Squadron, William could not resist the opportunity of trying to outshine his uncle as a yachtsman. He challenged the prince's racing cutter *Britannia* with his own yacht *Meteor* and won the Queen's cup.

Not content with that, on another occasion that week he challenged his uncle to a friendly race. All was going well when the wind suddenly dropped, and unless the race was abandoned it was unlikely that they would be back at Osborne that night for a full dress dinner Queen Victoria was giving in the Emperor's honour. Bertie consulted his suite and signalled to the emperor that he proposed abandoning the race and returning by train. William objected, saying that the race must be completed and it did not matter when they reached Cowes. In the end, all of them arrived at Osborne after the Queen had left the table and entered the reception room. As thick-skinned as ever, the Emperor greeted his glowering grandmother effusively and apologised for being late. Bertie entered in some consternation, stopping to take cover for a moment behind a pillar, wiping the perspiration from his brow and getting his breath back before summoning up courage to address his mother. She gave him a perfunctory nod, and he retreated behind the pillar again.

While the yachts were in full sail off Cowes, Duke Ernest of Saxe-Coburg was enjoying his last sport. He caught a chill while out shooting, and died on 22 August. His death was unlamented by his late brother's family. He had been an unrepentant supporter of Bismarck, even to the extent of joining in campaigns of vilification against Vicky. A notorious womaniser and father to several illegitimate children, Queen Victoria regarded him as such a threat to female chastity that only bachelor diplomats and ambassadors from England were deemed safe at his court.

Affie's naval career in England had just come to an end. On the day he left Devonport and relinquished his post as commander-in-chief, 3 June 1893, he was promoted to the rank of admiral of the fleet.

He took up his inheritance as Duke of Saxe-Coburg with little enthusiasm. The life at a small German court gave scant promise of responsibilities or excitement commensurate with that of his beloved navy; and, like Bertie, he thoroughly disliked and distrusted his imperial nephew. If Emperor Frederick III had lived, the German empire would have been on the best possible terms with England; under the unstable Emperor William II, the future of Anglo-German relations filled the family and British statesmen with alarm.

Affie's first few months were spoilt first by unfounded rumours that he had renounced the succession before Ernest's death in favour of his son Alfred, and secondly by unseemly wrangles in the English and German parliaments as to whether the new Duke of Coburg was still a British subject or not. If both countries went to war against each other, could he be indicted in England on a charge of high treason as a result of his acts as a German sovereign? Should he still be allowed to sit or speak in the House of Lords at Westminster, or retain his membership of the privy council? Not until the spring of 1894 was his rather confused nationality status finally clarified. He resigned from the council, and all his rights pertaining to the upper house; he relinquished the annuity granted to him in 1866, but kept the allowance granted on his marriage for the upkeep of Clarence House, which remained his London residence until his death. By English law, he retained (somewhat ambiguously) his British nationality, modified 'by his status as a German sovereign.'[15]

However, in April 1894 the normally sleepy town of Coburg was made the site of festivities such as had not been witnessed for many years. Affie's second daughter Victoria Melita ('Ducky') was to marry her first cousin Ernest, who had succeeded his father as Grand Duke of Hesse in March 1892. Queen Victoria paid her first visit to the duchy for eighteen years, and among the other guests were the Emperor William, Vicky, Bertie, Beatrice and Liko, plus representatives from almost every German court and European monarchy. While they were waving the bride and groom goodbye after the ceremony, four enterprising photographers ran into the courtyard square and frantically signalled to the assembled company not to move. Far from regarding this as an intrusion on their dignity, the distinguished gathering posed good-naturedly for several photographs. They were only just in time, for a few minutes later the April sunshine gave way to such violent thunderstorms that the town's evening illuminations had to be postponed.

Even as guests were arriving for the wedding, their minds were on another budding romance. Why was the tsarevich there, everybody wondered. It was common knowledge that he was passionately fond of Ernest's youngest surviving sister Alicky. But she took her religion seriously to a degree which few of the family could comprehend, and hesitated to join the Greek Orthodox church – which she would have to do if she was to marry the future Tsar. However the fact that she would now have to give precedence at Darmstadt to the extroverted, comparatively frivolous Ducky and probably suffer the presence of Ducky's domineering mother, helped her make up her mind. On the day after the wedding, her sister Ella excitedly went round telling everyone that Alicky and Nicky were engaged.

Everyone expected that they would have an apprenticeship of several years together before assuming the imperial crown, for Tsar Alexander III was not yet fifty and apparently in good health. He himself had done nothing to prepare his heir, whom he regarded as a 'mere boy' for the throne. However, in September Alexander suddenly fell ill with nephritis. Neither doctors nor the milder climate of the Crimea, at his summer palace at Livadia, could save him. Affie and Marie arrived just before he breathed his last on 1 November 1894, the latter distinguishing himself by the none-too-tactful greeting of 'Thank God I've arrived in time to see you once more.' Bertie and Alix had only reached Vienna before they heard that all was over. Bertie's recent relations with the Tsar had been difficult, and he could not forgive him for his cruel bullying of Sandro (who had died one year earlier, at the age of thirty-six), but he was touched by Alix's tears for her sister and brother-in-law. To George, he wrote that this was 'the most trying and sad journey I have ever undertaken.'[16]

Lord Rosebery, who had just succeeded the ageing Gladstone as prime minister, begged the Prince of Wales to seize the opportunity to woo the impressionable young tsar. Nicholas was stunned by having succeeded his father so unexpectedly, and other guests at the St Petersburg funeral described him as looking 'dreadfully pale and worn.' Bertie's tactful attention to his young nephew and niece at this trying time for them could not have been surpassed. He had persuaded the Queen to appoint the Tsar an honorary colonel of the Scots Greys, and in return he was made an honorary colonel of the 27th Dragoon regiment of Kiev. Charles Wynne-Carrington, Marquess of Lincolnshire, was startled to see 'a fat man in a huge shaggy greatcoat looking like a polar bear.'[17] Royalties, he added, looked dreadful in ill-fitting foreign uniforms, and the Prince of Wales was no exception.

Conditions in Russia gave the English considerable cause for alarm. While Bertie told his son that 'the opportunity to see the great capital is not one to be missed,' Vicky – who was not at the funeral, but had been there for Affie's wedding – called it 'another world – there is something so squalid and sad, suggesting poverty and loneliness, about the landscape and population, so much in contrast with the wealth of the imperial court, the money and jewels and the almost reckless extravagance with which some things are carried out and presents lavished on people.'[18]

Carrington was appalled at what he saw and told Bertie he thought a revolution was inevitable. The prince dismissed this as fanciful pessimism, but remarked that it was necessary everywhere to move with the times. To the Queen he wrote rather optimistically that there was great loyalty and affection for the tsar and his family among the people. If the new popular ruler proved to be tolerant to his subjects, and liberal in his views, 'a more popular ruler of this country could not possibly exist.' However Tsar Nicholas did not prove liberal in his views, and never became popular in Russia. It was not long before he described democratic ideals as senseless dreams. Bertie was not alone in his opinion that the young man was 'weak as water.'

On his return to London early in December, Bertie was received with congratulations by Lord Rosebery for his 'patriotic work' in Russia. 'Never has Your Royal Highness stood so high in the national esteem as today,' he said, 'for never have you had such an opportunity. That at last has come, and has enabled you to justify the highest anticipations, and to render a signal service to your country as well as to Russia and the peace of the world.'[19]

Bertie's diplomatic forays, for the most part successful, were in marked contrast to Arthur's military frustrations. After his return from India in 1890 the Duke of Connaught was appointed to the southern command, based at Portsmouth. After his time in the middle east he found the coastal town very unexciting. He thirsted for the post of commander-in-chief either in India or at home. Despite Queen Victoria's ardent championship of her favourite son's 'great and varied experiences . . . which, combined with HRH's characteristic conscientious zeal and his love for the service', neither hope was ever realised. In 1893 he was appointed to the more congenial Aldershot command, a post he held for five years, but his disappointment at not being made commander-in-chief of the British army was acute. In November

Queen Victoria, engraving
after a portrait by Franz Xaver
Winterhalter at the time of her
coronation, 1838

Albert, Prince Consort,
1861

Queen Victoria with Victoria, Princess Royal and Albert Edward, Prince of Wales, engraving after a portrait by Edwin Landseer, 1842

Osborne House, Isle of Wight

Balmoral Castle, the family home in the Scottish Highlands

Prince Alfred as a midshipman, *c.* 1858

Albert Edward, Prince of Wales, on horseback, *c.* 1846

rince Leopold and
rince Arthur, 1860

Princess Beatrice, 1860

Princess Alice, engraving after a photograph by John Jabez Edwin Mayall, 1860

Victoria, Princess Royal, engraving after a portrait by Franz Xaver Winterhalter, 1856

Albert Edward and Alexandra, Prince and Princess of Wales, with their two eldest children, Prince Albert Victor and Prince George, 1865

Princess Louise, *c.* 1870

The German Crown Prince and Princess Frederick William with their family, 187
Children, left to right: Prince Henry; Princess Margaret (with her father at the
back); Princess Victoria (seated at front); Princess Sophie; Prince Waldemar; Prin
William; Princess Charlotte

Prince Leopold, Duke of
Albany, *c.* 1882

Princess Beatrice, *c.* 1885

Crown Prince Frederick William, 1883

The Empress Frederick, the title by which the Princess Royal was known in widowhood, *c.* 1892

Queen Victoria with Prince and Princess Henry of Battenberg
(Princess Beatrice) and their two elder children, Princess Victoria Eugenie and
Prince Alexander, 1890

Arthur and Louise, Duke and Duchess of Connaught, with Princess Margaret,
Prince Arthur and Princess Patricia of Connaught, 1893

Alfred, Duke of Edinburgh and Duke of Saxe-Coburg Gotha, *c.* 1897

Princess Henry of Battenburg, with her daughter Princess Victoria Eugenie, and King Alfonso XIII of Spain, shortly after their engagement, and the King's mother, Dowager Queen Maria Christina, 1906

King Edward VII, one of the last-known photographs before his death in 1910

Princess Christian of Schleswig-Holstein, the title by which Princess Helena was known on her marriage, *c.* 1910

Arthur, Duke of Connaught, *c.* 1930

the seventy-six-year-old Duke of Cambridge retired, and Arthur was an obvious choice for his successor, but the government thought him too junior for the supreme command and appointed Lord Wolseley instead.

Unfulfilled hopes were one thing; unexpected death was another. At Windsor and Osborne, Liko was becoming increasingly frustrated by his dull existence. His official appointments as governor of the Isle of Wight and honorary colonel of the Isle of Wight Rifles did not, as he commented, 'present much scope for activity.' Sir Henry Ponsonby found him 'moping and miserable,' chafing at not being allowed to hunt after the death of a gentleman at court while out on the chase.

When he joined his elder brother Louis for a few days in Corsica while Beatrice and her mother were on holiday at Cannes, his wife had him fetched back smartly. Rumour had it that the Battenberg princes had gone to the Ajaccio carnival for some 'low company,' and unlike Alix, Beatrice was not prepare to sit by patiently while her husband was led into temptation. Later he joined a regiment of the volunteer battalion in Hampshire, and was delighted to spend a few days again sharing the camaraderie of a soldier's life. 'I feel like a fish in water,' he wrote, perhaps a little tactlessly, to Beatrice. 'Everyone seems to have confidence in me.' It was said that a certain lady at court had a good deal more than simple confidence in the handsome Prince Henry. Nobody had the courage to name her directly, but opinion suggested the restless Princess Louise.

In the autumn of 1895 an expeditionary force of West African troops and British army officers and men was assembled to restore order in the kingdom of Ashanti, north of the Gold Coast Protectorate. Helena's elder son Prince Christian Victor, who was commissioned in the King's Royal Rifles, was invited to join the force, and a few days later Liko told the Queen that he also wanted to go to Ashanti. Remembering the Prince Imperial's death in the Zulu war, and stressing to him the dangers from malaria, at first she would not hear of it. But Beatrice fully supported her husband, insisting that his brothers had all seen active service, and seeing that Liko was becoming excessively bored with his life of enforced inactivity. That, and Liko's determination to volunteer in a national cause to prove his devotion of his adopted country, persuaded the Queen. On 6 December, he took farewell of his mother-in-law at Windsor, as he and Beatrice left for Bagshot to stay the night with the Duke and Duchess of Connaught on his way to Africa.

From that continent, Liko wrote enthusiastically to Beatrice that he was 'really happy and pleased to have received permission to see all that is going on.' In fact, almost nothing was going on. King Prempeh and his chiefs decided not to fight but instead submit to British protection. Meanwhile the futile little expedition continued through the tropical heat, several men dying of fever on the way. Liko was among those to contract malaria, and the doctors ordered that he should be carried back to the coast at once. He lingered for a few days and died on 20 January 1896.

Two days later a telegram arrived at Osborne. Beatrice had been warned by one earlier that he had fever, and she expected it to contain the news that he had arrived safely at Madeira to convalesce, so would she go out and join him. 'The life is gone out of me,' she said to her mother in a trembling voice, stunned by the blow. The Duchess of Connaught led her gently to her room.

With the possible exception of Fritz's tragic death in 1888, no loss had affected Queen Victoria so deeply since the death of her husband. Liko had entered her life at a time when she was still mourning John Brown and the Duke of Albany. His sense of humour and obvious enjoyment of life had rejuvenated her, and introduced a breath of fresh air into the old-fashioned court. By giving her another four grandchildren, he had reminded her how it felt to have a young family around her – and a family to which she could be (and was) far more indulgent than she had ever been towards her own children.

Beatrice's sisters arrived to comfort her, although one succeeded in doing exactly the opposite. With an extraordinary display of malice, Louise told Beatrice that she had been Liko's confidante, and his wife was nothing to him. The Duchess of Teck arrived at Osborne to find that the mischievous marchioness had made no end of trouble, being equally unkind to the Duchess of Albany and then trying to set Bertie against Lenchen. 'Charming behaviour truly – The whole place is ringing with it.'

Louise still suffered regular pain in her neck as a result of the sleigh accident in Canada, since when her aversion to her mild-mannered husband had been increasingly evident. As a result of her infatuation with Liko she had become jealous of Beatrice. Marie Adeane, a lady-in-waiting, did not trust her; 'never have I come across a more dangerous woman, to gain her end she would stick at nothing. One would have given her a wide berth in the sixteenth century; happily she is powerless in the nineteenth.'[20]

But her complex nature had its more positive side. Louise, said Sir Henry Ponsonby (who had died in November 1895), made evening parties particularly pleasant in her own way; 'Whatever people say of her I must say she is charming and I don't know what I should do at these long dreary evening parties if it were not for her. With such a sweet smile and soft language she says such bitter things!'[21]

She would often say what other people were thinking but dared not put into words. To the Queen's physician, she said that her mother was no longer fit to reign as her people were 'learning to do without her and the government tells her very little'. It would only be fair of the Queen to abdicate in favour of her son and heir, she maintained, as she was 'reducing the future role of the Prince of Wales to a nonentity.'[22]

At times her attitude bordered on persecution mania. She thought her sisters were intriguing against her, ingratiating themselves with the Queen in order to exclude her. To Reid, her ever-faithful if sometimes weary confidant, she complained that the Queen, Princesses Christian and Beatrice were all being unkind to her. 'They had laid their heads together to ruin her position here [at court], and had succeeded.'[23]

Vicky hurried over from Germany to condole with Beatrice. An incident just before her arrival brought a measure of sorely-needed relief to their existence. Frederick Ponsonby, an equerry who would shortly be taking over the functions discharged by his father Sir Henry, was met by a German who told him in broken English that he wished to see the Empress Frederick the moment she stepped ashore. Visions of an anarchist attempt on her life filled his mind and he detailed a police officer to watch the man carefully. When Vicky was about to arrive next day the man reappeared, asking persistently to see her. Beatrice was convinced he must be a lunatic and thought Ponsonby should have had him locked up. They were amazed when they saw Vicky wave cheerily to the man and blow him a kiss as she passed him in her carriage. He was an eminent sculptor from Berlin and a close friend of hers. She had told him she would see him as soon as she set foot in England and he took her words literally.

The Empress Eugenie thought Beatrice would benefit from a complete break, and offered her her villa at Cap St Martin in the south of France for a few weeks. Louise came to visit her and apologise for her bad behaviour. As a further mark of penitence, she executed a memorial to Liko which was placed on his tomb at Whippingham Church. Her statue of Queen Victoria overlooking the Round Pond at Kensington Gardens, unveiled on 28 June 1893, had been much admired (and still is by London visitors to this day). On her return Beatrice took up residence at Osborne Cottage, where Sir Henry Ponsonby had lived. Yet it was no more than a token new start, for her life still revolved around the Queen and her fatherless children. They were suddenly very lonely without a father to join in their games, for Beatrice was as unmaternal as her own mother, and could never enter into the spirit of their pastimes or their 'romping.'

Vicky was still desperately lonely in Germany, but the tensions between her and her eldest son had eased with time, and the fighting spirit in her led her to make the most of what she still had in life. In 1889 she acquired a country estate near Kronberg, west of Berlin, comprising 250 acres and a small villa. The latter she had demolished, and set about building herself a house to be named Friedrichshof in her husband's memory. Her architect was the half-English Herr Ihne, whom she sent to make a study of English country houses before planning his commission. In particular she asked him to base it on Flete, an imposing Devonshire mansion about ten miles from Plymouth. The family home of Mary Bulteel, wife of Sir Henry Ponsonby, she had paid a visit there while staying in Britain after the jubilee in 1887.

She moved into her new home in 1894, and within weeks its contents rivalled those of a museum and national library. Hundreds of books collected since childhood, many carefully annotated in her own hand; her mother's letters mounted and bound in half-leather; every scrap of paper on which Fritz had written after he could no longer speak; portfolios of her paintings and sketches; photograph albums; arrangements of medallions, curios and antiques, dismissed by her daughters as 'dirty, ugly, horrid old rubbish,' all found their place at Friedrichshof. 'One loves one's own possessions,' she told her guests; 'one strokes them with one's eyes.'

The house quickly became a centre of hospitality to artists, writers and scientists from all over Germany. At Kronberg she established a hospital and public library, and helped to organise the renovation of the town church. She was thrilled when an old fresco was uncovered and restored in the process.

Helena and Christian proved ever supportive of the Queen as she grew older, but Helena was distressed by Louise's jealousy, and her normally robust health showed signs of giving way. Reid, a close confidant of Louise, was unsympathetic to her, called her 'a great bore', and was inclined to dismiss her complaints about neuralgia and other illnesses as 'imaginary ailments', as hypochondria. She took refuge in opium and laudanum, much to the alarm of her husband and mother, until Reid intervened, told her she was malingering, and withdrew her drugs altogether. The shock treatment evidently worked, for from then on her general health improved.

Queen Victoria passed a landmark on 23 September 1896, the day on which she had reigned longer than any other British sovereign, thus beating the record of her grandfather King George III. Though she received several messages of congratulations, it was decided that the celebrations should be deferred until the following year – her diamond jubilee, or as she called it, her 'swan song'.

On 24 May 1897 she would complete her seventy-eighth year, and with the increasing infirmity of old age she would not even contemplate trying to entertain or receive legions of kings, emperors and their vast suites, or accommodate them at Windsor and Buckingham Palace. She readily accepted a suggestion from Joseph Chamberlain, now her colonial minister, for turning the jubilee first and foremost into a 'Festival of Empire.' Fifteen premiers from the colonies would be invited to London, but certainly no crowned heads. The Emperor William considered himself the exception to every rule, and was sure that a little well-timed bullying of his relatives would secure his place in London for the occasion. His grandmother decided otherwise. Would her private secretary Sir Arthur Bigge kindly tell the Prince of Wales that there was not the slightest fear of her giving way about the emperor coming in June; 'it would *never* do.'

All her surviving children and children-in-law joined her and took part in the procession through London in brilliant sunshine on 22 June 1897; 'a never-to-be-forgotten day,' she recorded in her journal. 'No-one ever, I believe, has met with such an ovation as was given to me.' Yet the presence of whose who had passed away since the first jubilee – Fritz, Liko, Louis of Hesse and 'poor dear Eddy' – was sorely missed.

Throughout her adult life, Vicky had suffered from chronic ill-health, regular attacks of excruciating pain which she described variously as rheumatism, neuralgia, colic, lumbago and sciatica. They were often accompanied by dark red blotches, rashes or blisters, malarial fever, and inflammation of the eyes. Modern research[24] suggests that she might have inherited the porphyria which had blighted the life of her great-grandfather King George III. The year after the jubilee, an even worse disease struck her. In September 1898 she was out riding when her horse shied at the approach of a traction engine and threw her to the ground. At first she suffered no more than concussion and bruising, and would not let it interfere with her plans to visit London and Balmoral later that month. When increasing pain forced her to consult a specialist, it was to receive a grim diagnosis – cancer of the spine. Had she suspected her symptoms six months earlier an operation might have saved her, but because of the delay she had perhaps two years to live. Though some of her closest friends sense that she seemed to derive a small measure of satisfaction in having a similar disease to that which had claimed her husband, it was with sadness that she declined an invitation to join the family in May 1899 for Queen Victoria's eightieth birthday dinner at Windsor.

Vicky was not the only one under sentence of death. Affie's health had been deteriorating ever since the diamond jubilee, if not earlier. Like Vicky, he had known but little happiness for the last few years. His marriage to Marie had been increasingly difficult, and in his own words Coburg was 'deadly dull'. To exchange the responsibilities and camaraderie of naval life for the tedious existence at the head of a German duchy had made him appreciate how bored Liko became in his last months at home. Moreover, he was increasingly alarmed at the Emperor William's expansion of the German fleet, and he trembled to think of the consequences that this Anglo-German rivalry at sea might have in the future.

Even as a young bachelor, Affie had always been inclined to drink more than was good for him. In his declining years, the bottle was one of his few consolations. Sir Arthur Sullivan was deeply worried at what was happening to his old friend, and kept his distance because of the 'distinctly hostile element risen up against me, which made me feel very uncomfortable'. The composer could hardly blame him 'if he sought a little 'soulagement' in a resource which was neither right nor healthy.'[25] He was not the only one to express concern. Several of the Duke's staff reported on the worrying extent of his drinking habits, particularly his secretary, Condie Stephen, who reported that his kidneys were already affected, and that it was imperative he cut down on his drinking.

However Affie had little to live for, particularly after the tragic death of his only son and heir. 'Young Alfred' had apparently contracted a marriage with a commoner, argued violently with his mother who had ordered annulment of the union, and shot himself. The Duchess was furious with him, and embarrassed at having him under her roof while she was receiving guests and delegations for her and her husband's silver wedding celebrations. Brushing aside the objections of doctors who implored her not to let him be moved, she sent him off to convalesce at Meran in the Tyrol. A week later he was dead.

After his funeral there were endless heated discussions about the Coburg succession. As Queen Victoria's third son, the Duke of Connaught should have automatically become heir to the duchy, but he made no secret of his intense reluctance to give up his army career (he still cherished ambitions of becoming commander-in-chief at home) and uproot his family. Charles, the young Duke of Albany, was therefore selected for the dubious honour. Affie wanted to adopt Charles and have him in his household, but Helen knew that he was totally unfit company for a boy of fourteen. By now Affie was a broken man, drinking more heavily than ever, holding Marie responsible for the tragedy of their son and spending as little time with her as possible.

From South Africa yet another shadow fell to darken Queen Victoria's last years. In October 1899 war broke out between the British and the Boers. For the first two months defeat followed defeat, and the Queen entered the new year and new century 'full of anxiety and fear of what may be before us'. As Britain gradually regained lost ground, so did her popularity plunge on the continent. On a train journey through Brussels in April Bertie and Alix were shot at and narrowly escaped assassination, and Queen Victoria was forced to abandon her customary spring holiday on the Riviera. Increasing fatigue, indigestion and failing eyesight made her irritable, though by midsummer she was in better spirits. However her resistance to bad news in the family was low, and she was in no state for the blow which befell her in July.

In May Affie had gone to take the waters in Herculesbad, ostensibly (so the press reported) for attacks of rheumatism. He had distanced himself so much from Marie that she had little idea how ill he was. In June a group of specialists held a consultation in Vienna and discovered a carcinomatous growth at the root of the tongue, so advanced as to render any operation useless. He had no more than six months left. The Queen's family were anxious to spare her further upsets. Not until 25 July did she receive a telegram (initially withheld from her, probably on Beatrice's instructions) from the physicians saying that her second son's condition was hopeless.

That weekend the doctors prepared to give him a tracheotomy to facilitate his breathing, but it was too late. Like his father, Affie did not 'cling to life.' On the evening of 30 July he passed away in his sleep.

'Oh, God! my poor darling Affie gone too!' the Queen mourned when Helena and Beatrice broke the news to her at Osborne the next morning. The court was already shocked by the assassination, twenty-four hours earlier, of King Humbert of Italy. 'One sorrow, one trial, one anxiety, following another! It is a horrible year, nothing but sadness and horrors of one kind and another.'[26] The Queen forgot how she had often censured and argued with Affie, who had never been her favourite son, since the Prince Consort's death. Her lady-in-waiting Marie Mallet (formerly Adeane), who helped to comfort her, felt that she could only remember the Duke of Coburg as a happy, laughing youngster, swimming on the beach or talking excitedly about going to join the navy. He had always been Helena's favourite brother, except briefly during the *Sultan* affair of 1878; she was upset and angry that the news had been kept from them for so long, blaming Beatrice through her tears. If only she had known, she told Marie Mallet, she would have gone to Germany to see him once more. On 2 August they received news of an attempt on the shah of Persia's life, which made the Queen fear for the safety of her sons and grandsons on their way to Coburg for the funeral.

Bertie arrived back from the obsequies in a mood of black depression, having learnt beyond doubt that Vicky – too ill to attend – was dying. She was rarely well enough to rise from her bed at Friedrichshof, dictating most of her letters as it was difficult to find a period free from pain long enough in which to write. Sometimes her attacks of agony were so severe that it was feared she might predecease her mother.

Still the miseries of this 'horrible year' were not complete. Affie's death was only a momentary distraction from Helena's and the Queen's worries about Princess Marie Louise, unhappily married to Prince Aribert of Anhalt, who wanted to divorce her on the grounds that she was too fond of her native England and had borne him no children. The marriage was annulled later that year, by which time the family was in mourning again. Helena's eldest son Christian Victor had survived the Ashanti campaign, only to succumb to fever in South Africa that October. Queen Victoria felt her decision not to allow the Duke of Connaught to go on active service against the Boers amply vindicated, despite his protests.

Christmas 1900 was the saddest the family had known since that of 1861. Shortly before the festive season, Beatrice and bereaved Helena had been to see Vicky, knowing it might be for the last time. Most of her letters were now dictated to her daughters Charlotte and Mossy, for it was agony to hold a pen or pencil for long. At Osborne, Helena's elder daughter Thora wrote the Queen's journal for her, while Beatrice wrote her mother's letters. As the Queen could hardly sleep, Beatrice experimented with sitting beside her reading aloud, but this only kept her more awake than ever. She would fall asleep in the small hours and wake at midday, cross at having 'wasted' the morning.

On 27 December the Queen dictated a letter to Vicky, thanking her for the gift of a magnifying glass. Condoling with her on her illness, she added bravely that she had not been very well herself, 'but nothing to cause you alarm . . . I have been able to get out a little most days.'[27]

On new year's day 1901 she went with Arthur to visit convalescing soldiers, leaving Helena and Beatrice to answer telegrams, letters and cards of congratulation for the new year. She did not look forward to it; 'Another year begun and I am feeling so weak and unwell that I enter upon it sadly.'[28] On 13 January she dictated what was to be the final entry in her journal, thus closing a record of her life kept faithfully throughout sixty-nine years.

It was evident to those around her that Queen Victoria's 'extraordinary fund of vitality' was close to exhaustion. On 17 January she had a mild stroke, and both her sons were alerted. Her daughters, except for Vicky, were already at Osborne, and several grandchildren joined them. Bertie had been dividing his time since Christmas between London and Sandringham, and reached the gathering on 19 January. Arthur, who was on better terms with the German Emperor than the others, was in Berlin taking part in celebrations for the bicentenary of the Hohenzollern dynasty. When he received the telegram and told William, the latter immediately postponed the rest of his programme and said he would come to England as well.

In vain did the Duke of Connaught suggest tactfully that he might not be welcome; William was sure that his place was by his grandmother's side. Throughout the journey to London he was in unbearably high spirits, his excuse being that 'Uncle Arthur is so downhearted we must cheer him up.'[29] Only when he met the anxious relations in the deathly hush of Osborne did his breezy demeanour give way to a more respectful air. With uncharacteristic humility he said that he only wanted to see Grandmama before she died, but if that was impossible he would understand. The family gracefully allowed him in.

On the morning of 22 January, it was clear that Queen Victoria was fading away. The family assembled in her room, and for brief periods she seemed quite conscious of everyone around her. Oxygen was administered to help her breathe more easily. She confused Willy with his father, but she clearly recognised Bertie. Both men knelt beside her, the German Emperor helping to support her with his good right arm. Her last audible word was 'Bertie', at which he was so overcome that he burst into tears and had to leave the room hurriedly to regain his composure. Bishop Davidson, Dean of Windsor, and the vicar of Whippingham, were called to read prayers and recite hymns. At 6 p.m. the doctors warned the family that the end was near. Each one present walked up to her and said their names. Thirty minutes later, as the Bishop read another prayer and pronounced the blessing, her face assumed a look of complete calm. After thirty-nine years, she had been granted her wish. She was going to rejoin Prince Albert.

Helena told the Bishop her mother 'knew she was beyond the Border Land – & had seen & met all her loved ones. In death she was so beautiful, such peace & joy on her dear face – a radiance from heaven.'[30]

Denied the solace of being with her brothers and sisters, Vicky was desperate when Mossy broke the half-expected yet almost unbelievable news next day: 'Oh, my beloved Mama! Is she *really* gone? Gone from us all to whom she was such a comfort and support. To have lost her seems so impossible . . .'[31] Though Bertie's inexperience in matters of statecraft had only been alleviated during the last few years of his mellowing mother's reign, his grief was no less sincere. Much as she had disapproved of his way of life, with her increasing age they had drawn closer in a way which nobody could have imagined nearly forty years before. Even Louise, the non-conformist of the family, wrote ruefully that she could never realise that her mother was gone, 'only that for a bit I cannot see her. The desire to write to her, and feeling she expects news, is still on me. She was always wanting to hear and know.'[32]

Yet on none did Queen Victoria's death fall more severely than on her widowed eldest daughter and great confidante, Beatrice: 'No one knows what the daily missing of that tender care and love is to me, coming as it does on top of that other overwhelming loss, so that my heart is indeed left utterly desolate. If it were not for the dear children, for whom I have alone to live now, I do not know how I should have the courage of struggling on.'[33]

5

The Twentieth Century 1901–44

It was inevitable that Queen Victoria's death would mean a weakening of the bonds between the six of her nine children who outlived her. King Edward VII (the style he chose for himself, despite his mother's wish that he should reign with the rather un-English title of King Albert Edward) had never been very close to his younger brothers and sisters. His favourite sister, Alice, and favourite brother, Affie, were dead, as was Leopold, the one loved best by Queen Alexandra. After Alice's death, the bonds between Bertie and Vicky had become stronger than ever before, but as he recognised, his sorely-tried elder sister's sufferings would soon be over.

One month after his accession, he made his first expedition abroad as King. For reasons of court mourning there was no question of any state visits to foreign capitals for several months. This was purely a private journey to Germany in order to see Vicky at Friedrichshof for the last time. Among the King's suite were Dr Francis Laking and Sir Frederick Ponsonby, now his assistant private secretary. Laking had been brought by King Edward in the hope that he could persuade the German physicians to give larger and more frequent injections of morphia to the dying Empress, but he soon realised that his German colleagues strongly resented his presence. In the aftermath of Sir Morell Mackenzie, feelings about British medical science still ran high in Germany.

King Edward had requested an absence of formality on his visit, and he was exasperated when the Emperor received him at Frankfurt station in the uniform of a Prussian general. He had not been put in the best of moods by arriving at Flushing to the sound of a 'hymn' being sung over and over again. On enquiry, it turned out that the tune was the Boer national anthem.

But the weather was unusually fine that February, with snow-clad pine forests around Friedrichshof glistening in the winter sun. Cheered by her brother's visit, Vicky marked the occasion by venturing into the fresh air for the first time in several weeks. Her attendants wheeled her in a bath chair along the sheltered paths in the castle park as she and her three younger daughters talked to the King.

According to Ponsonby, dinner each evening was hardly lively, though the Emperor kept small talk going. Sophie and Mossy would cut in tactfully 'if the conversation seemed to get into dangerous channels, and one always felt there was electricity in the air when the Emperor and King Edward talked.'[1] One night the superstitious King was alarmed to find that thirteen people had sat down to dinner, but later he told Ponsonby it was all right as Princess Frederick Charles (Mossy) was *enceinte.* In fact time was to reveal that they had been safer than they thought, for in July the princess gave birth to a second set of twins.

After they had been at Friedrichshof for three days, Ponsonby was summoned to go and see the Empress, who was his godmother. On his arrival in her sitting room he found her propped up with cushions, looking 'as if she had just been taken off the rack after undergoing torture.' After half an hour of conversation about England, King Edward's position, and the war in South Africa, Vicky asked him if he would take charge of her letters and take them back to England. She did not want anybody to know they had been taken away, and on no account must the emperor have them – or even know of their whereabouts. At one o'clock that morning four servants brought two large portmanteaux, newly tied up with cord, into Ponsonby's room and left without saying a word. He was thunderstruck, having imagined lightheartedly that her reference to letters implied a couple of small packets. More in hope than expectation, he wrote on one, 'China with care', and on the other, 'Books with care', praying that the military police who guarded Friedrichshof at every corner would not suspect anything. Fortunately his plan worked and the correspondence was smuggled to safety across the North Sea as its owner had intended.

The Empress Eugenie invited Beatrice to stay at Cap St Martin, as she had done after Liko's death, in the spring. On 14 April, her forty-fourth birthday and the first without her mother, she wrote to Marie Mallet how she was 'thankful to be well away from everything and to have still some time before me were I see all the old places again.' In June Beatrice and her children went with Marie to Kissingen in Germany. She was surprised to see how unmaternal the princess was. Her second son Leopold, like his namesake uncle whom he had never known, was haemophilic, and confined to his bed at the Kissingen hotel. But Beatrice seemed at a loss as to how to deal with sick children, and unlike her sisters she did not possess the nursing instinct. Perhaps hers was a practical turn of mind; nothing could be done, so her son should be made comfortable and left in peace and quiet, with suitable medical attention at hand – and as few anxious relatives as possible.

Later that summer they went to Kronberg, where Vicky's unquenchable spirit still kept her alive and conscious though she could barely eat or sleep. By now she was a pitiful sight. Though she was taken out for a drive in the open air every afternoon, her face had become quite misshapen with disease; 'every feature and limb distorted and that charming countenance quite unrecognisable, her mouth drawn up, her teeth project, her nostrils are dilated by her terrible struggle for breath which makes her nose bleed constantly, and the whole face yellow.'[2] She could no longer speak coherently, and nobody could understand what she said, but she liked being read aloud to – particularly English novels and travels.

As the periods of consciousness became shorter and more intermittent, the doctors notified her closest relations. Moretta, Sophie and Mossy had kept a regular vigil for months on end, and Willy and Dona joined them just before the end. Of late mother and son had grown closer to each other than they had been since Willy was a boy; her forgiving nature excused him the misery he had caused his parents, realising that he had been misled by Bismarck and his coterie. On his visits to her in the last few months, he could not but feel remorse for the mental suffering he had caused. Yet there was no formal deathbed reconciliation. When he arrived for the last time, she was in a coma and had barely thirty-six hours to live.

On 5 August Canon Teignmouth-Shore, a friend of several years' standing, was asked to come and say farewell to her as the end could not be far off. He was shown into the library while waiting, and by coincidence he selected a volume of diplomatic reminiscences which opened at a passage describing the young Princess Royal and 'the bright intelligent face, flushed with the joy of life.' What a contrast, he felt with sadness, to the face of the aged woman upstairs, 'sanctified with the sacrament of pain and sorrow.'[3] At six o'clock that afternoon he was called to the bedside to read a few prayers, and he could see the faint movement of her lips. A white butterfly, the symbol of the resurrection and life eternal, flew in through the open window, circled round her head and then out again. As it disappeared from view, her heart stopped.

Patience and suffering had brought their own reward. The Empress Frederick was mourned by grieving crowds who came to pay their last respects, filing solemnly past her coffin at the Kronberg church. Much as her enemies at court had tried to blacken her name (above all Bismarck, whose own death in July 1898 had been scarcely lamented), the ordinary people had loved her. They appreciated her unstinting work for the wounded in wartime, her devotion to artistic, educational and charitable causes, her work for the rights of women in German society, and defiance of anti-Semitism and other reactionary causes which had been taken for granted for so long in Prussia. She was the first person of royal birth to read Karl Marx's *Das Kapital*, and though she disagreed with his philosophy of an international socialist economy she was intrigued enough to ask a mutual acquaintance to send her a full report on the author. Misunderstood and often feared during her lifetime, she had made a lasting impact on Germany, though it would be some years before that impact was fully recognised. For all her faults, notably poor judgement of character and a certain impulsiveness, in some ways she was as talented and remarkable a character as Queen Victoria herself.

It was not only a tragedy for her and her husband, but also a disaster for Europe, that Emperor Frederick III died before his time and she was relegated to a bitter, often inactive widowhood. Though she found a measure of fulfilment in organising her schools, hospitals and charities throughout Germany during the last years, the nation was the poorer in being denied the full potential of her abilities. In a happier world, King Edward VII would have been congratulated on his accession by the Emperor and Empress Frederick, and a more stable Crown Prince William. An English declaration of war on Germany in August 1914, under such circumstances, would have been inconceivable.

Vicky was under no illusion as to the disastrous course on which Germany was set. In 1892 she had gloomily predicted with foresight worthy of the medieval prophet Nostradamus that the absolute sovereignty practised by her son ran the risk of leading the empire 'down the steep path which leads to a Republic or even a Socialist state. The latter could never last, there would be chaos, then reaction, dictatorship and God knows what further damage.'[4]

The death of 'my dearly beloved and gifted sister is a terrible loss for me,' King Edward wrote to Lady Londonderry, 'but her sufferings were so great that we could not have wished her life prolonged. She has now at last the rest and peace she wished.'[5] He and Queen Alexandra attended the funeral at Potsdam on 13 August, the latter bringing a bunch of flowers from Windsor to lay on the grave in the Friedenskirche mausoleum where widow, husband and their shortlived younger sons were at last reunited. Much to their irritation, the Emperor had planned grandiose military displays at Homburg and Potsdam. 15,000 men lined the streets on their way to the castle and took part in a march past – a ceremonial 'courtesy' which the King and

Queen felt in poor taste on such a sad occasion. But it was an almost unrecognisable William who, pale and trembling as he arranged the wreath on his mother's coffin at the altar, fell to his knees and buried his face in the folds of the pall as he silently broke down.

Queen Victoria's death had left Bertie with five residences – the state properties of Windsor Castle, Buckingham Palace, and the private estates at Sandringham, Balmoral and Osborne. The first two were essential, because of their place in the nation's heritage, and he was intent on spending more time in London than his mother, therefore Buckingham Palace would be used much more than formerly. Sandringham was secure in his affections, and Balmoral was valuable as a base for entertaining his Scottish friends and for shooting. Despite the Queen's wish that Osborne should remain as a sacred family possession, it was the odd one out.

The other four children of Queen Victoria had their own properties. Arthur and his family had moved into Clarence House after Affie's death; Helena and Christian had Cumberland Lodge, Windsor Park, and Queen Victoria had left them Schomberg House, Pall Mall, in her will; and Louise had Kent House, just outside the grounds of Osborne, though she spent more time in Scotland, Kensington Palace, or on the continent. Beatrice was the one most attached to the Osborne estate and all it stood for. She had been married at Whippingham Church and her husband had been laid to rest there; she had succeeded him in the honorary post of Governor of the Isle of Wight; and, with the Duke of Connaught and Sir Fleetwood Edwards, Keeper of the Privy Purse, she was a co-executor of Queen Victoria's will. Would she consent to relinquishing the family claim on the house she and her mother had loved the most?

King Edward VII sought legal advice on the wording of his mother's will. The estate of Osborne, he was informed, was his to retain, dispose of or alter as he thought fit, as long as his heir did not wish to live there when he ascended the throne. The Duke and Duchess of York (created Prince and Princess of Wales on 9 November 1901, his father's sixtieth birthday) replied that they did not.

To what practical use, therefore, could the house and grounds be put? Lord Esher, Secretary to the Office of Works, had two suggestions which appealed to the King. One was to establish a new naval college for cadets, to replace the old training ship *Britannia* at Dartmouth; the Medina shipyard and the Solent were both conveniently close. No other place was immediately available and the Board of Admiralty welcomed the idea. So did the Duke of York, who had abandoned his naval career with great regret and retained an abiding affection for the service. At the same time there was a pressing need for a rest home to accommodate convalescing officers. The Netley Naval and Military Hospital was already used for those who returned from active service abroad as individuals, but it was inadequate for those who needed a prolonged period of recuperation.

Much as the King favoured these schemes, he knew that there would be opposition from at least one of his sisters. As expected Helena raised little objection, for she and Christian spent most of their time in London, and as an indefatigable committee member for various charities she was willing to sacrifice family sentiment in a good cause. Louise, who chafed so often at the handicap of being born royal, did not mind. Like her brother, she was perhaps a little relieved at being rid of irksome family memories.

Unlike them, needless to say, Beatrice regarded Osborne as sacred. As the daughter who had always remained closest to her mother, the house built by her parents had always been home. To her, Lord Esher's proposals were nothing short of sacrilege. For the last few years of her mother's life, she had been the Queen's unofficial private secretary, reading letters to her mother and writing her personal replies, in addition to helping handle minor day-to-day family problems. It had often fallen to her to pass disagreeable news or commands, relating to domestic trifles, from her mother to her eldest brother, who was understandably a little jealous of her closeness to Mama. Now all that was gone, and her home was about to go too.

Bertie had been fully prepared for this. In order to respect their mother's wishes, he decided that the rooms she and his father had occupied should be kept closed. Five apartments were to be sealed off; only the family and a few trusted staff would be allowed to see them. Beatrice had been bequeathed her own home on the estate, Osborne Cottage, which despite its name was a very imposing Tudor-style villa. At first she resented the idea of she and her children having to make their home in an outbuilding which she had always regarded as a guest cottage, but she knew that it would be impossible for her or the government to maintain Osborne as it was, with herself the sole adult resident. A break with the past had to be made, and as a compromise the grounds of her new home would be enlarged in order to give her sufficient privacy from the cadets.

After negotiations with the government, the gift of Osborne to the nation took effect on Coronation Day. King Edward opened the Royal Naval College on 4 August 1903, and for the rest of his days he took a keen interest in its progress. The two most illustrious cadets from the first years were his grandsons Edward and Albert, eldest children of the Prince and Princess of Wales. They would be regularly entertained to tea on Sundays by their great-aunt Beatrice.

King Edward VII wanted his coronation to be an occasion of national rejoicing, and in order that it should not be overshadowed by the Boer war it was not scheduled until the end was in sight and victory assured. 26 June 1902 was the date chosen.

The fears for his health of those closest to him, notably Queen Alexandra and Mrs George Keppel, the latest and most discreet in a long line of female companions, were not unfounded. Mrs Keppel was one of those rare women blessed with a sense of tact and humour, and without an enemy in the world. When the King chided her one evening at bridge for muddling her cards, she excused herself prettily by admitting she could never 'tell a King from a Knave.' While he took his work, his responsibilities and his programme of opening buildings and launching new battleships as seriously as his station demanded, his already prodigious appetite for good food, vintage wine and strong cigars increased in proportion. His clothes suddenly ceased to fit; he grew more irritable than ever; and he would drop off to sleep from exhaustion at the theatre, opera and even at meals. On 14 June he was taken seriously ill with stomach pains, but he protested angrily to his doctors that he would attend his coronation later that month if it killed him. They warned him that it almost certainly would. His condition worsened, and after he had driven in semi-state to Buckingham Palace in some agony, it was clear that the ceremony would have to be postponed. Meanwhile he was to undergo an operation for appendicitis.

For the second time in his life Bertie was in grave danger, but for the second time his exceptional will to live triumphed. The operation was a complete success, and it was an impatient but more relaxed, much slimmer King Edward VII who was crowned at a curtailed ceremony in Westminster Abbey on 9 August. 'Good morning, children,' he greeted his wide-eyed grandchildren genially before leaving Buckingham Palace for the Abbey, attired in his ceremonial finery. 'Am I not a funny-looking old man?'

'We cannot pretend that there is nothing in his long career which those of us who respect and admire him would wish otherwise,' *The Times* wrote rather grandly on his accession. Memories of the unlamented King George IV flooded back, and there were not a few who doubted King Edward's fitness to occupy the throne. Ten years earlier, in the wake of Tranby Croft and the Lady Brooke scandal, there had been sanctimonious mutterings that God would never allow such a wicked man as the Prince of Wales to become King.

Yet the new monarch soon disarmed his critics and detractors. Admittedly, his conception and style of sovereignty were very different to those of his mother. By his use of Buckingham Palace as a regular London residence he was seen far more often, and was regarded as more accessible, than Queen Victoria. The people appreciated his love of pagentry, demonstrated at the first state opening of parliament in his reign, very different from occasions when a reluctant Queen in deepest mourning had been persuaded to show herself, and by numerous royal progresses throughout the kingdom. Old traditions for their own sake were ruthlessly discarded. Dreary afternoon 'drawing-rooms' were replaced by glittering evening courts in the palace ballroom.

Another break with tradition was to be found in the exemplary relations between King Edward and his heir. Determined not to make the same mistake as his mother, the King kept no official secrets from Prince George, and treated him more like a junior business partner than a son. Aged sixty and not in the best of health, he realised that he could die suddenly at any time; and moreover the Prince of Wales was a diffident personality, lacking in self-confidence which ill-befitted a future King of England. Sad to relate, the lesson was lost on the latter. When he ascended the throne, King George V deliberately kept his own sons at arm's length.

With his brothers and sisters, Bertie had no specially close relationship as King. Queen Alexandra, according to her nephew Lord Carisbrooke, was said to be so jealous of the English royal family that she would never invite any of her sisters-in-law to Sandringham, but instead fill the place with her Danish relations.[6]

Louise was the only one who got on well with him, and the only one invited to Sandringham. She was more broad-minded, and her lively if sometimes sharp-tongued conversation appealed to him. He teased her about the role of her attendant Madame Klepac, and the strict diet and exercise to which she adhered. Louise pointed out that she would never get overweight like her mother or sisters, and that she would outlive them all. On both counts she was right, for she lived to a greater age than any of them, and kept her figure to the end. During the last years of Queen Victoria's reign, the household appreciated it when she took Beatrice's place at dinners and functions, because she was 'capital at entertaining strangers.' Not even her worst enemy could accuse the Duchess of Argyll with her loud, penetrating laugh of ever being dull. She was tireless in her speeches, meetings and letters to the press on behalf of the National Union for Higher Education of Women, whose first president she had become in 1872, much to her mother's disapproval. (Abhorrence of women's rights was one of the few subjects on which Queen Victoria and Gladstone were at one). Sculpture still occupied much of her time. In addition to her mother's statue in Kensington Gardens and Liko's memorial, she executed a monument in St Paul's Cathedral to Canadian soldiers who fell in the South African conflict.

Louise, her niece Alice of Albany told the biographer Nina Epton many years later, was on very good terms with the Germer emperor – 'indeed, with any man – she ran after anything in trousers.'[7] Her husband Lord Lorne, who had succeeded to the peerage as Duke of Argyll in 1900, was said by some to be not immune to the trait. His friendship with a few notorious homosexuals, notably Lord Ronald Gower, a fellow Scottish Member of Parliament, added to a certain effeminacy of manner, is accepted by some biographers as proof of the love that dare not speak its name, though not by others. It was rumoured that Louise had to have a window bricked up at Kensington Palace to prevent him from slipping out into Hyde Park at dead of night for secret meetings with good-looking guardsmen. His other idiosyncrasies were more endearing. He had a habit of wearing his old Norfolk jacket on formal occasions, and absent-mindedly sporting his Order of the Garter at breakfast. Those who knew the Argylls thought that his good-natured reluctance to be firm with his wife had been a contributory factor to the failure of their marriage. A more masterful man (with more normal inclinations) might have succeeded with her.

Bertie had never had very much in common with Helena, and for political reasons Alix was none too friendly with her or her husband. As Princess of Wales, she never relished their visits to Sandringham. 'Old Christian', she complained, did nothing but eat and shoot other people's pheasants. In 1891

Arthur had inadvertently shot Christian through the eye, which subsequently had to be removed under chloroform. As a result Christian amassed a wonderful range of glass eyes, and when conversation flagged at his dinner parties, he would ask the footman to bring the tray containing his collection to the table. Then he would explain the history and functions of each one at unnecessary length to his guests, his favourite reputedly being a bloodshot one he wore when he had a cold.

After the family upheavals of 1901 in which she lost her mother and then her eldest sister, Helena saw relatively little of her surviving siblings. She and Christian continued to lead an unexciting life supporting the monarchy and her various charities. In 1894 she had founded the Princess Christian District Nurses, and eight years later she undertook to expand it with a medical and surgical nursing home which she dedicated to the memory of Christian Victor, the elder son whom they had lost in South Africa. It was a proud moment for her in February 1904 when the Princess Christian Nursing Home opened in Windsor. Meanwhile, despite his advancing years, Christian played his part in various ceremonial functions, notably in 1906 when he represented the King at Emperor William's silver wedding celebrations in Berlin.

Within their own family, the Christians had known more than a little sadness. None of their three surviving children were destined to find happiness in marriage. Marie Louise still considered herself married, though her father-in-law had declared her empty wedded union with Aribert of Anhalt null and void, while her elder sister Helena Victoria remained a spinster throughout her seventy-eight years. Only Albert gave them a grandchild, but is doubtful whether they were fully aware of his liaison with a mistress and the birth of a daughter in Hungary on 3 April 1900 who was raised by Jewish foster parents.[8]

In 1901 almost every European major country was a monarchy, with the exception of France, and nearly every monarch or consort was related to King Edward VII. He was uncle to the

German Emperor William II and to Alexandra, Tsarina of Russia; brother-in-law to King George of Greece; son-in-law to King Christian IX of Denmark (who in his bachelor days had been considered as a suitor for the young spinster Queen Victoria); second cousin to Leopold II, King of the Belgians; and linked by more distant ties of blood to King Carlos of Portugal and Prince Ferdinand of Bulgaria. Another niece Marie was married to Crown Prince Ferdinand of Roumania, who ascended the Balkan throne in 1914; his youngest daughter Maud was married to Prince Charles of Denmark, who was elected King of newly-independent Norway in 1905 and assumed the title of King Haakon VII; and had the Habsburg heir Crown Prince Rudolf not shot his mistress and himself at Mayerling in 1889, another distant Coburg cousin, King Leopold's daughter Stephanie, would have eventually become Empress of Austria and Queen of Hungary.

Five years after his accession, King Edward VII – already uncle of Europe several times over – saw yet another kingdom linked to his by marriage. In June 1905, the young bachelor King Alfonso XIII of Spain paid a state visit to England. King Edward had already offered the hand of friendship by sending the Duke of Connaught to bestow the Order of the Garter on Alfonso. It was hoped that the gesture would draw Spanish attention to the Duke's unmarried daughter Patricia, as indeed it did. Photographs of her began to appear in Spanish magazines with embarrassing frequency.

However, once in London, King Alfonso and Patricia made no headway with each other. Beatrice was the first to find out that the young monarch had set his heart on her daughter Ena. The engagement brought objections in Madrid, where the idea of a Queen from England (and one born of stock as lowly as the morganatic Battenbergs) was frowned on by Spanish conservatives, and in London, on account of religious difficulties and the instability of the Hispanic throne. But disapproval was swept aside, Ena was received into the Roman Catholic church, and preparations were made for the wedding in Madrid on 31 May 1906. Among the guests who travelled to Spain were the bride's mother and brothers, the Prince and Princess of Wales, and Marie, Dowager Duchess of Saxe-Coburg Gotha.

Beatrice's two eldest brothers had narrowly escaped death from the bullets of would-be assassins, one in Australia and one in Belgium. Now she, and the rest of the royal gathering, were all about to know how it felt to escape a violent end by a hair's breadth. As bride and groom drove in procession from the church of San Jeronimo after a three-hour wedding ceremony, the coach suddenly stopped. Queen Ena asked why, and her husband answered that it was probably a delay caused by those ahead alighting at the palace. Just then a large bouquet of flowers was thrown from the window opposite, landing in front of the carriage. One second later there was a sheet of flame, a pungent whiff of gunpowder, a thick black cloud of smoke and the terrified screams of people and horses. Twelve people lay dead or dying and over a hundred were wounded. Ena's dress and shoes were spattered with blood. For a dreadful moment, her husband thought she was among the casualties. Mateo Morales, an anarchist, was later apprehended and shot himself as he was led to prison. He had been narrowly prevented from slipping into the church with his floral weapon. Had he succeeded, he would have perpetrated the most horrific assassination yet seen in Europe.

Queen Victoria had only paid one state visit to a foreign court – to Paris in 1855. She had thus made no conscious attempt to influence foreign affairs with ambassadorial journeys abroad. But Bertie had been a tireless traveller as Prince of Wales, and as King he gladly seized the opportunity to try and improve Britain's relations with European powers by means of personal appearances.

Never was his success more marked than in Paris during the spring of 1903. Anglo-French relations had deteriorated with the British occupation of Egypt in 1882, with English condemnation of French corruption and anti-Semitism during the Colonel Dreyfus scandal, and above all during the Boer War. The King's arrival in Paris on 1 May, after expeditions to Rome and Lisbon, was greeted with angry cries of '*Vivent les Boers!*' After a series of effusive speeches, and attendance at theatres and racecourses, he turned the tide, and it was a case of '*Vive le Roi! Vive l'Angleterre!*' Hostility was swept aside almost overnight. Two months later President Loubet of France made an equally well-received visit to London. Since reaching maturity, King Edward had maintained that European interests could best be served by an *entente* between England and France, and the signing of an Anglo-French agreement in April 1904 owed far more to the spirit of goodwill in France created by the King than his ministers cared to admit.

It was regrettable but not surprising that he failed to create the same favourable impression in Britain's traditional ally Germany. Emperor William's provocative behaviour precluded anything more than half-hearted attempts between sovereigns and statesmen to bring about a lasting rapprochement between their two nations. King Edward would have gladly done what he could to safeguard European peace by improving Anglo-German relations, but with his unstable and untrustworthy nephew on the imperial throne it was impossible. And his heart ached to recall that, but for the cruelty of fate, he would have been entertained at the German court by his beloved sister and brother-in-law.

Nonetheless the German Emperor and his virulently Anglophobe wife had to be honoured with a state visit to Windsor in November 1907. It was an ordeal the English hosts were almost spared. A scandal at Berlin in which some of the emperor's closest friends were accused by their press of indulgence in unnatural vices had left him badly shaken, and he telegraphed to England that an attack of influenza prevented him from coming. That same day the British ambassador saw him riding at a gallop near his palace, obviously in the best of health, and after his miraculous recovery he could hardly refuse pressure on all sides to withdraw his cancellation. The King and Queen of Spain, plus a galaxy of other European royalties, were also staying at Windsor, and a packed week of shooting and other entertainments was laid on, but nobody was sorry to see the emperor and his suite depart. 'Thank God he's gone!' muttered the King crossly as he watched his nephew leave.

In April 1908 King Edward and Queen Alexandra paid a state visit to Copenhagen, their first since the accession of the Queen's brother as King Frederick VIII of Denmark. For King Edward, who had always been bored by the quiet homely atmosphere of his wife's country, the only thing he could remember afterwards was a visit to Hvidøre, a small seaside villa Queen Alexandra and the Dowager Tsarina of Russia had bought jointly as a retirement residence. It was so inadequately heated that he kept his coat on all the time.

From Copenhagen they embarked on expeditions to the other two Scandinavian capitals, Stockholm and Christiania. Both were of special family interest, as in Sweden the Duke of Connaught's eldest daughter Margaret was married to Gustav Adolf, elder son of the Crown Prince. In Norway, the democratic court seemed a little too informal even for the King and Queen of England. King Haakon and Queen Maud thought that the best way of combating republicanism was 'to go as much as possible among the people' and use trams instead of driving everywhere in a motor car. Ponsonby told Haakon to 'get up on a pedestal and remain there.' His subjects were bound to be disappointed if they saw him going about his business like any one of them.

During the summer they made the first state visit ever paid by a ruling British monarch to a Tsar of Russia, a move which was unpopular at home and abroad. In England, left-wing members of parliament objected strongly to their King's hobnobbing with 'a tyrant and common murderer.' King Edward was particularly incensed that one of his most vehement critics was Arthur Ponsonby, then Liberal member for Stirling, feeling that a son of the late Sir Henry Ponsonby should know better, and demanded an apology from him before admitting him to court again. In view of the revolutionary state of Russia, and the prevalence of anarchist attempts on royalty (the King and Crown Prince of Portugal had joined the growing list of assassination victims in

Lisbon in February 1908), the visitors were advised not to go ashore. King and Tsar therefore met each other and their respective families on board their yachts *Standart* and *Polar Star*, anchored off Reval. The King delighted his nephew by creating him Admiral of the Fleet.

In Germany, the Russian visit was viewed with alarm by Emperor William, who was almost hysterical at what he saw as the threat of anti-German encirclement. The German nations felt slighted by the continual postponement of a state visit from the King, and it was not until February 1909 that one took place. By this time, relations between the European countries were in a fragile state. King Edward had been on the best of terms with the Austrian Emperor Francis Joseph, and was therefore astonished when Austria annexed the Balkan territories of Bosnia and Herzegovina without warning him. Germany's increased naval programme was seen as a threat to British interests and continental stability. It was an anxious King who arrived in Berlin. Suffering from a bronchial chill, he dozed off at the opera only to wake up suddenly and see the stage apparently in flames. He was furious to find the firemen doing nothing about it, and was only pacified with difficulty when the empress explained patiently that it was part of the performance.

Later that week the King nodded off at a family dinner party, and after a luncheon at the British embassy he suffered such a violent attack of coughing that the company were horrified lest he might succumb to a heart attack. 'My God, he is dying!' exclaimed Princess Daisy of Pless. 'Why not in his own country?' The Emperor had tried to make the British visit a success, and he recognised that his uncle's health was failing, but by this time Anglo-German relations had almost reached the point of no return. The English entourage returned home despondently, under no illusions; the German nation disliked and distrusted them.

The nearest King Edward ever came to a family rift during his reign was an argument with his brother. Though he was often a little jealous of the Duke of Connaught, who had been Queen Victoria's favourite and listened to much more than he ever was, he respected Arthur's military career and abilities, and always gladly supported any effort to advance his position and standing in the armed service. When a committee appointed to report on reorganisation of the war office proposed in January 1904 to abolish the office of commander-in-chief and replace it with the post of inspector-general, the King was gratified when the Duke was appointed.

Three years later the Duke of Connaught was chosen as high commissioner and commander-in-chief of all British garrisons in and around the Mediterranean, with headquarters at Malta. He was reluctant to accept a post which he thought superfluous and the result of an ill-planned strategy, but King Edward – supported by the war office – persuaded him that it would be a valuable step in 'the military federation of the Empire by a process of gradual development.' In 1909 the Duke informed his brother that the experiment had proved a failure, and that the Mediterranean command, a source of inefficiency in peacetime, would be a positive danger in war. His position, he felt, was equivalent to that of a fifth wheel on a coach, and he intended to resign and return home.

The King argued that his brother had taken so much home leave that the experiment had not been given a fair chance, and the Duke and Duchess replied acidly that he had wanted them out of England because they were too popular at home. Annoyed at Arthur's 'persistent obstinacy,' the King declared that he 'must now consider his military career at an end.'[9] The post was accordingly conferred on a reluctant Lord Kitchener, who convinced his sovereign that the Malta command was 'a damned rotten billet.' By way of apology he secured his brother's appointment to a much more congenial post – governor-general of Canada.

Towards the end of his life, King Edward made a point of taking the cure at Biarritz each spring. He suffered increasingly from bronchitis, and after a winter in England the clear air of the continent helped his breathing. But by 1910 not even Biarritz could save him. Considering his chronic lack of fitness, his refusal to cut down on eating and smoking, and his two severe illnesses in 1871 and 1902, it was remarkable that he attained the age of sixty-eight.

King Edward had always vowed to work to the very end, and he kept his promise. Though suffering from bronchitis and exhausted by his journey when he returned from Biarritz to London on 27 April, he refused to consider cutting back on his programme of state business and audiences. A weekend visit to Sandringham, inspecting recent improvements to the estate in howling wind and heavy rain, resulted in a chill. By the time he was back at Buckingham Palace, he was showing signs of heart trouble and had difficulty in breathing properly. Queen Alexandra and Princess Victoria had gone to Corfu and Venice, but were summoned back to England at once. They arrived at Victoria Station on 5 May, and only when the Prince and Princess of Wales met them, instead of the King himself, did it begin to dawn on the Queen that his condition must be serious.

Friends and visitors had been urging the increasingly ashen-faced sovereign to rest, but he brushed their concerns aside. By the morning of 6 May he was clearly struggling, but still insisted that his valet should dress him in frock coat and formal clothes before receiving two of his friends. That afternoon he collapsed, and at last it was clear that he could no longer resist attempts to put him to bed. Though only semi-conscious throughout the afternoon, he was cheered a little when the Prince of Wales told him that his horse Witch of the Air had won the 4.15 race at Kempton Park, he nodded, muttering, 'Yes, I have heard of it. I am very glad.'[10] They were his last coherent words. Shortly afterwards he fell into a coma, and at 11.45 that night he passed away.

The new King, George V, noted in his diary that 'I have lost my best friend and the best of fathers. I never had a word with him in my life. I am heartbroken and overwhelmed with grief . . .'[11]

Tributes were paid by family, friends, courtiers and ministers alike. There had been much uncertainty about the future on Queen Victoria's death, and in a similar fashion, unease was voiced after that of her eldest son. In nine years he had made an inestimable impact on British relations with the continent. His reputation as a peacemaker King may have been exaggerated, for it was beyond the ability of any one man to dispel the mutual suspicion which existed between the main powers and the instability of the Balkan states, which ultimately led to conflict four years later. Yet on his accession King Edward VII had been all too aware that Britain's 'splendid isolation' could not last, and he soon effortlessly established himself as the pre-eminent sovereign of his time in Europe. His only rivals for such a title were the impossibly remote Emperor Francis Joseph of Austria–Hungary, and the showy, vainglorious, unstable German Emperor William II. An astute judge of character, the King had as good as foreseen the catastrophe for which his imperial nephew in Berlin was heading some five years before his death. William, he had told Marquis Luis de Soveral, the Portuguese ambassador in London, was vain, cowardly, and would not have the courage to talk any sense into the sycophants around him, but would obey them cravenly instead. 'It is not by his will that he will unleash a war, but by his weakness.'[12]

'Good old Teddy' was intensely human, and blessed with his share of weaknesses. On 20 May, the day of his funeral, the diarist Wilfrid Scawen Blunt noted in his journal that he hoped the country would soon 'return to comparative sanity, for at present it is in delirium.' Yet he acknowledged the towering reputation enjoyed by the late King throughout his own dominions and indeed the continent of Europe, a man who 'liked to be well received wherever he went', who 'wanted an easy life, and that everybody should be friends with everybody'.[13] As the Earl of Granville had remarked during his mother's lifetime, 'Prince Albert was unloved, because he possessed all the virtues which are sometimes lacking in the Englishman. The Prince of Wales is loved because he has all the faults of which the Englishman is accused.'[14] His diffident son and heir knew that he could hardly hope to equal his father's position on the European stage.

The four surviving children of Queen Victoria all lived through the European family tragedy of the First World War; all but one of them witnessed the outbreak of Hitler's conflict. It was fortunate for Vicky, Alice and Affie that they had all died at a comparatively early age, for the heartbreak of being at war with the country of their birth would surely have been too heavy a burden to bear. As it was, there would be distressing divisions of loyalty among the next generation. Charles, Duke of Saxe-Coburg Gotha, and Ernest, Grand Duke of Hesse and the Rhine, were sovereign princes in the Fatherland. Like Prince and Princess Henry of Prussia, they were on much more friendly terms with their easy-going relations in England than with the German Emperor and his sabre-rattling entourage at the unbearably military Berlin court. But family ties counted for as little in 1914 as they had during Bismarck's ascendancy. Again, 'every family feeling was rent asunder.'

In 1912 Beatrice sold Osborne Cottage and moved into Carisbrooke Castle, a few miles south. She was there in July 1914, when the Austrian government was demanding satisfaction from Serbia after the assassination of Archduke Francis Ferdinand and his wife at Sarajevo. On the advice of Louis of Battenberg, now First Sea Lord, she made urgent preparations to move back to the mainland. On 4 August, the day Britain declared war on Germany, she phoned Helena to say she was returning to London forthwith. At a family luncheon it was arranged that Beatrice and Helena's divorced daughter Marie Louise should stay together for the time being at Kensington Palace. Louise had been widowed in May, when the Duke of Argyll succumbed to pneumonia at Kent House. He was remembered less for his marriage and political career than for his books, including volumes of Canadian and Scottish memoirs illustrated by his wife, plus biographies of Palmerston and – inevitably – Queen Victoria.

Everyone believed that this arrangement would last for just a few weeks. Had anybody prophesied that the conflict would drag on for four miserable years, they would not have been believed.

On 12 August Beatrice's three sons left for the front. Even so, she was not spared the general abuse and hatred directed at those in England with German connections. An aggressive letter demanded to know what part she was playing in the war. As she was actively engaged in planning hospitals and raising funds for the wounded, as were her sisters, she was justifiably angered. She answered that her sons were in the army, and she had lost her husband on active service in the cause of defending the British Empire; she did not see what more she could do. Two months later Maurice, her youngest son, was mentioned in despatches for having shown outstanding gallantry in leading his men of the 60th Rifles into action. On 28 October he fell fighting a gallant rearguard action at Ypres during the retreat from Mons.

If the shy and retiring Beatrice kept her thoughts on the German emperor to herself, her surviving sisters did not. In the first few weeks of the war, Helena wrote to a friend that her nephew 'must be quite mad to have lit such a conflagration', while on a visit to Kensington Palace one of Louise's nephews found her 'most violent against the Kaiser'.[15] The Duke of Connaught shared their 'mad' verdict, writing to Louise of his amazement at William's order to his troops 'for want of dignity, fine feeling and personal animosity'.[16] As patriotic as any of his countrymen, he lambasted the Germans as 'savage', while the Duchess, a Hohenzollern princess herself, called the war 'the deed of the Devil'.[17]

Helena and Christian had also known the grief of losing a son in wartime. They now had another cross to bear, in the shape of their surviving son Albert. With their consent, he had been chosen as heir to his uncle, the dispossessed Duke Frederick, but this had necessitated his adopting German nationality and being brought up in Germany. On Frederick's death in 1880 he had succeeded to the duchy of Schleswig-Holstein, inheriting estates in Silesia. Naturally he was commissioned in the Germany army, and though on the retired list when war was declared in 1914, he was in honour bound to place his services at the German Emperor's disposal. With his stipulation that under no circumstances would he serve on the western front, the Emperor concurred. He therefore appointed his cousin to serve under a general, whose mother was also English, in charge of defence at Berlin. Yet it pained his parents greatly that he should have to serve in any capacity in hostilities against their country.

By the outbreak of war Helena had a formidable list of achievements in the field of charity work to her credit. She was president of the Royal British Nurses' Association, whose Royal Charter she had helped to obtain; she took a particular interest in the Society for the Prevention of Cruelty to Children, and had helped to establish a children's holiday home near Cumberland Lodge; and she was an enthusiastic patron and visitor to hospitals in the borough of Windsor. Despite his advancing years and loss of one eye, Christian pursued his sporting activities with vigour until he was over eighty. He was known within the family as an indefatigable walker, an ardent follower of hounds, and a keen annual visitor to deer hunts in the forests of Silesia and Hungary.

On 5 July 1916 Helena and Christian celebrated their golden wedding. Considering that the age difference between them (fifteen years) was greater than that in any other marriage among Queen Victoria's children, it was remarkable that they were the only couple to reach such an anniversary. The event could not pass unnoticed, even in wartime. A thanksgiving service in the chapel at Windsor Park was held in the morning, followed by the reception of endless messages of congratulations from the family and neighbourhood. Christian was High Steward of the royal borough of Windsor, and there were deputations from the town. In the afternoon, while entertaining King George and Queen Mary to tea, Helena was handed a telegram from Emperor William that had been sent through their cousin Margaret, Crown Princess of Sweden, one of the countries which was still neutral. Even in the midst of war, he still wanted to convey his 'loyal and devoted good wishes' to his aunt and uncle on their anniversary. They were deeply moved that he should have remembered at such a crucial time.

Christian lived just long enough to see his name swept into oblivion, as far as Britain was concerned, along with those of Teck, Battenberg, and above all the dynastic name of Saxe-

Coburg Gotha. Complaints from socialists about the 'alien and uninspiring court' had provoked the King's memorable retort that 'I may be uninspiring but I'll be damned if I'm alien!'[18] German titles were accordingly eliminated from the royal house, which henceforth became the house of Windsor. The Battenbergs became Mountbattens except for Princess Henry of Battenberg who became simply, once again, Princess Beatrice; the princes and princesses of Schleswig-Holstein likewise reverted simply to being known by their first names. The senior one of all, eighty-six-year-old Christian, died peacefully at Schomberg House after a short illness in October 1917. To the end he remained keenly interested in the war's progress. His last words to King George, as he asked about the battle of Caporetto, were: 'George, what about those damned Italians?'

Life in the Connaught household was enlivened by the companionship of Leonie Leslie, a younger sister of Lady Randolph Churchill. It was the most respectable of friendships, fully endorsed by the shy Duchess of Connaught who admitted freely if a little naïvely that 'Arthur and I never had any fun until we met Leonie.' Arthur, it was noticed, became less stiff and awkward, and more informal in his demeanour, under her influence. Lady Cynthia Asquith judged him to be 'the only gentleman royalty with manners and presence.' When Mrs Leslie had a crisis of conscience, and suggested that she should 'fold up her tent Arab-fashion,' terminating their relationship, the Duchess besought her by letter not to – 'the very idea has made the Duke miserable.' All three exchanged notes and letters regularly, one of the most touching of Arthur's being his description in May 1910 of Queen Alexandra taking him to gaze on his brother's face for the last time, 'so calm and beautiful and natural.' Leonie knew what a poignant occasion it must have been, made more so by the memory of heated arguments between the brothers.

When it was confirmed that the Duke of Connaught had been appointed to the governor-generalship of Canada, there were some dissentient voices. Remembering Lord and Lady Lorne's faults, a few critics foresaw 'a rigid and arbitrary etiquette, the trappings of a Court.' The Duke let it be known that he intended to be a democratic governor-general and did not propose to establish a royal court in the dominion. This egalitarianism may not have accorded with his personal views, for he was as conservative as most of his generation. In private, he regarded the Beaverbrook and Rothermere press as 'poisonous and ultra socialist', while Lloyd George and trade unionism were 'dangerous'. To cheers of *'Vive le Duc!'* and *'Vive Connaught!'* the Duke and Duchess arrived at Quebec in October 1911. They made a popular couple, assiduous in their attention to the administrative duties and social functions at Ottawa and Montreal.

But their five-year tenure of office was overshadowed by the Duchess's failing health. In June 1912 she fell ill with peritonitis, and after a period of rest she resumed her activities before recovering completely. Early the following year she was taken ill again, and as soon as she could travel across the Atlantic she went back to London for two serious operations. At one stage it seemed unlikely that she would ever return to Canada, but by the autumn she was pronounced sufficiently strong to go back. However, she did not long survive her farewell to the dominion in October 1916. Shortly after returning to Clarence House she contracted influenza and bronchitis. Leonie Leslie visited them regularly, joining the Duchess of Argyll and Queen Alexandra in trying to look after the Duchess and comfort her husband.

On 12 March 1917 Mrs Leslie noted in her diary that she was much worse: 'Only a miracle can save her . . . He seems stunned. I tell him there is no hope – he is so silent and patient in his grief – does not want anyone with him . . . he is the loneliest man I have ever seen – God knows what he will do without her.'[19] On 14 March the Duchess died. Three years later the grief-stricken widower suffered another bereavement when his eldest daughter Margaret, Crown Princess of Sweden, died suddenly after complications following an inflammation of the eyes and erysipelas.

The princesses had spent four years organising charity bazaars, planning and visiting hospitals and convalescent homes, and raising donations for the war effort, when the armistice was signed in November 1918. No tragedy had affected the royal family in England more than the horrific fate of the dethroned Romanovs in Russia, the Tsar, Tsarina and their haemophilic son and four daughters, savagely butchered by Bolsheviks in the cellar of Ekaterinburg. For those of an older generation who remembered their niece Alicky of Hesse as a merry little girl in the nursery at Darmstadt, it was a nightmare that could never be forgotten.

Shortly after her seventy-seventh birthday at Schomberg House in May 1923 Helena, who had pursued her charitable causes faithfully to the last, fell ill with influenza. After lingering for a few days she died on 9 June. As *The Times* commented, 'she had not lived a "showy" life, but an extremely useful one. Her services, given personally, directly, and ungrudgingly over many years to nursing and to kindred causes, were of a highly practical kind, and their results could not have failed to give her pleasure as she contemplated them in old age.'[20] She was followed to the grave a couple of years later by that other royal benefactress with whom she had little in common, Queen Alexandra. Alix's last years had been clouded by total deafness and partial blindness. She died at Sandringham on 20 November 1925, aged eighty.

Sir Frederick Ponsonby's removal of the dying Vicky's letters to safety had its sequel in the post-war world. For over a quarter of a century he hesitated to reveal them to the world. But the continued publication of books presenting a grossly distorted portrait of the Empress Frederick as a scheming Englishwoman who despised her deformed son and ruthlessly dominated her husband forced his hand. The last of these works, a biography by Emil Ludwig (published in English translation as *Kaiser Wilhelm II* in 1926) was particularly damaging to her reputation – but nonetheless as successful in Britain as it was in Germany.

The following year, Ponsonby asked King George V if he might publish some of the Empress Frederick's letters. The

King was doubtful, and advised him to consult the Empress's surviving brother and sisters. Only Beatrice disapproved, presumably on the grounds that she had been the most closely-involved as a result of the Battenberg marriage controversy, and also as she was averse to the idea of opening old wounds. The past was something she would rather forget. King George therefore withdrew his half-hearted opposition and recommended that Ponsonby should exercise his own judgement. Accordingly, he devoted several months to reading through the letters, bound in some sixty volumes of about four hundred pages each. He selected some for typing, and wrote a commentary to link them. On the advice of his publisher Sir Frederick Macmillan, he invoked the aid of S.F. Markham, who had completed the second volume of Sir Sidney Lee's officially-commissioned biography of King Edward VII after Lee's death. Markham corroborated Ponsonby's work and letters with material from other recent books, including Ludwig's biography, the memoirs of Bismarck's colleagues, and speeches of the Emperor William himself.

The result, *Letters of the Empress Frederick*, was published in October 1928. As expected it was welcomed with keen interest by press and public alike. The royal family were strangely divided on its merits. King George did not express an opinion until his unmarried sister Victoria said she thought it one of the most dreadful books ever published; Beatrice saw extracts in the papers and joined in their condemnation without reading it for herself. Queen Mary thought Ponsonby was right in publishing the letters, though he should have been more selective in his choice of material. Louise and Arthur firmly supported him, the latter pointing out that Ludwig's book and the ex-Emperor's accounts would form history unless adequately contradicted, and he was never in any doubt that his much-maligned sister had intended Ponsonby to publish the letters anyway. Vicky's two youngest daughters likewise wrote Ponsonby charming letters for having carried out their mother's wishes so faithfully. Ludwig recanted his previous views on the Empress's character and admitted that, had

Letters of the Empress Frederick been published earlier, it would have 'caused substantial changes to be made' in his book.[21]

From his exile at Doorn in Holland, the ex-Emperor was infuriated and embarrassed. He tried to have the book withdrawn, on the grounds that he was head of the family and his mother's letters therefore belonged to him, but his efforts to pursue a case against Ponsonby for theft fell on stony ground. He accordingly purchased the German publishing rights and wrote an introduction in which he attempted to defend himself by explaining that the Empress was very sensitive and everything wounded her; 'she saw everything in shadows, everything hostile, saw want of sympathy and coolness where there was only a helpless silence, and her temperament made her use bitter words about everybody.'[22]

Quite apart from her annoyance at seeing her sister's letters published, Beatrice found little comfort in her declining years. The princess whose childhood had been overshadowed by the Prince Consort's death and Queen Victoria's protracted mourning, had lost her husband and youngest son on active service. Her second son Leopold succumbed in 1922 to haemophilia, the scourge of her daughter Queen Ena's married life. Like her ill-fated cousin Alexandra in Russia, the superstitious subjects of her husband firmly believed that the English princess's deformed male offspring signified divine retribution for changing her religion. Ena could not hold the love and devotion of her restless husband, who blamed them both for their sickly sons, and sought comfort in a playboy lifestyle. Unstable Spanish politics sealed their fate; republicans made significant gains in the elections of 1931, and rather than provoke civil war King Alfonso abdicated. He died in Rome ten years later, Ena living on until 1969. Had she survived another seven years, she would have seen Spain's monarchy fully restored, with her grandson Juan Carlos proclaimed King.

In January 1931 Beatrice slipped on a mat at Kensington Palace and broke two bones in her left arm. Bronchitis followed, and at one point the doctors despaired for her life.

Her recovery was slow, and for the rest of her days she was very lame. Cataracts gave her trouble and she was almost blind until an operation partially restored her sight. Yet she could no longer read music, and had to turn on the radio for enjoyment of the works she used to play herself on the piano.

By the 1930s, old age had gradually driven the longest-lived of the Victorian princes and princesses into retirement from public life. At home their conversational powers remained undimmed, and as an adult the young Princess Elizabeth of York, later Queen Elizabeth II, would later recall how the elderly Louise and Beatrice talked 'until their audience was stunned by the outpouring of words.'[23]

Queen Mary's acquisitive instincts, when it came to persuading owners of or custodians of items of art and furniture to part with them, were legendary, but Louise was proof against these. On a visit to Kensington Palace the Queen made her way towards a clock on the mantelpiece, her admiration all too transparent. Standing between clock and Queen, she said firmly, 'The clock is here, and here it remains.'[24]

Louise enjoyed excellent health to the end, and from time to time she could be seen reviewing the Argyll and Sutherland Highlanders, whose colonel-in-chief she had been made in 1919. Her last major public appearance was at Kensington Town Hall in the summer of 1935, when she welcomed King George V and Queen Mary to a reception during their silver jubilee celebrations. Always the most modern-minded of the family, she welcomed new theories on education: 'Luckily the habit of moulding all children to the same pattern has gone out of fashion. It was deplorable. I know, because I suffered from it. Nowadays, individuality and one's own capabilities are recognized.'[25] As for preserving the sanctity of her father's spotless reputation, she would have none of it. After the author Percy Colson had written and published a rather critical account of him, she invited him for tea and greeted him with the words, 'You were very naughty, but it is all true.'[26]

With increasing old age and frailty she longed to be left alone. On her eighty-ninth birthday in March 1937, she remarked to the Dowager Marchioness of Milford Haven that she was irritated by the fuss people were making of her. Much as she was touched by the thoughtfulness of people who sent flowers and messages, it seemed a case of 'lots of silly people . . . doing silly things meaning to be kind but really to please themselves.'[27]

By the time the Second World War broke out, she was fading away gently. On 30 November 1939 a friend brought her some carnations, and from her bed she told him gently with a smile that he need never bring her any more flowers. Shortly afterwards she slipped into a coma, and died three days later. She was ninety-one years of age. Unorthodox to the last, she had left instructions that her body should be cremated. It was an appropriate ending for the princess who, in the words of her obituary, was 'the least bound by convention and etiquette of any of the Royal Family.'[28] The ceremony took place at Golders Green, her boxed ashes were put in a coffin, and taken to Windsor for the funeral at St George's Chapel. Three months later, her final resting place was ready. At a short ceremony in March 1940, to a refrain piped by her beloved Argyll and Sutherland Highlanders, her remains were buried in the Royal Cemetery at Frogmore.

The Duke of Connaught was always on excellent terms with his nephew King George, and when he died in January 1936, had high hopes for the reign of King Edward VIII. During his last months, when he was gravely worried about his son and heir's relationship with Wallis Simpson, King George had asked 'uncle Arthur' to intervene, though it is unlikely that the elder man ever did. Throughout the abdication crisis he was deeply sympathetic towards King Edward, though in his letters to Louise he wondered whether their embattled sovereign had 'even thought what we must be feeling at "the Queen"!! he is going to introduce into our family?' After the accession of King George VI in December, he shared the family's general relief, though saddened at the sudden end of the reign of 'poor David', the great-nephew 'we all hoped would make a model though rather too modern King . . . Wrong-headed as I think he was in his friendships, and in his loves, we must always remember that he was but human.'[29] He thought it an imaginative gesture of King George VI to create the ex-King Duke of Windsor: 'I so thoroughly approve of the title and I am sure that all at Windsor will be proud to have him as their Duke.'[30]

In his later years he derived much pleasure from gardening. His villa in southern France, '*Les Bruyères*', was noted for its colourful display of lovingly-tended flowers. When he had to give up travelling abroad he spent his winters in Bath and Sidmouth, the town in which his soldier grandfather had breathed his last, and he was gratified when the latter's town councillors named one of its great scenic attractions 'Connaught Gardens' in his honour.

Leonie Leslie remained his devoted friend to the last, though as he became slower and more deaf, she regarded her weekly visits to Bagshot as rather a chore. Sometimes she took her grandchildren with her to see him, and one of them remarked on a drive back afterwards that she had liked the Duke's tartan dressing gown. At this Leonie snapped crossly that nothing looked shabbier than tartan. Everybody was 'sick of that old dressing gown. He is so obstinate about it!'[31]

Like other members of the family who lived to a great age, he became increasingly lonely as he outlived his closest relations, including not only his wife but two of their three children. His only son, another Arthur, died suddenly in 1938. Like Louise, he was in his ninety-second year when he passed away peacefully at Bagshot on 16 January 1942, thus attaining a record age for male members of the royal family.

Beatrice, the last to be born and the last to die, still had two important tasks to undertake. Queen Victoria had bequeathed her all her private journals, with instructions to modify or destroy any passages she thought not suitable to preserve for posterity. Accordingly she set to work on transcribing passages in her own hand, substantially altering much and destroying a good deal more. When eye operations called a temporary halt to her work, she delegated it to her niece Thora. Amongst passages apparently consigned to the flames was a description by Queen Victoria of her wedding night, that night which Charles Greville had thought strangely short at the time.

Beatrice's second job was to translate extracts from the diary of Queen Victoria's great-grandmother Augusta, Duchess of Saxe-Coburg Saalfeld. The resulting volume was published in 1941 as *In Napoleonic Days*, with proceeds going to war charities.

She spent the last two years of her life quietly at Brantridge Park, Balcombe, Sussex, a country house belonging to her nephew and niece the Earl and Countess of Athlone, where she was joined by Helena's daughters Helena Victoria and Marie Louise. During the winter of 1943 she suffered increasingly from bronchial asthma. As her daughter-in-law Irene, Marchioness of Carisbrooke, wrote, 'she struggled so hard to "carry on" in spite of all her sufferings with supreme courage but it was very painful for those who loved her'. [32] The tide of war was turning in favour of Britain and her allies in the autumn of 1944 when she became ill for the last time. Ena, living in Switzerland at the time, was warned of her mother's condition, and the British government sent a converted bomber to bring her back to England.

She arrived just in time, for early on the morning of 26 October Beatrice died in her sleep, aged eighty-seven. After the funeral at St George's Chapel, Windsor, her body was temporarily housed in the royal vaults. The following year, after peace was declared, her sole surviving son Alexander, Lord Carisbrooke, asked and received permission from King George VI for her body to be brought to the Isle of Wight and be buried beside that of her husband at Whippingham Church. Over a century had elapsed since the birth of Queen Victoria's first child. Now it was time for the youngest to return home and find eternal rest.

Queen Victoria and Prince Albert both left an indelible impression on the nineteenth century in a way that no other British monarch and her (or his) consort had done, or even come close to doing. All nine princes and princesses inherited much of their parents' strength of personality, talent for organisation and unshakeable resolve to be of service. (The same could hardly be said for the voluminous family of King George III and Queen Charlotte.)

The princes made their contribution in differing but no less valuable ways. As heir to the throne and later sovereign, King Edward VII proved himself a born statesman whose intellectual shortcomings were more than balanced by his tact, charm and sound judgement of character. The Dukes of Edinburgh and Connaught aspired to the heights of the navy and army respectively through hard work and determination, not merely because of their exalted birth; and the Duke of Albany's patronage, during his short life, of the arts and education was substantial.

The princesses likewise did much to establish and run hospitals, schools and welfare organisations at home and abroad. Though the two eldest encountered considerable resistance and prejudice in their efforts in Germany, they would not be swayed from their intentions, and they set an example which was gratefully appreciated by the poorer people if not in official circles. Whether they married and lived at home or in Europe, none of Queen Victoria's children was content to be a mere Royal Highness. They all personified the sentiments echoed by King Edward VII in the rhetorical question he is reputed to have asked within a day or two of his death: 'Of what use is it to be alive if one cannot work?'[33]

The House of Hanover

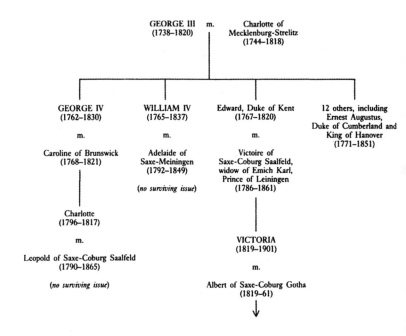

The House of Saxe-Coburg Saalfeld and Saxe-Coburg Gotha

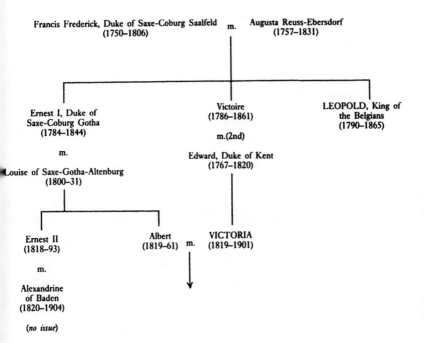

The House of Hohenzollern

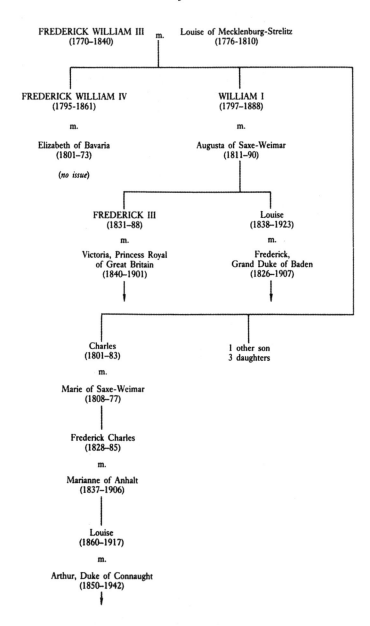

FREDERICK WILLIAM III
(1770–1840)
m.
Louise of Mecklenburg-Strelitz
(1776-1810)

FREDERICK WILLIAM IV
(1795-1861)

m.

Elizabeth of Bavaria
(1801–73)

(no issue)

WILLIAM I
(1797–1888)

m.

Augusta of Saxe-Weimar
(1811–90)

FREDERICK III
(1831–88)

m.

Victoria, Princess Royal
of Great Britain
(1840–1901)

Louise
(1838–1923)

m.

Frederick,
Grand Duke of Baden
(1826–1907)

Charles
(1801–83)

m.

Marie of Saxe-Weimar
(1808–77)

Frederick Charles
(1828–85)

m.

Marianne of Anhalt
(1837–1906)

Louise
(1860–1917)

m.

Arthur, Duke of Connaught
(1850–1942)

1 other son
3 daughters

The House of Hesse and the Rhine;
the House of Battenberg

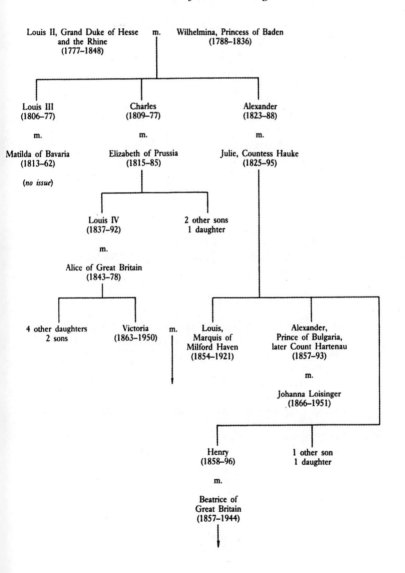

Queen Victoria's Children and Grandchildren

1. VICTORIA Adelaide Mary Louise, Princess Royal, later German Empress, born 21 November 1840, died 5 August 1901. Married Prince Frederick William of Prussia, later German Emperor Frederick III (1831–88; reigned March to June 1888), 25 January 1858. Children:
    (1) William II, German Emperor (1859–1941; reigned 1888–1918)
    (2) Charlotte, Duchess of Saxe-Meiningen (1860–1919)
    (3) Henry of Prussia (1862–1929)
    (4) Sigismund of Prussia (1864–66)
    (5) Victoria, Princess Adolf of Schaumburg-Lippe and later Mrs Alexander Zubkov (1866–1929)
    (6) Waldemar of Prussia (1868–79)
    (7) Sophie, Queen of the Hellenes (1870–1932; her husband King Constantine reigned 1913–17 and 1920–22)
    (8) Margaret, landgravine of Hesse (1872–1954)

2. Albert EDWARD, Prince of Wales, later King Edward VII (reigned 1901–10), born 9 November 1841, died 6 May 1910. Married Princess Alexandra of Denmark (1844–1925), 10 March 1863. Children:
    (1) Albert Victor, Duke of Clarence and Avondale (1864–92)
    (2) King George V (1865–1936; reigned 1910–36)
    (3) Louise, Duchess of Fife (1867–1931; Princess Royal from 1905)
    (4) Victoria of Wales (1868–1935)
    (5) Maud, Queen of Norway (1869–1938; her husband King Haakon VII reigned 1905–57)
    (6) Alexander John of Wales (6–7 April 1871)

3. ALICE Maud Mary, later Grand Duchess Louise of Hesse and the Rhine, born 25 April 1843, died 14 December 1878. Married Prince Louis of Hesse and the Rhine, later Grand Duke (1837–92; reigned 1877–92), 1 July 1862. Children:

    (1)   Victoria, Princess Louis of Battenberg, later Mountbatten,
              Marchioness of Milford Haven (1863–1950)
    (2)   Elizabeth, Grand Duchess Serge of Russia (1864–1918)
    (3)   Irene, Princess Henry of Prussia (see 1. (3) above)
              (1866–1953)
    (4)   Ernest, Grand Duke of Hesse and the Rhine (1868–1937;
              reigned 1892–1918)
    (5)   Frederick William of Hesse and the Rhine (1870–73)
    (6)   Alix, Tsarina of Russia (1872–1918; her husband Tsar
              Nicholas II reigned 1894–1917)
    (7)   May of Hesse and the Rhine (1874–78)

4.   ALFRED Ernest Albert, later Duke of Edinburgh, Earl of Ulster
      and Kent, later Duke of Saxe-Coburg Gotha, born 6 August
      1844, died 30 July 1900. Married Marie, Grand Duchess of
      Russia (1853–1920), 23 January 1874. Children:
    (1)   Alfred of Saxe-Coburg Gotha (1874–99)
    (2)   Marie, Queen of Roumania (1875–1938, her husband
              King Ferdinand reigned 1914–27)
    (3)   Victoria Melita, Grand Duchess of Hesse and the Rhine
              (see 3. (4) above; marriage dissolved) and later Grand
              Duchess Kyril of Russia (1876–1936)
    (4)   Alexandra, Princess Ernest of Hohenlohe-Langenburg
              (1878–1942)
    (5)   Beatrice, Infanta of Orleans (1884–1966)
              A stillborn son was born to Alfred and Marie in 1879

5.   HELENA Augusta Victoria, later Princess Christian of Schleswig-
      Holstein, born 25 May 1846, died 9 June 1923. Married Prince
      Christian of Schleswig-Holstein (1831–1917), 5 July 1866.
      Children:
         (1)   Christian Victor of Schleswig-Holstein (1867–1900)
         (2)   Albert, Duke of Schleswig-Holstein (1869–1931;
                reigned 1880–1918)
         (3)   Helena Victoria of Schleswig-Holstein (1870–1948)
         (4)   Marie Louise, Princess Aribert of Anhalt (until
                marriage dissolved) (1872–1956)
         (5)   Harold of Schleswig-Holstein (12–21 May 1874)

6.   LOUISE Caroline Alberta, later Marchioness of Lorne and
      Duchess of Argyll, born 18 March 1848, died 3 December 1939.
      Married John Campbell, Marquis of Lorne, later 9th Duke of
      Argyll (1845–1914; Duke 1900–14), 21 March 1871. No issue.

7.   ARTHUR William Patrick Albert, later Duke of Connaught and Strathearn, born 1 May 1850, died 16 January 1942. Married Princess Louise of Prussia (1860–1917), 13 March 1879. Children:
  (1)   Margaret, Crown Princess of Sweden (1882–1920)
  (2)   Arthur of Connaught (1883–1938)
  (3)   Patricia, Lady Patricia Ramsay (1886–1974)

8.   LEOPOLD George Duncan Albert, later Duke of Albany, Earl of Clarence, and Baron Arklow, born 7 April 1853, died 28 March 1884. Married Princess Helen of Waldeck-Pyrmont (1861–1922), 27 April 1882. Children:
  (1)   Alice, Countess of Athlone (1883–1981)
  (2)   Charles, Duke of Albany, later Duke of Saxe-Coburg Gotha (1884–1954; reigned 1900–18)

9.   BEATRICE Mary Victoria Feodora, later Princess Henry of Battenberg, born 14 April 1857, died 26 October 1944. Married Prince Henry of Battenberg (1858–96), 23 July 1885. Children:
  (1)   Alexander, Marquis of Carisbrooke (1886–1960)
  (2)   Victoria Eugenie, Queen of Spain (1887–1969; her husband King Alfonso XIII reigned 1886–1931)
  (3)   Leopold of Battenberg, later Mountbatten (1889–1922)
  (4)   Maurice of Battenberg (1891–1914)

Reference Notes

PROLOGUE (pp. 1–13)
1. Queen Victoria, *Girlhood* I 136
2. Greville I 412
3. Queen Victoria, *Letters* I i 48; *Girlhood* I 160
4. Queen Victoria, *Letters* I i 49
5. ibid. I i 178
6. Victoria, *Girlhood* II 262
7. Longford, *Victoria R.I.* 143
8. Charlot 195
9. Longford, *Victoria R.I.* 153

CHAPTER 1 (pp. 14–47)
1. Queen Victoria, *Dearest Child* 165
2. Anon., *Empress Frederick: A Memoir* 4
3. Queen Victoria, *Dearest Child* 168
4. Longford, *Victoria R.I.* 160
5. Albert, *Letters of the Prince Consort* 135
6. Longford, *Victoria R.I.* 217
7. ibid. 266
8. ibid. 262
9. Albert, *Letters of the Prince Consort* 288
10. Magnus, 26
11. Wortham 57
12. Bennett, Vicky 69
13. Queen Victoria, *Dearest Child* 134

14. McClintock 25
15. Stanley 206
16. ibid. 214
17. Corti 63
18. Queen Victoria, *Letters* I iii 413
19. Corti 64
20. Stanley 85
21. Magnus 51
22. Martin V 415
23. Longford, *Victoria R.I.* 298
24. Queen Victoria, *Letters* I iii 473

CHAPTER 2 (pp. 48–87)
1. Queen Victoria, *Dearest Mama* 30
2. Corti 81
3. Queen Victoria, *Dearest Mama* 85
4. Magnus 59
5. Queen Victoria, *Dearest Mama* 172–3
6. Kennedy 214
7. Lee, *Edward VII* 1 256
8. Battiscombe 78
9. Queen Victoria, *Letters* III 296
10. *Alice: Biographical sketch and letters* 122–3
11. Queen Victoria, *Your Dear Letter* 81
12. Corti 153
13. Queen Victoria, *Your Dear Letter* 192, 200

14. ibid. 70
15. Zeepvat 61
16. Longford, *Victoria R.I.* 364–5
17. ibid. 364–5
18. Queen Victoria, *Your Dear Letter* 200–01
19. Longford, *Victoria R.I.* 376
20. Magnus 102
21. Ponsonby, A. 71
22. Epton 128
23. Queen Victoria, *Your Dear Letter* 114
24. Epton 126
25. Longford, *Victoria R.I.* 368
26. Queen Victoria, *Letters* II i 632–33
27. Longford, *Victoria R.I.* 386
28. Battiscombe 116–17
29. Ponsonby, A. 98
30. Battiscombe 118

CHAPTER 3 (pp. 88–127)
1. Magnus 119
2. Röhl 97
3. Queen Victoria, *Darling Child* 39
4. Marie Louise 17
5. Bennett, *Queen Victoria's Children* 125
6. Hough 90
7. Zeepvat 138
8. Hibbert 400
9. Noel 224
10. ibid. 231
11. Epton 154
12. Queen Victoria, *Letters* II ii 655
13. Victoria, Princess, *Letters of the Empress Frederick* 172
14. Aston 145
15. Queen Victoria, *Beloved Mama* 36
16. Alice, *For my Grandchildren* 15
17. Longford, *Victoria R.I.* 448

18. Queen Victoria, *Beloved Mama* 162
19. Longford, *Victoria, R.I.* 478
20. Corti 225–6
21. Duff, *Shy Princess* 128; Queen Victoria, *Beloved Mama* 195
22. Weintraub 475

CHAPTER 4 (pp. 128–170)
1. Queen Victoria, *Letters* III i 320
2. Marie, Queen of Roumania I 38
3. Queen Victoria, *Letters* III i 355
4. Victoria, Princess, *Letters of the Empress Frederick* 315–6
5. Pakula 497
6. Queen Victoria, *Letters* III i 423
7. ibid. III i 440–1
8. ibid. III i 504
9. ibid. III i 526
10. St Aubyn, *Edward VII* 115
11. Battiscombe 182
12. Magnus 227
13. ibid. 239
14. Ponsonby, A. 359
15. Van der Kiste & Jordaan, *Dearest Affie* 154; *The Times*, 9.2.1894
16. Magnus 246
17. ibid. 247
18. Victoria, Princess Royal, *Empress Frederick writes to Sophie* 281
19. Crewe II 474
20. Mallet 50
21. Epton 177
22. Reid 102
23. ibid. 103
24. Röhl, Warren & Hunt 133

25. Longford, *Darling Loosy* 242–3
26. Queen Victoria, *Letters* III ii 579–80
27. Duff, *Shy Princess* 195–6
28. Queen Victoria, *Letters* III iii 637
29. Aston 223
30. Mullen & Munson 147
31. Victoria, Princess Royal, *Empress Frederick writes to Sophie* 343
32. Epton 222
33. ibid. 224

CHAPTER 5 (pp. 171–203)
1. Ponsonby, F. 110
2. Epton 225
3. Teignmouth-Shore 307
4. Corti 343
5. Lee, *Edward VII* II 124
6. Vickers 50
7. Epton 243
8. Packard 319
9. Lee, *Edward VII* II 497
10. ibid. 717
11. Nicolson 105
12. Brook-Shepherd 255
13. Blunt 721–2
14. Bülow I 336
15. Wake 396
16. Longford, *Darling Loosy* 286
17. ibid. 79
18. Nicolson 308
19. Leslie 216
20. *The Times*, 11.6.1923
21. Ponsonby, F. 113
22. ibid. 114–15
23. Hough 50
24. Wake 410
25. Epton 227
26. Colson 56
27. Wake 410
28. *The Times*, 4.12.1939
29. Longford, *Darling Loosy* 306–7
30. Wheeler-Bennett 295
31. Leslie 218
32. Dennison 204
33. Redesdale 32–3

Bibliography

This is partly a list of volumes used in the text, and also a guide to standard lives and editions of letters, arranged thematically. Relevant works on Queen Victoria's children-in-law are given under the names of the respective children.

Queen Victoria, Prince Albert and the family in general

Aronson, Theo. *Grandmama of Europe: the crowned descendants of Queen Victoria*, Cassell, 1973

Ashdown, Dulcie M. *Queen Victoria's family*, Robert Hale, 1975

Bennett, Daphne. *King without a crown*, Heinemann, 1977

—— *Queen Victoria's children*, Victor Gollancz, 1980

Benson, E.F. *Daughters of Queen Victoria*, Cassell, 1939

Buchanan, Meriel. *Queen Victoria's relations*, Cassell, 1954

Charlot, Monica. *Victoria, the young Queen*, Blackwell, 1991

Epton, Nina. *Victoria and her daughters*, Weidenfeld & Nicolson, 1971

Fulford, Roger. *The Prince Consort*, Macmillan, 1949

Hibbert, Christopher. *Queen Victoria: a Personal Portrait*, Harper Collins, 2000

James, Robert Rhodes. *Albert, Prince Consort*, Hamish Hamilton, 1983

Lee, Sir Sidney. *Queen Victoria: a biography*, Smith, Elder, 1902

Longford, Elizabeth. *Victoria R.I.*, Weidenfeld & Nicolson, 1964

Martin, Sir Theodore. *The Life of HRH The Prince Consort*, 5 vols. Smith, Elder, 1875–80

Mullen, Richard, & Munson, James. *Victoria: Portrait of a Queen*, BBC, 1987

Packard, Jerrold. *Victoria's daughters*, Sutton, 1999

Röhl, John C.G., Warren, Martin, & Hunt, David, *Purple Secret: Genes, 'Madness' and the Royal Houses of Europe*, Bantam, 1998

St Aubyn, Giles. *Queen Victoria: a Portrait*, Sinclair-Stevenson, 1991

Van der Kiste, John, *Sons, Servants and Statesmen: The men in Queen Victoria's life*, Sutton, 2006

Weintraub, Stanley, *Victoria: Biography of a Queen*, Unwin Hyman, 1987

Woodham-Smith, Mrs Cecil. *Queen Victoria, her Life and Times*, Vol. 1, 1819–1861, Hamish-Hamilton, 1972

BIBLIOGRAPHY

Royal letters and diaries

Alice, Grand Duchess of Hesse. *Biographical sketch and letters*, John Murray, 1884

Hough, Richard, sel. *Advice to a grand-daughter: letters from Queen Victoria to Princess Victoria of Hesse*, Heinemann, 1975

Longford, Elizabeth, ed. *Darling Loosy: Letters to Princess Louise, 1856–1939*, Weidenfeld & Nicolson, 1991

Victoria, Queen. *The Girlhood of Queen Victoria: a selection from Her Majesty's Diaries between the years 1832 and 1840*, ed. Viscount Esher, 2 vols, John Murray, 1912

—— *The Letters of Queen Victoria: a selection from Her Majesty's Correspondence between the years 1837 and 1861*, ed. A.C. Benson & Viscount Esher, 3 vols, John Murray, 1907

—— *The Letters of Queen Victoria, second series: a selection from Her Majesty's Correspondence and Journal between the years 1862 and 1885*, ed. G.E. Buckle, 3 vols, John Murray, 1926–8

—— *The Letters of Queen Victoria, third series: a selection from Her Majesty's Correspondence and Journal between the years 1886 and 1901*, ed. G.E. Buckle, 3 vols, John Murray, 1930–2

—— *Leaves from the Journal of Our Life in the Highlands, from 1848 to 1861*. Smith, Elder, 1868

—— *More leaves from the Journal of a Life in the Highlands, from 1862 to 1882*. Smith, Elder, 1884

Victoria, Queen, and Victoria, Princess Royal, later Crown Princess of Prussia, later German Empress. *Dearest Child: letters between Queen Victoria and the Princess Royal, 1858–61*, ed. Roger Fulford, Evans Bros, 1964

—— *Dearest Mama: letters between Queen Victoria and the Crown Princess of Prussia, 1862–64*, ed. Roger Fulford, Evans Bros, 1968

—— *Your dear letter: private correspondence between Queen Victoria and the Crown Princess of Prussia, 1865–71*, ed. Roger Fulford, Evans Bros, 1971

—— *Darling Child: private correspondence between Queen Victoria and the Crown Princess of Prussia, 1871–78*, ed. Roger Fulford, Evans Bros, 1976

—— *Beloved Mama: private correspondence between Queen Victoria and the Crown Princess of Prussia, 1879–85*, ed. Roger Fulford, Evans Bros. 1981

—— *Beloved and Darling Child: last letters between Queen Victoria and her eldest daughter, 1886–1901*, ed. Agatha Ramm, Sutton, 1990

—— *Further letters of Queen Victoria, from the Archives of the House of Brandenburg-Prussia*, ed. Hector Bolitho, Thornton Butterworth, 1938

Victoria, Princess Royal, later Crown Princess of Prussia, later German Empress. *Letters of the Empress Frederick*, ed. Sir Frederick Ponsonby, Macmillan, 1928

—— *The Empress Frederick writes to Sophie, her Daughter, Crown Princess and later Queen of the Hellenes: Letters 1889–1901*, ed. Arthur Gould Lee, Faber, 1955

Other royal biographies

Hough, Richard. *Louis and Victoria: The first Mountbattens*, Hutchinson, 1974

Nicolson, Harold. *King George the Fifth: His life and reign*, Constable, 1952

Pope-Hennessy, James. *Queen Mary, 1867–1953*, Allen & Unwin, 1959

Röhl, John C.G. *Young Wilhelm: The Kaiser's early life, 1859–1888*, Cambridge University Press, 1998

Vickers, Hugo. *Alice, Princess Andrew of Greece*, Viking, 2000

Wheeler-Bennett, John W. *King George VI: His Life and Reign*, Macmillan, 1958

Court and associated biographies, memoirs and letters

Blunt, Wilfrid Scawen. *My Diaries: Being a Personal Narrative of Events, 1888–1914*, Martin Secker, 1919

Bülow, Prince von. *Memoirs*, 4 vols. Putnam, 1931

Colson, Percy. *Victorian portraits*, Rich & Cowan, 1932

Crewe, Marquis of. *Lord Rosebery*, 2 vols. John Murray, 1931

Downer, Martyn, *The Queen's Knight: The extraordinary life of Queen Victoria's most trusted confidant* [Sir Howard Elphinstone], Bantam, 2007

Greville, Charles C.F. *The Greville diary*, including passages hitherto withheld from publication, Philip Whitwell Wilson, ed. 2 vols. Heinemann, 1927

Kennedy, A.L., ed. '*My dear Duchess*': *Social and Political Letters to the Duchess of Manchester, 1858–1869*, John Murray, 1956

Lyttelton, Sarah. *The correspondence of Sarah, Lady Lyttelton*, ed. The Hon. Mrs Hugh Wyndham, John Murray, 1912

McClintock, Mary Howard. *The Queen thanks Sir Howard*, John Murray, 1945

Mallet, Victor, ed. *Life with Queen Victoria: Marie Mallet's letters from court, 1887–1901*. John Murray, 1968

Ponsonby, Arthur. *Henry Ponsonby, Queen Victoria's Private Secretary: His Life from His Letters*, Macmillan, 1942

Ponsonby, Sir Frederick. *Recollections of three reigns*, Eyre & Spottiswode, 1951

Ponsonby, Mary. *Mary Ponsonby: a Memoir, some Letters, and a Journal*, ed. Magdalen Ponsonby. John Murray, 1927

Reid, Michaela. *Ask Sir James: Sir James Reid, Personal Physician to Queen Victoria and Physician-in-Ordinary to three monarchs*, Hodder & Stoughton, 1987

Stanley, Lady Augusta. *Letters of Lady Augusta Stanley: A Young Lady at Court*, ed. The Dean of Windsor and Hector Bolitho, Gerald Howe, 1927

Teignmouth-Shore, T. *Some Recollections*, Hutchinson, 1911

Princess Victoria, later Empress Frederick

Anon. *The Empress Frederick: a Memoir.* James Nisbet, 1913

Barkeley, Richard. *The Empress Frederick, daughter of Queen Victoria*, Macmillan, 1956

Bennett, Daphne, *Vicky, Princess Royal of England and German Empress.* Collins Harvill, 1971

Corti, Egon Caesar Conte. *The English Empress: a study in the relations between Queen Victoria and her eldest daughter, Empress Frederick of Germany*, Cassell, 1957

Pakula, Hannah. *An uncommon woman: the Empress Frederick*, Weidenfeld & Nicolson, 1996

Sinclair, Andrew. *The other Victoria: The Princess Royal and the Great Game of Europe*, Weidenfeld & Nicolson, 1981

Taylor, Lucy, *'Fritz' of Prussia: Germany's Second Emperor*, Nelson, 1891

Tisdall, E.E.P. *She Made World Chaos: The Intimate Story of the Empress Frederick of Prussia*, Stanley Paul, 1940

Van der Kiste, John. *Dearest Vicky, Darling Fritz: Queen Victoria's Eldest Daughter and the German Emperor*, Sutton, 2001

—— *Frederick III: German Emperor 1888*, Sutton, 1981

Prince Albert Edward, later King Edward VII

Battiscombe, Georgina, *Queen Alexandra*, Constable, 1969

Brook-Shepherd, Gordon. *Uncle of Europe: The Social and Diplomatic Life of Edward VII*, Collins, 1975

Cowles, Virginia. *King Edward VII and his Circle*, Hamish Hamilton, 1956

Hibbert, Christopher, *Edward VII: A portrait*, Viking, 1976

Lee, Sir Sidney. *King Edward VII: a biography*, 2 vols. Macmillan, 1925–7

Leslie, Anita. *Edwardians in Love*, Hutchinson, 1972

Magnus, Philip. *King Edward the Seventh*, John Murray, 1964

Redesdale, Algernon, Baron. *King Edward VII: a Memory*, Ballantyne, 1915

St Aubyn, Giles. *Edward, Prince and King*, Collins, 1979

Weintraub, Stanley, *The importance of being Edward: King in waiting*, John Murray, 2000

Princess Alice

Duff, David. *Hessian tapestry: The Hesse family and British royalty*. Frederick Muller, 1967; David & Charles, 1979

Noel, Gerard. *Princess Alice: Queen Victoria's forgotten daughter*. Constable, 1974

Prince Alfred

Marie, Queen of Roumania. *The story of my life*, 3 vols. Cassell, 1934–5

McKinlay, Brian. *The first royal tour 1867–68*. Robert Hale, 1971

Van der Kiste, John, & Jordaan, Bee. *Dearest Affie: Alfred, Duke of Edinburgh, Queen Victoria's second son*. Sutton, 1984

Princess Helena

Baird, Diana, arr. *Victorian days and a royal friendship*. Littlebury, 1958

Marie Louise, Princess. *My memories of six reigns*. Evans Bros, 1956

Princess Louise

Duff, David. *The life story of HRH Princess Louise, Duchess of Argyll*. Stanley Paul, 1940; Cedric Chivers, 1971

Wake, Jehanne. *Princess Louise: Queen Victoria's Unconventional Daughter*, Collins, 1988

Prince Arthur

Aston, Sir George G. *HRH The Duke of Connaught and Strathearn*. Harrap, 1929

Frankland, Noble. *Witness of a Century: The Life and Times of Prince Arthur, Duke of Connaught*, Shepheard Walwyn, 1993

BIBLIOGRAPHY

Prince Leopold

Alice, Countess of Athlone. *For my grandchildren: Some Reminiscences of HRH Princess Alice, Countess of Athlone*, Evans Bros, 1966
Aronson, Theo. *Princess Alice, Countess of Athlone*. Cassell, 1981
Zeepvat, Charlotte, *Prince Leopold*, Sutton, 1998

Princess Beatrice

Dennison, Matthew, *The last princess: The devoted life of Queen Victoria's youngest daughter*, Weidenfeld & Nicolson, 2007
Duff, David. *The shy Princess*. Evans Bros, 1958; Frederick Muller, 1974
Sara, M.E. *The Life and Times of Princess Beatrice*. Stanley Paul, 1945

Index

Abbreviations used: E – King Edward VII; PC – Albert, Prince Consort; QV – Queen Victoria; V – Victoria Princess Royal and German Empress. Crowned heads are of England unless stated otherwise. Nicknames are only given if mentioned in the text.

INDEX